TOEFL® MAP

MAP New TOEFL® Edition

Reading

Intermediate

DARAKWON

TOEFL® MAP New TOEFL® Edition

Reading Intermediate

Publisher Chung Kyudo
Editor Cho Sangik
Authors Michael A. Putlack, Stephen Poirier, Allen C. Jacobs
Proofreader Talib Din
Designers Park Narae, Jung Kyuok

First published in November 2022
By Darakwon, Inc.
Darakwon Bldg., 211, Munbal-ro, Paju-si, Gyeonggi-do 10881
Republic of Korea
Tel: 82-2-736-2031 (Ext. 250)
Fax: 82-2-732-2037

ISBN 978-89-277-8030-4 14740
978-89-277-8025-0 14740 (set)

www.darakwon.co.kr

Photo Credits
Shutterstock.com

Components Main Book / Answers and Explanations
10 9 8 7 6 5 4   24 25 26 27 28 29

Introduction

Studying for the TOEFL® iBT is no easy task and is not one that is to be undertaken lightly. It requires a great deal of effort as well as dedication on the part of the student. It is our hope that by using *TOEFL® Map Reading Intermediate* as either a textbook or a study guide, the task of studying for the TOEFL® iBT will become somewhat easier for the student and less of a burden.

Students who wish to excel on the TOEFL® iBT must attain a solid grasp of the four important skills in the English language: reading, listening, speaking, and writing. The Darakwon *TOEFL® Map* series covers all four of these skills in separate books. There are also three different levels in all four topics. This book, *TOEFL® Map Reading Intermediate*, covers the reading aspect of the test at the intermediate level. Students who want to read passages, learn vocabulary terms, and study topics that appear on the TOEFL® iBT will have their wishes granted by using this book.

TOEFL® Map Reading Intermediate has been designed for use both in a classroom setting and as a study guide for individual learners. For this reason, it offers a comprehensive overview of the TOEFL® iBT Reading section. In Part A, the different types of questions that are found on the TOEFL® iBT Reading section are explained, and hints on how to answer these questions properly are also provided. In Part B, learners have the opportunity to build their background knowledge of the topics that appear on the TOEFL® iBT by studying the reading passages of varying lengths that are found in each chapter. Each passage is followed by the types of questions that appear on the TOEFL® iBT. Each chapter also has a vocabulary section, which enables learners to test their knowledge of vocabulary that is specific to the particular topics covered in each chapter. Finally, in Part C, students can take two TOEFL® iBT practice tests. These are passages that have the same numbers and types of questions that appear on actual TOEFL® iBT Reading section passages. Combined, all of these should be able to help learners prepare themselves to take and, more importantly, to excel on the TOEFL® iBT.

TOEFL® Map Reading Intermediate has a great amount of information and should prove to be invaluable as a study guide for learners who are preparing for the TOEFL® iBT. However, while this book is comprehensive, it is up to each person to do the actual work. In order for *TOEFL® Map Reading Intermediate* to be of any use, the individual learner must dedicate him or herself to studying the information found within its pages. While we have strived to make this book as user friendly and as full of crucial information as possible, ultimately, it is up to each person to make the best of the material in the book. We wish you luck in your study of both English and the TOEFL® iBT, and we hope that you are able to use *TOEFL® Map Reading Intermediate* to improve your abilities in both of them.

Michael A. Putlack
Stephen Poirier
Allen C. Jacobs

TABLE
OF
CONTENTS

Part A | Understanding Reading Question Types

Part B | Building Background Knowledge of TOEFL Topics

Chapter 01 *History*

Chapter 02 *The Art*

How Is This Book Different?

When searching for the ideal book to use to study for the TOEFL® iBT, it is often difficult to differentiate between the numerous books available on a bookstore's shelves. However, *TOEFL® Map Reading Intermediate* differs from many other TOEFL® iBT books and study guides in several important ways.

Many TOEFL® iBT books arrange the material according to the types of questions on the test. This often results in learners reading a passage on history, followed by a passage on economics, and so on. Simply put, there is little cohesion except for the questions. However, *TOEFL® Map Reading Intermediate* is arranged by subject. This book has eight chapters, all of which cover subjects that appear on the TOEFL® iBT. For instance, there are a chapter on history, a chapter on the arts, a chapter on life sciences, and a chapter on physical sciences. By arranging the chapters according to subjects, learners can read passages related to one another all throughout each chapter. This enables them to build upon their knowledge as they progress through each chapter. Additionally, since many vocabulary terms are used in certain subjects, learners can more easily recognize these specialized terms, understand how they are used, and retain the knowledge of what these terms mean. Finally, by arranging the chapters according to subjects, learners can cover and become familiar with every TOEFL® iBT question type in each chapter rather than just focus on a single type of question.

TOEFL® Map Reading Intermediate, unlike many other TOEFL® iBT books and study guides, does not have any translations into foreign languages within its pages. All too often, learners rely on translations in their native language. They use these translations to help them get through the material. However, the actual TOEFL® iBT has no translations, so neither does this book. This will better prepare learners to take the test the test by encouraging them to learn difficult terms and expressions through context, just as native speakers of English do when they encounter unfamiliar terms and expressions. Additionally, learners will find that their fluency in English will improve more rapidly when they use *TOEFL® Map Reading Intermediate* without relying on any translations.

Finally, the passages in *TOEFL® Map Reading Intermediate* are based on topics that have appeared on the actual TOEFL® iBT in the past. Therefore, learners can see what kinds of topics appear on the TOEFL® iBT. This will enable them to recognize the difficulty level, the style of TOEFL® iBT passages, and the difficulty of the vocabulary on the test. Second, learners can enhance their knowledge of topics that have appeared on the TOEFL® iBT. By knowing more about these topics when they take the actual test, test takers will be sure to improve their scores. Third, learners will also gain knowledge of the specialized vocabulary in particular topics, which will help them more easily understand passages on the actual test. Finally, many topics appear multiple times on the TOEFL® iBT. Thus, students who study some of these topics may be pleasantly surprised to find the same topic when they take the actual TOEFL® iBT. That will no doubt help them improve their test scores.

How to Use
This Book

TOEFL® Map Reading Intermediate is designed for use either as a textbook in a classroom in a TOEFL® iBT preparation course or as a study guide for individuals who are studying for the TOEFL® iBT on their own. *TOEFL® Map Reading Intermediate* has been divided into three sections: Part A, Part B, and Part C. All three sections offer information which is important to learners preparing for the TOEFL® iBT. Part A is divided into 10 sections, each of which explains one of the question types that appear on the TOEFL® iBT Reading section. Part B is divided into 8 chapters. There is a chapter that covers each of the four subjects that appear on the TOEFL® iBT. Part C has 2 complete practice tests that resemble those which appear on the TOEFL® iBT.

Part A   Understanding Reading Question Types

This section is designed to acquaint learners with each question type on the TOEFL® iBT Reading section. Therefore there are 10 sections in this chapter—one for each question type. Each section is divided into 4 parts. The first part offers a short explanation of the question type. The second part shows the ways in which questions of that particular type often appear on the test. The third part provides helpful hints on how to answer these questions correctly. The fourth part has one or two short passages followed by a question. At the end of Part A, there is a full-length Reading passage with questions from every type that is asked on the Reading section.

Part B   Building Background Knowledge of TOEFL Topics

The purpose of this section is to introduce the various subjects that most frequently appear on the TOEFL® iBT. There are 8 chapters in Part B. Each chapter covers a single subject and contains 7 Reading passages of various lengths as well as vocabulary words and exercises. Each chapter is divided into several parts.

Introduction

This is a short description of the subject of the chapter. The purpose of this section is to let learners know what fields of study people focus on in this subject.

Mastering the Question Types

This section contains 3 Reading passages that are between 250 and 300 words in length. Following each passage, there are 3 Reading questions. Each question is identified by type. All 10 question types are covered in this section. In addition, there is a short summary of each passage after the questions with four blanks for learners to fill in.

Mastering the Subject

This section contains 3 Reading passages that are between 400 and 450 words in length. To the side of each passage are several long notes that provide additional information meant to help learners better understand the passage. Following each passage, there are 4 Reading questions. These questions may be from any of the 10 types of Reading questions. In addition, there is a short summary of each passage after the questions with four blanks for learners to fill in.

TOEFL Practice Test

This section contains 1 Reading passage that is between 500 and 550 words in length. The passage has 10 Reading questions of any type. The purpose of this section is to acquaint learners with the types of passages they will encounter when they take the TOEFL® iBT.

Star Performer Subject Topics, Word Files, and Vocabulary Review

This section contains 12 short passages about topics related to the chapter. These can provide learners with additional information that can help them become more familiar with the subject of the chapter. It also contains around 80 vocabulary words that are used in the passages in each chapter. The words include nouns, verbs, adjectives, and adverbs. Definitions are provided for each word. There are also 20 questions that review the vocabulary words that learners cover in each chapter. The purpose of this section is to teach learners specific words that often appear in passages on certain subjects and to make sure that learners know the meanings of these words and how to use them properly.

Part C Experiencing the TOEFL Actual Tests

This section contains 7 long TOEFL® iBT Reading passages and questions. The purpose of this section is to let learners experience long Reading passages and to see if they can apply the knowledge they have learned in the course of studying TOEFL® Map Reading Intermediate.

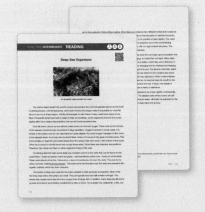

Part **A**

Understanding Reading Question Types

Vocabulary questions require the test taker to understand the meanings of words and phrases in the passage. These questions highlight a word or phrase in the text. Then, they ask the test taker to choose another word or phrase with a similar meaning. The highlighted words are always important to the passage. Knowing their meanings is crucial to understanding the passage. Many times, highlighted words have several meanings. The test taker needs to be aware of the different meanings of these words. Then, the test taker will be able to select the correct meanings of the words or phrases.

Vocabulary questions often appear on the test like this:

→ The word "X" in the passage is closest in meaning to

→ In stating "X", the author means that

Vocabulary questions often require these skills:

◆ Many words and phrases in English have multiple meanings. The most common meaning of a word is not always the correct answer. Do not choose an answer simply because it is the most common meaning of a word.

◆ Focus on how the word or phrase is used in the sentence itself.

◆ All answer choices can be substituted for the highlighted word or phrase in the passage. Try putting every answer choice into the passage. That may help determine which answer choice is correct.

◆ Carefully read the sentence the highlighted word is in. In addition, read the other sentences both before and after the one with the highlighted word. Many times, there are contextual clues in the passage. These clues can help you find the meanings of some words.

Examples

The first four planets in the solar system all share several characteristics with one another. For this reason, people refer to them as the terrestrial planets. These four planets—Mercury, Venus, Earth, and Mars—are all relatively close to the sun. They are also all rocky planets. This makes them unlike the other four planets, which are gas giants. The terrestrial planets orbit the sun quickly as they all take fewer than two years to do so.

Finally, the terrestrial planets have a small number of moons. Mercury and Venus have none, Earth has one, and Mars has two.

Q The word "characteristics" in the passage is closest in meaning to

(A) facts

(B) abilities

(C) traits

(D) personalities

⭐ **Explanation of the above question and answer:**

Choice (C) has the closest meaning to the highlighted word. Characteristics can often refer to abilities, traits, and personalities. However, planets have no abilities or personalities. People do. So Choice (B) and Choice (D) are incorrect. Choice (A) is incorrect because characteristics are not facts.

One of the leaders of ancient Greece was the city-state of Athens. Even today, people are aware of its greatness. One reason for Athens's lasting fame is the many accomplishments made by its citizens. Its people made contributions in the fields of science, philosophy, history, politics, and even warfare. Perhaps the most famous Athenian of all was the philosopher Socrates. Socrates himself never actually recorded any of his own thoughts. Instead, his student Plato saved them for posterity in his own writings. Plato would later go on to become one of the greatest philosophers in all of Western history.

Q The word "recorded" in the passage is closest in meaning to

(A) repeated

(B) wrote down

(C) considered

(D) kept track of

⭐ **Explanation of the above question and answer:**

Choice (B) has the closest meaning to the highlighted word. When a person records something, that individual often writes it down. In the passage, the author mentions, "Plato saved them for posterity in his own writings." This indicates that Plato recorded, or wrote down, Socrates's thoughts. Choices (A), (C), and (D) are all incorrect.

Reference questions require the test taker to understand the relationships between certain words and what they refer to in the passage. These questions highlight a word in the text. The word is typically a pronoun such as *he*, *she*, *it*, or *they*. It may also be other words such as *his*, *hers*, *its*, or *theirs*. Demonstrative pronouns such as *this*, *that*, *these*, or *those* may be highlighted as well. The test taker must then determine which word or phrase the highlighted word is referring to. Nowadays, these questions seldom appear. Many passages have no Reference questions after them.

Reference questions often appear on the test like this:

→ The word "X" in the passage refers to

Reference questions often require these skills:

◆ The case and the number of the pronoun and its antecedent must be the same. If the highlighted word is singular, ignore any plural answer choices. Likewise, if the highlighted word is plural, ignore any singular answer choices.

◆ Try substituting the highlighted word with each answer choice. See which of the answer choices makes the most sense. This process can help eliminate some of the answer choices as possibilities.

◆ The answer choices use the same words or phrases that appear in the passage. They also appear in the same order that they are written in the passage. Some answer choices consist of a single word. Others may be phrases.

◆ Most of the time, the correct answer appears before the highlighted word. Sometimes, however, the correct answer choice comes after the highlighted word.

Examples

The American westward movement began in earnest in the early 1800s. This was when President Thomas Jefferson made the Louisiana Purchase. For fifteen million dollars, he bought a vast area of land from France in 1803. The Louisiana Territory covered the land west of the Mississippi River to the Rocky Mountains and from the Gulf of Mexico up to Canada. The French did not really want to sell it. But they were fighting wars in Europe. So Napoleon needed the money. They also suspected that the United States would eventually seize the land. So they wanted to get something for it before that happened.

Q The word "it" in the passage refers to

(A) the Louisiana Territory

(B) the Mississippi River

(C) the Gulf of Mexico

(D) Canada

★ **Explanation of the above question and answer:**

Choice (A) is what "it" refers to. Pay attention to the sentence the highlighted word is in. It is about the French selling something. They were selling the Louisiana Territory to America. Thus the correct answer is (A). Choices (B), (C), and (D) are incorrect since the French were not trying to sell the Mississippi River, the Gulf of Mexico, or Canada.

Another aspect is that people in cities often have no need for personal vehicles. Many still drive. Yet large numbers of people do not. The main reason for this is the existence of public transportation systems in urban centers. Most cities have extensive bus systems. These provide cheap, convenient, and swift travel throughout cities and their suburbs. Larger cities typically have subway systems as well. An extra benefit of these is that they do not have to stop for traffic at all. Instead, they speed through underground corridors and take their passengers to their destinations in a predictable amount of time.

Q The word "these" in the passage refers to

(A) extensive bus systems

(B) cities and their suburbs

(C) larger cities

(D) subway systems

★ **Explanation of the above question and answer:**

Choice (D) is what "these" refers to. The important phrase in the sentence is "they do not have to stop for traffic at all." Since "these" is something that is moving, Choice (B) and Choice (C) can be eliminated. Choice (A) would result in a factually incorrect sentence. It was also discussed earlier in the paragraph. That leaves Choice (D) as the correct answer. Reading the sentence following the one with the highlighted word will further confirm it as being correct.

03 | Factual Information

Factual Information questions require the test taker to understand all of the facts that are covered in the passage. These questions typically ask about details, definitions, explanations, and other similar data. The facts that these questions ask for are often covered in one part of the passage. They may be found in one or two sentences, not an entire paragraph. Answering these questions does not require a complete understanding of the entire passage. The test taker only needs to understand the section that contains the important information.

Factual Information questions often appear on the test like this:

→ According to the paragraph, which of the following is true of X?

→ The author's description of X mentions which of the following?

→ According to the paragraph, X occurred because . . .

→ According to the paragraph, X did Y because . . .

→ According to the paragraph, why did X do Y?

→ Select the TWO answer choices from paragraph 1 that identify X. *To receive credit, you must select TWO answers.*

Factual Information questions often require these skills:

◆ Focus on all of the facts that are mentioned in the passage.

◆ Do not trust your memory to answer these questions properly. Most passages have a large number of details. Instead, go back through the passage to confirm the information that you need.

◆ Read the answer choices closely. Answer choices frequently contain information that is partially correct. However, one or two words—often adverbs such as *always*, *usually*, or *never*—may change the meaning of the answer choice and make it an incorrect statement.

◆ Answer choices sometimes have correct information that was not covered in the passage. These answer choices are incorrect. Be sure that the information in the answer choice you select can be found in the passage.

Examples

[1]→ Nowadays, most astronomers agree that the solar system has only eight planets. Whereas once there were nine, Pluto has been removed from that group. Rather than being a planet, Pluto is now a dwarf planet instead. There are several requirements for a celestial body to be considered a dwarf planet. First, it must orbit the sun and not be the satellite of another body. It must have a roughly spherical shape as well. However, a dwarf planet is not large enough to have a strong gravitational pull. So it has not cleared other objects from its path. Finally, dwarf planets travel around the sun in elliptical orbits. At present, there are several known dwarf planets. Pluto is one, and Ceres, a massive asteroid found between Mars and Jupiter, is another. Eris, which is even farther from the sun than Pluto, is yet another dwarf planet.

Q In paragraph 1, the author's description of dwarf planets mentions which of the following?

  (A) Why they are close to other planets

  (B) How their gravity makes planets move

  (C) What shape they have

  (D) How many there are in the solar system

❓ Explanation of the above question and answer:

> Choice (C) is the only statement that is mentioned in the passage. The answer is found in the sentence that mentions that dwarf planets "must have a roughly spherical shape." Since dwarf planets must be roughly spherical, then they are "somewhat round." Choice (A) is incorrect since there is no mention of how close dwarf planets are to other planets. Choice (B) is incorrect since dwarf planets' gravitational forces are so weak that they cannot make other objects move. And Choice (D) is not mentioned in the passage.

[2]→ While television advertisements can be effective, they are also expensive. A thirty-second spot on American primetime television may cost hundreds of thousands or even a couple of million dollars. For big events, such as the Super Bowl or the season finale of a popular program, an ad might cost several million dollars. So companies must spend their advertising dollars wisely. One way is to be aware of the demographics of the people watching the shows they advertise on. By knowing the average age of the viewers, companies can be more selective in advertising their products. For instance, older people tend to watch the news on television. Therefore, ads for healthcare products often run on these shows. They are unlikely to appear on ads during cartoons, which are viewed by children and teenagers. Instead, ads for candy, fast-food restaurants, and toys are more likely to air.

Q According to paragraph 2, companies want to know the demographics of television programs' viewers because

    Ⓐ they want to advertise their products on the correct shows

    Ⓑ they are the most interested in advertising to children and teenagers

    Ⓒ the elderly are the most influenced by television advertisements

    Ⓓ some programs attract many viewers while others do not

✪ Explanation of the above question and answer:

Choice Ⓐ completes the sentence properly. In the passage, the author notes that companies that know the demographics of various programs "can be more selective in advertising their programs." So these companies want to be able to advertise their products on the correct shows. Choice Ⓑ is incorrect because the passage does not mention which demographic companies want to advertise to. Choice Ⓒ is incorrect since the effectiveness of advertisements is not covered. And Choice Ⓓ is incorrect since the ratings of programs are not covered as well.

04) Negative Factual Information

Negative Factual Information questions require the test taker to understand all of the facts that are covered in the passage. These questions typically ask about details, definitions, explanations, and other similar data. In this way, they are similar to Factual Information questions. However, these questions require the test taker to identify incorrect information. Three of the answer choices contain correct information. The answer choice with the incorrect information is the one that the test taker must choose.

Negative Factual Information questions often appear on the test like this:

→ According to the passage, which of the following is NOT true of X?

→ The author's description of X mentions all of the following EXCEPT:

→ In paragraph 2, all of the following questions are answered EXCEPT:

Negative Factual Information questions often require these skills:

◆ Focus on all of the facts that are mentioned in the passage.

◆ Do not trust your memory to answer these questions properly. Most passages have a large number of details. Instead, go back through the passage to confirm the information that you need.

◆ The information in these answer choices is often found in a single paragraph or occasionally in two paragraphs. The question will identify the paragraph or paragraphs the information is in, so focus only on the identified section to find the answer.

◆ The correct answer is often the opposite of information that appears in the passage. At other times, the correct answer may contain information that is not included in the passage. And in some instances, the correct answer may be a truthful statement but may refer to something else in the passage rather than the topic of the question.

Examples

[3]→ As feudalism declined in Europe, many nations began to look for a new economic system. Several settled upon mercantilism. It would dominate European economies from the 1500s to the 1700s. One of its most important features was the government's role in the economy. In mercantilism, a government had a major role in the economy of the entire nation. What mercantilist governments were most interested in was acquiring wealth. This was often in the form of bullion, such as gold and silver. This was one of the reasons the Europeans competed against one another so much in the Americas. The New World was rich in gold and silver. By plundering the New World, European countries could grow richer. Many rulers sent adventurers to the

Americas. Their instructions were simple: Acquire as much treasure as possible. And do it any way possible.

Q According to paragraph 3, which of the following is NOT true of mercantilism?

- Ⓐ It was later replaced by feudalism in Europe.
- Ⓑ One of its features was the amassing of gold.
- Ⓒ It was practiced by some European countries.
- Ⓓ Governments had major roles in mercantilist economies.

✪ Explanation of the above question and answer:

Choice Ⓐ is the only statement in the passage that is NOT true. The passage mentions that feudalism was on the decline, so European countries were on the lookout for a new economic system. It is therefore not true that mercantilism was replaced by feudalism. In fact, the opposite is true. This makes Choice Ⓐ an incorrect statement. Choices Ⓑ, Ⓒ, and Ⓓ are all correct statements, so they should not be chosen.

²➔ Among nature's most unusual mammals are marsupials. Kangaroos are the best-known species. Others among them are opossums and wombats. For the most part, marsupials reside in North America and Australia. The manner in which they give birth is what sets them apart from other mammals. When most mammals give birth, their babies are fully developed. Many, such as human babies, are virtually helpless, but they can survive in the outside world. This is not the case for marsupials. At birth, they are extremely undeveloped. So marsupial females have a pouch in which their young remain and continue to develop outside the womb. Inside the pouch, the young stay attached to their mother's teat, which nourishes them. After they develop, they leave the pouch. However, many often return there to seek both safety and to move from place to place with their mothers.

Q In paragraph 2, all of the following questions are answered EXCEPT:

- Ⓐ What are some animals that are considered to be marsupials?
- Ⓑ What is the purpose of the pouch a female marsupial has?
- Ⓒ Why do most marsupials live either in Australia or North America?
- Ⓓ How are mammal babies and marsupial babies different at birth?

✪ Explanation of the above question and answer:

Choice Ⓒ is the only question in the passage that is NOT answered. The passage reads, "For the most part, marsupials reside in North America and Australia." However, it does not explain why most marsupials live in those two places. This means that the question in Choice Ⓒ is not answered. The questions in Choices Ⓐ, Ⓑ, and Ⓓ are all answered, so they should not be chosen.

05 Sentence Simplification

Sentence Simplification questions require the test taker to look at a sentence in the passage that has been highlighted. Then, the test taker must choose the sentence that best restates the highlighted one. These questions require the test taker to pay attention to the main points in the sentence. The test taker must be sure that all of the main points are mentioned in the simplified sentence. The answer choices use words, phrases, and grammar that differ from the highlighted sentence. So these questions also check the test taker's knowledge of vocabulary and grammar. When they are asked, there is only one Sentence Simplification question per passage.

Sentence Simplification questions often appear on the test like this:

→ Which of the sentences below best expresses the essential information in the highlighted sentence in the passage? *Incorrect* answer choices change the meaning in important ways or leave out essential information.

Sentence Simplification questions often require these skills:

◆ The highlighted sentences often have two or more separate clauses. Make sure you know what the main point or idea of each clause is.

◆ Make sure that the answer choice you select covers all of the essential information in the highlighted sentence.

◆ Make sure that the answer choice you select has no information that disagrees with or is in opposition to the main sentence.

◆ Do not select answer choices that omit essential information. Some answer choices may have accurate information but may leave out an important point from the highlighted sentence. These are incorrect, so do not choose them.

Example

After the caterpillar eats a sufficient amount of food, it is ready to enter the third stage of its life cycle. This is known as the pupa stage. First, the larva, as the caterpillar is called, must find an ideal spot for pupation. While the larva typically finds a twig on a tree or bush to enter the third stage, the site could be any other place so long as it is hidden from the view of predators. The reason is that, while in the pupa stage, the butterfly is extremely vulnerable. So camouflage is its only protection. Once it has secured a site, the larva begins to spin a cocoon. It essentially entombs itself inside a fairly hard shell. While inside, a transformation occurs as the caterpillar changes into a butterfly. Most of its body parts literally dissolve. They are then re-formed into new parts. These include wings, limbs, organs, and tissue. The pupa stage usually lasts around two weeks for most butterflies. However, if the butterfly undergoes its transformation in winter or in cold climates, it may take even longer. Once the metamorphosis is complete, the butterfly is ready to enter its fourth, and final, stage of life.

Q Which of the sentences below best expresses the essential information in the highlighted sentence in the passage? *Incorrect* answer choices change the meaning in important ways or leave out essential information.

- (A) The larva often looks for a twig or some other place that is concealed from hunters while it transforms.
- (B) The third stage of its life cycle requires the larva to find a twig in order to hide from predators.
- (C) By staying out of view of predators, a larva is able to locate a tree branch to hide on during its metamorphosis.
- (D) A larva that does not hide from predators on a twig will most likely be eaten before it can undergo a change.

✪ Explanation of the above question and answer:

Choice (A) best restates the important information from the highlighted sentence. The highlighted sentence has two parts: 1) the larva looks for a twig or something similar to enter the third stage, and 2) the place it finds needs to be hidden from predators. Choice (A) includes both of these pieces of information. Choice (B) is incorrect because a larva is not required to find a twig; it can find another site instead. Choice (C) is incorrect because the order of the actions is reversed. The larva finds a place to hide to stay out of the view of predators. It does not stay hidden from predators and then find a place to hide. Choice (D) is incorrect because there is nothing in the sentence about the larva getting eaten.

06 — Inference

Inference questions require the test taker to understand certain arguments that the author of the passage is making. These questions require the test taker to think about the information in the passage and then come to various conclusions about it. The answers to these questions are never stated in the passage. Instead, the answers are implied. So the test taker must infer the author's intent. Many Inference questions ask about cause and effect. Others ask the test taker to make comparisons between two things, ideas, events, or people.

Inference questions often appear on the test like this:

→ Which of the following can be inferred about X?

→ The author of the passage implies that X . . .

→ Which of the following can be inferred from paragraph 1 about X?

Inference questions often require these skills:

◆ Learn to read between the lines. The author's words often have a second meaning. These meanings are not stated though. The author merely hints at them.

◆ Many passages have cause-effect relationships. Think carefully about these. When the author describes an event, idea, or phenomenon, consider what some possible effects of one of them may be.

◆ The correct answer will never contradict the main point of the passage. Avoid answer choices that do not agree with the central idea of the passage.

◆ Some answer choices may contain words that appear in the passage. Be careful of them because they are often intentionally misleading.

Examples

2→ Movie directors try to create the most realistic films possible. To do this, many employ special effects. This is especially true of directors of action films. Special effects can be either audio or visual in nature. They can be small-scale effects such as the sounds of cars driving or a simple background view of a city. They can also be large-scale effects. Examples of these are exploding buildings or flying spaceships. Today, many special effects are done with computers. They are generated electronically and then inserted into the film. Yet the use of computers is a relatively recent practice. In the past, special effects artists had to be creative. For instance, they painted backgrounds for scenes in the films. They used puppets, especially when filming aliens, monsters, or other nonhuman creatures. Sometimes they built small models of large objects and filmed them from very close up.

Q In paragraph 2, the author implies that special effects

- Ⓐ are relatively expensive to create
- Ⓑ are convincing when done by computers
- Ⓒ are commonly used in action films
- Ⓓ can make aliens and monsters look realistic

❓ Explanation of the above question and answer:

Choice Ⓒ is implied about special effects. The author writes, "To do this, many employ special effects. This is especially true of directors in action films." By writing "especially true," the author implies that action films require a great number of special effects. It can therefore be inferred that action films commonly use special effects. There is nothing written about cost in the passage, so Choice Ⓐ is incorrect. Computers are mentioned, but their effectiveness at making special effects is not hinted at, so Choice Ⓑ is incorrect. And there is nothing mentioned about how realistic aliens and monsters look because of special effects. This makes Choice Ⓓ incorrect.

3→ The levels of oceans, seas, and other large bodies of water are not constant but instead rise and fall periodically. These changes are called tides. Tides are mostly the result of the force of gravity on the water. In the Earth's case, tides are caused not only by the Earth's gravitational forces but also by those of the sun and the moon. Acting in concert, they cause the tides to rise and fall throughout the day. As a general rule, tides occur twice a day. There are both high tide, when the water reaches its highest point, and low tide, when it reaches its lowest point. The levels reached at high tide and low tide vary over time. The alignment of the Earth, the sun, and the moon affects these levels. During new and full moons, the alignment of all three bodies causes the tides to reach their greatest levels.

Q Which of the following can be inferred from paragraph 3 about the tides?

(A) When they are going to occur is not possible for people to predict.

(B) They are very low at the halfway point between the new and full moon.

(C) They might be higher than normal depending on the season.

(D) High tide may occur up to three times in one day.

❷ Explanation of the above question and answer:

Choice (B) can be inferred about the tides. The author writes, "During new and full moons, the alignment of all three bodies causes the tides to reach their greatest levels." Since the tides are at their highest during both the new moon and the full moon, it can be inferred that they are at their lowest point halfway between the two events. Choice (A) is incorrect. The passage includes nothing about predicting when the tides will occur. Choice (C) is incorrect since there is no mention of the seasons in the passage. Choice (D) is incorrect as well. The passage notes that the tides generally occur twice a day. But there is no hint that there may be "up to" three high tides in one day.

07 | Rhetorical Purpose

Rhetorical Purpose questions require the test taker to understand the author's reason for mentioning something in the passage. These questions ask the test taker to consider the reasoning behind the inclusion of certain information in the passage. To answer these questions properly, the function of the material is the most important aspect. The actual meaning of the information is not important to answering these questions correctly. The information asked about in these questions can be found either in entire paragraphs or in individual sentences.

Rhetorical Purpose questions often appear on the test like this:

→ The author discusses X in paragraph 2 in order to . . .

→ Why does the author mention "X"?

→ The author uses X as an example of . . .

Rhetorical Purpose questions often require these skills:

◆ Find the part of the passage that includes the topic being asked about. Then, consider how that topic relates to the passage as a whole.

◆ There are often clues in the passage that help identify the author's purpose in including the information. Pay attention to words such as *definition*, *example*, *illustrate*, *explain*, *contrast*, *compare*, *refute*, *note*, *criticize*, or *function*.

◆ Many times, the question does not concern the topic as a whole. So you only need to consider the section that mentions the topic of the question and figure out why the author mentioned it in that one section.

Examples

[4]→ Many scientists rely upon fossils to learn more about the Earth's past. They are not terribly interested in the fossils themselves. However, the fossils can tell them about how the land has changed over time. For instance, there are many places where fossils of sea creatures can be found on land. Once the age of a fossil is determined, a geologist will know that the area where it was found was underwater at that time. In addition, the types of fossils that are discovered can tell scientists about the past. For instance, the woolly mammoth lived in cold regions in the Northern Hemisphere during the last ice age. When mammoth fossils are found and dated, climatologists can be assured that the area where the fossil was unearthed—no matter how warm it is now—was once cold enough for mammoths to live in.

Q The author discusses "the woolly mammoth" in paragraph 4 in order to

- Ⓐ compare fossils of it with those of sea creatures
- Ⓑ prove that it used to live in cold climates
- Ⓒ mention that it was still alive during the last ice age
- Ⓓ show that fossils can be used to learn about past weather conditions

✪ Explanation of the above question and answer:

Choice Ⓓ best describes why the author discusses the woolly mammoth. The final sentence in the paragraph provides the reason. It mentions that the presence of woolly mammoth fossils in a region is evidence that the area "was once cold enough for mammoths to live in." Choice Ⓐ is incorrect because there is no comparison of the woolly mammoth and sea creature fossils made. Choice Ⓑ is incorrect because this is a minor fact. The author merely mentions that the woolly mammoth lived in cold climates. Choice Ⓒ is incorrect because it too is a minor fact.

3→ Some of the greatest developments of the Industrial Revolution were in transportation. At first, steam engines—such as the Newcomen steam engine—were used in factories to operate equipment. But then people realized they could use steam engines for transportation. During the first decade of the 1800s, both locomotives and steamships were invented. Trains could transport people and goods over land faster than any other mode of travel. Steamships were the same for water travel. The first successful steamship, *the Clermont*, was designed by Robert Fulton. However, many people called her "Fulton's Folly." These individuals were doubtful that steam engines would ever work in ships. Yet they did, and they transformed the world. Steamships could cross the ocean much faster than sailing ships. Eventually, by the end of the 1800s, sailing ships were a relic of the past.

Q In paragraph 3, why does the author mention "*the Clermont*"?

- Ⓐ To give the name of the first successful steamship
- Ⓑ To praise the man who designed the ship
- Ⓒ To mention that it crossed the ocean very quickly
- Ⓓ To claim that it should have been named *Fulton's Folly*

✪ Explanation of the above question and answer:

Choice Ⓐ best explains why the author mentions the *Clermont*. The passage notes that both trains and steamships were first invented in the early 1800s. Then, the author mentions the *Clermont* and notes that it was "the first successful steamship." Choice Ⓑ is incorrect because there is no praise for Robert Fulton. Choice Ⓒ is incorrect because the passage does not mention whether or not the *Clermont* ever crossed the ocean. Choice Ⓓ is incorrect because the nickname is merely mentioned. The author does not note whether or not it was appropriate.

08 Insert Text

Insert Text questions require the test taker to determine where in the passage a new sentence should be placed. These questions require the test taker to consider a number of different aspects. These include grammar, logic, connecting words, and flow. Insert Text questions do not always appear in a passage. When they are asked, there is only one Insert Text question per passage. No matter where in the passage the black squares appear, Insert Text questions are always the second-to-last question asked. Nowadays, there is almost always one Insert Text question for every passage.

Insert Text questions often appear on the test like this:

→ Look at the four squares [■] that indicate where the following sentence could be added to the passage.

[You will see a sentence in bold.]

Where would the sentence best fit?

Insert Text questions often require these skills:

◆ Try putting the new sentence in all four places in the passage where there are squares. Then, read the passages with the new sentence. This will often help you find the correct place for the sentence.

◆ Connecting words can be crucial to answering these questions. Their presence can affect the flow of the passage. Some common connecting words used are *therefore*, *similarly*, *in contrast*, *for example*, *for instance*, *finally*, *meanwhile*, *on the other hand*, and *as a result*.

◆ The new sentence must fit logically with the other sentences in the passage. Pay attention to any facts or opinions that are in the new sentence. Then, see how they relate to the other sentences in the passage.

Example

When a tropical storm begins to intensify, it may become a hurricane. Once a storm's winds reach speeds of 119 kilometers per hour, it is considered a hurricane. Oddly, the amount of rain a storm drops is irrelevant to it being a tropical storm or a hurricane. Hurricanes vary in intensity, so meteorologists have created five classifications for them. They are categories 1, 2, 3, 4, and 5. The weakest hurricanes are Category 1. The strongest are Category 5. Hurricanes also weaken or strengthen at various times. So they often change categories depending upon the speed of their winds. In general, Category 1 hurricanes cause the least amount of damage. That is not to say that they are harmless. **1** They can still cause flooding and damage the land. **2** Category 5 hurricanes have winds blowing at least 251 kilometers per hour. **3** These hurricanes can cause large amounts of flooding, especially from their storm surges as they move inland. **4** Their winds can blow down trees. And they can dump massive amounts of rain in a short period of time. Citizens living in coastal areas are always advised to flee in the face of a Category 5 hurricane. Fortunately, they are fairly rare events.

Q Look at the four squares [■] that indicate where the following sentence could be added to the passage.

For example, in 2005, Hurricane Katrina's winds briefly reached 289 kilometers per hour, making it a short-lived Category 5 hurricane.

Where would the sentence best fit?

Click on a square [■] to add the sentence to the passage.

● Explanation of the above question and answer:

The sentence best fits after the third square. The sentence before the third square reads, "Category 5 hurricanes have winds blowing at least 251 kilometers per hour." The new sentence also mentions wind speed. It notes that Hurricane Katrina was a Category 5 hurricane. And it begins with the connecting words "for example." This makes it a perfect fit after the third square. As for the other three sentences, they all concern the danger hurricanes pose or the damage they can cause. There is no mention in the new sentence of the damage that Hurricane Katrina did. That makes all three of those locations inappropriate for the new sentence.

09 Prose Summary

Prose Summary questions require the test taker to know what the main idea of the passage is and then to be able to choose sentences that focus on the main idea. These questions include a sentence that functions as a thesis statement for the entire passage. The main points of the passage are included in this sentence. Then, there are six sentences that include information from the passage. The test taker must choose the three sentences that most closely describe the main points that are mentioned in the introductory sentence. The other three sentences are about minor points, contain incorrect information, or have information not mentioned in the passage. These are always the last question asked about a reading passage, but they do not always appear. Instead, a Fill in a Table question may appear. However, nowadays, Prose Summary questions are much more common than Fill in a Table questions.

Prose Summary questions often appear on the test like this:

→ **Directions:** An introductory sentence for a brief summary of the passage is provided below. Complete the summary by selecting the THREE answer choices that express the most important ideas of the passage. Some sentences do not belong because they express ideas that are not presented in the passage or are minor ideas in the passage. ***This question is worth 2 points.***

Prose Summary questions often require these skills:

- ◆ The introductory sentence always covers the main themes or ideas of the passage.

- ◆ Look for answer choices that refer to the main themes or ideas.

- ◆ Do not choose answer choices that refer to minor themes or ideas.

- ◆ Some answer choices have correct information about the main themes or ideas. However, this information is not mentioned in the passage. Do not choose these answer choices. All correct answer choices contain information that is found in the passage.

The Stone Age

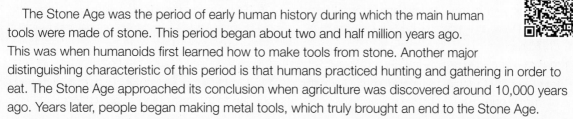

The Stone Age was the period of early human history during which the main human tools were made of stone. This period began about two and half million years ago. This was when humanoids first learned how to make tools from stone. Another major distinguishing characteristic of this period is that humans practiced hunting and gathering in order to eat. The Stone Age approached its conclusion when agriculture was discovered around 10,000 years ago. Years later, people began making metal tools, which truly brought an end to the Stone Age.

When the first human made a stone tool is debatable. However, the evidence points to around two and half million years ago. Archaeologists have found stones that humans had obviously shaped to be used for specific purposes. Common stone tools were weapons such as spears and, later, arrowhead tips. Domestic tools included stone knives for cutting and tools that early man used for grinding. Early humans commonly used flint, basalt, and sandstone for making tools since they were easy to shape. They used harder stones, including granite, to shape the softer stones into tools.

Stone Age humans were hunter-gatherers. They lived in bands that roamed the landscape in search of food. Typical food sources included fruits and berries, wild grains, fish from seas or rivers, and any animals they managed to kill. These early humans expended the majority of their energy on finding enough food to survive. This changed with the discovery of agriculture. It enabled humans to settle down and to develop civilization. In addition, the development of metallurgy and metal tools, starting with copper, and then bronze and iron, signified an end to the Stone Age.

Yet the Stone Age did not end everywhere at the same time. Agriculture and metallurgy were discovered in different places all around the world. Some people began emerging from the Stone Age around 10,000 years ago. Still, other societies did not end their use of stone tools and hunter-gatherer lifestyles until much later. One example is the Aborigines of Australia. When the Europeans arrived there in the 1700s, the Aborigines were still living in a Stone Age culture.

Q **Directions:** An introductory sentence for a brief summary of the passage is provided below. Complete the summary by selecting the THREE answer choices that express the most important ideas of the passage. Some sentences do not belong because they express ideas that are not presented in the passage or are minor ideas in the passage. **This question is worth 2 points.**

Drag your answer choices to the spaces where they belong.
To remove an answer choice, click on it. To review the passage, click on **View Text**.

The Stone Age was characterized by the use of stone tools by humans as well as by the hunter-gatherer lifestyle.

-
-
-

Answer Choices

1. Agriculture had not been discovered, so people had to collect or capture all of the food that they ate.

2. Humans learned how to use hard stones such as granite to shape softer ones into tools they could use.

3. The Stone Age finally ended once people learned how to make tools from metal instead of from stone.

4. Humans managed to create tools such as the points of weapons as well as tools that could cut and grind.

5. Beginning around 2.5 million years ago, the Stone Age only recently ended for people in some parts of the world.

6. Humans first began to learn how to farm the land around 10,000 years ago, and this is what led to the beginning of civilization.

✪ Explanation of the above question and answer:

Choices 1, 2, and 4 are all correct. Choice 1 mentions that people did not farm but instead collected or captured their food. This refers to the hunter-gatherer lifestyle people led. Choice 2 describes the toolmaking method people used. And Choice 4 describes the types of tools people in the Stone Age had. These both refer to the part of the sentence that mentions humans using stone tools. Choices 3, 5, and 6 are incorrect. Choice 3 is partially correct but is a minor point. Choice 5 is correct, but it is also a minor point. And Choice 6 is another minor point.

10 Fill in a Table

Fill in a Table questions require the test taker to understand all of the information that is presented in the passage. These questions typically break down the passage into two or three main points or themes. Then, they include a number of sentences or phrases concerning the main points or themes. The test taker must match each sentence or phrase with the correct main point or theme. These questions often ask the test taker to consider cause and effect, to compare and to contrast, or to understand theories or topics that are covered in the passage. These are always the last question asked about a reading passage, but they do not always appear. Instead, a Prose Summary question may appear. Nowadays, Fill in a Table questions are much lesson common than Prose Summary questions.

Fill in a Table questions often appear on the test like this:

→ **Directions:** Select the appropriate phrases from the answer choices and match them to the type of X to which they relate. TWO of the answer choices will NOT be used. *This question is worth 3 [4] points.*

Fill in a Table questions often require these skills:

◆ Know what the main points or themes of the passage are. Be aware of any significant differences between them.

◆ Cause-effect passages and compare-contrast passages frequently have Fill in a Table questions. Pay close attention to the facts mentioned about the main points or themes in these passages.

◆ Take notes on the main ideas or themes. Focus on the major points rather than the minor points. Fill in a Table questions have statements about the main points while ignoring the minor ones.

◆ These questions also have two incorrect answer choices. These answer choices are not connected to either of the two or three categories. Do not select them.

Yellow Dwarfs and Red Giants

Astronomers classify stars based on their sizes, masses, colors, and heat as well as the stages of their lives they are undergoing. Two types of stars are yellow dwarfs and red giants. In actuality, they are merely two stages in a star's life. Yellow dwarf stars are ones that are in the primes of their lives as they convert hydrogen to helium and give off intense light and heat. Eventually, though, they begin to die as they run out of hydrogen. Then, they expand and become red giant stars.

Yellow dwarf stars are not the smallest in the universe, but they have been given that name to distinguish them from other types of stars. The sun is an example of a yellow dwarf. Most other yellow dwarfs are slightly smaller or bigger than the sun. They are not particularly hot as far as stars go. They have surface temperatures that range between 5,300 and 6,000 degrees Kelvin. Most yellow dwarfs live around ten billion years. Eventually, they burn up all of the hydrogen they contain. When that happens, they expand, become red giants, and then leave behind a planetary nebula, which is a colorful cloud of gas.

A red giant is a star that is at the end of its life. Red giants form from stars such as yellow dwarfs. A red giant typically forms once all of the hydrogen in a star is consumed. Then, the star swells and becomes many times the size of a star such as the sun. The star's heat gets spread over a wider area, thereby lowering its surface temperature to between 3,700 and 5,000 degrees Kelvin. The enlarging of the star also causes a shift in its visible color spectrum. So the star's color changes to red. Red giants typically last for only a few million years. After that, they become planetary nebulas. At the end of the red giant phase, the core of the original star shrinks, whereupon it is called a white dwarf.

Q *Directions:* Complete the table below to summarize the information about yellow dwarfs and red giants. Match the appropriate statements to the star it applies to. *This question is worth 3 points.*

Drag your answer choices to the spaces where they belong.
To remove an answer choice, click on it. To review the passage, click on **View Text**.

Answer Choices	STAR
1 It is greatly enlarged in size.	**Yellow Dwarf**
2 It is a star near the end of its life.	•
3 It is the smallest star astronomers have discovered.	•
4 It is among the hottest of all stars.	**Red Giant**
5 The sun is this type of star.	•
6 It has exhausted its supply of hydrogen.	•
7 It can last for billions of years.	•

✪ Explanation of the above question and answer:

The fifth and seventh answer choices refer to the yellow dwarf. The fifth choice notes that the sun is a yellow dwarf. The seventh choice mentions the number of years a yellow dwarf can live. The first, second, and sixth answer choices refer to the red giant. The first choice states that the red giant is greatly enlarged. The second choice mentions that it is near the end of its life. And the sixth choice declares that a red giant no longer has any hydrogen to burn. The third and fourth choices do not refer to either type of star.

Practice

Old and Young Mountain Ranges

Mountain ranges come in all shapes and sizes. The biggest—and most obvious—difference between them is height. Some, such as the Himalayas in southern Asia, stand high above the clouds. They are rocky, **craggy** piles of stone, snow, and ice rising to heights where humans cannot survive for long. Other mountain ranges, such as the Appalachians in the eastern United States, are low, rounded, tree-covered mounds. The mountains' formation, their ages, and the effects of erosion on them help account for the differences between these two ranges.

2→ Mountains form in several manners. Some are volcanoes. So they are created when molten rock pushes through the crust. Others are the result of soft rock eroding around harder rock, which leaves a mountain behind. Still others come from molten, **igneous** rock that pushes up from under the ground yet does not break through to form volcanoes. Finally, plate tectonics accounts for many. Scientists have determined that the Earth's crust is not solid but is instead made up of several pieces, or plates, that fit together like a puzzle. The plates rest atop the semi-solid mantle, the layer below the crust. The mantle is in constant, albeit extremely slow, motion. Over millions of years, the plates on the crust have moved around. So the shape of the Earth's surface and its features have changed. Two plates may push against one another. This causes mountain ranges to form. Over millions of years, the land buckles, folds, and pushes up. Land that was once the bottom of the sea can become the tops of mountains, as evidenced by scientists finding rock formations containing fossils of sea creatures on high mountains.

3→ Plate tectonics created some mountain ranges hundreds of millions of years ago and others more recently. Newer mountain ranges—those with greater altitudes—are located on the edges of plates that have been active in the relatively recent past. The Himalayas, for instance, formed when the plate containing the Indian subcontinent pushed into southern Asia around forty to fifty million years ago. The Himalayas are among the world's youngest mountain ranges. Other young ranges are the South American Andes and the North American Rockies. **1** Each formed on a long plate boundary on the eastern edge of the Pacific Ocean. **2** Meanwhile, older mountain ranges tend to be found in areas with less recent plate tectonic activity. **3** The Appalachians, for example, were formed almost 500 million years ago, when the plate they are on was more active. **4** Another aspect related to plate tectonics concerns earthquakes. They are a result of the movements of plates and are much less common in the Appalachians than they are in the western United States, where the Rocky Mountains are.

4→ Another reason why mountains have different shapes and heights is erosion. The effects of the wind, rain, and ice on many older mountain ranges have reduced them to rounded mounds. The movements of glaciers and the recent—geologically speaking—ice ages also played a role in reducing the sizes of some mountains through erosion. Finally, if a mountain is low enough, it may be warm enough for trees to grow on it. This too can contribute to the eroding of mountains. Today, the highest mountain in the Appalachians is fewer than 2,100 meters above sea level whereas many peaks in the Himalayas rise over 8,000 meters. No one knows if the Appalachians were once as high as the Himalayas. However, hundreds of millions of years of erosion have clearly reduced them in size. It is highly likely that the Appalachians once towered to heights much greater than what they rise to today.

5➜ The Himalayas are still growing by a few millimeters a year. This is the result of the Indian plate continuing to push north, which is increasing the height of the land in the Tibetan Plateau. Geological time passes slowly, but it is inevitable that the process will stop. Then, the Himalayas will cease growing. Eventually, they will begin decreasing in size. It may take tens of millions of years, but at some point in the future, Mount Everest will no longer be the world's highest mountain. Instead, a newer, younger mountain will rise above it.

Glossary

craggy: rough; rugged

igneous: produced from intense heat, such as that of magma or lava

---

• Answers and Explanations •

1 Which of the sentences below best expresses the essential information in the highlighted sentence in the passage? *Incorrect* answer choices change the meaning in important ways or leave out essential information.

Ⓐ Scientists believe that most mountaintops were once underwater, and they can prove this with fossils that they have found on mountains.

Ⓑ Most sea creature fossils have been discovered not on the bottom of the sea but instead on the tops of mountains.

Ⓒ The discovery of fossilized sea creatures on mountains has proven that land underwater can rise and turn into mountain peaks.

Ⓓ There is as yet no explanation as to why fossils of sea creatures have been unearthed on mountains but not underwater.

1
Sentence Simplification Question
(0-1 question per passage)

Ⓒ I The highlighted sentence notes that the discovery of fossils of sea creatures on mountains has shown that land underwater can rise to become mountains. This is best described in answer choice Ⓒ.

2 In paragraph 2, the author's description of mountain formation mentions all of the following EXCEPT:

Ⓐ How plate tectonics can create mountains

Ⓑ The ability of earthquakes to form mountains

Ⓒ The manner in which volcanoes can make mountains

Ⓓ The ability of erosion to create mountains

2
Negative Factual Information Question
(0-2 questions per passage)

Ⓑ I There is no mention in the passage of earthquakes creating mountains.

3 According to paragraph 2, which of the following is true of plate tectonics?

Ⓐ It is the reason why the mantle is in constant motion.

Ⓑ It has created the greatest number of mountain ranges.

Ⓒ It is responsible for the creating of volcanoes.

Ⓓ It results in some plates colliding with one another.

3
Factual Information Question
(1-3 questions per passage)

Ⓓ I The author declares, "Two plates may push against one another."

4 In paragraph 3, why does the author mention "the North American Rockies"?

   Ⓐ To explain how they were created

   Ⓑ To compare them with the Andes Mountains

   Ⓒ To focus on their geographic location

   Ⓓ To name a young mountain range

5 The word "they" in the passage refers to

   Ⓐ plate tectonics

   Ⓑ earthquakes

   Ⓒ the movements of plates

   Ⓓ the Appalachians

6 According to paragraph 4, why have some mountain ranges decreased in size?

   Ⓐ The forces of erosion have worn them down.

   Ⓑ They had too many trees growing on their peaks.

   Ⓒ Earthquakes caused their foundations to crumble.

   Ⓓ Warm temperatures have caused them to shrink.

7 The word "inevitable" in the passage is closest in meaning to

   Ⓐ possible

   Ⓑ considerable

   Ⓒ unavoidable

   Ⓓ determined

8 Which of the following can be inferred from paragraph 5 about the Tibetan Plateau?

   Ⓐ It is the name of the Indian tectonic plate.

   Ⓑ It is the location of the Himalaya Mountains.

   Ⓒ It is slowly being eroded by natural forces.

   Ⓓ It was created tens of millions of years ago.

4
Rhetorical Purpose Question
(0-2 questions per passage)

Ⓓ | The author writes, "Other young ranges are the South American Andes and the North American Rockies."

5
Reference Question
(0-2 questions)

Ⓑ | The "they" that are less common in the Appalachians are earthquakes.

6
Factual Information Question
(1-3 questions per passage)

Ⓐ | It is written, "Another reason why mountains have different shapes and heights is erosion. The effects of the wind, rain, and ice on many older mountain ranges have reduced them to rounded mounds."

7
Vocabulary Question
(1-3 questions per passage)

Ⓒ | Something that is inevitable is unavoidable.

8
Inference Question
(0-2 questions per passage)

Ⓑ | The passage reads, "The Himalayas are still growing by a few millimeters a year. This is the result of the Indian plate continuing to push north, which is increasing the height of the land in the Tibetan Plateau. Geological time passes slowly, but it is inevitable that the process will stop. Then, the Himalayas will cease growing." It can therefore be inferred that the Himalaya Mountains are in the Tibetan Plateau.

9 Look at the four squares [■] that indicate where the following sentence could be added to the passage.

Both of them have some of the highest peaks found in the Americas.

Where would the sentence best fit?

Click on a square [■] to add the sentence to the passage.

10 *Directions:* Select the appropriate phrases from the answer choices and match them to the mountain range to which they relate. TWO of the answer choices will NOT be used. *This question is worth 3 points.*

Drag your answer choices to the spaces where they belong.
To remove an answer choice, click on it. To review the passage, click **View Text**.

Answer Choices

1. Have eroded so that their tops are rounded
2. Have some of the world's highest peaks
3. Were created around half a billion years ago
4. Are susceptible to many powerful earthquakes
5. Can be found in the western United States
6. Are fairly young mountains
7. Were formed by the actions of an Indian tectonic plate

MOUNTAIN RANGE

Himalayas
-
-
-

Appalachians
-
-

9

**Insert Text Question
(0-1 question per passage)**

*Always appears just in front of the last Reading to Learn question

■ I The sentence before the first square mentions the Andes and Rocky mountains. The sentence to be inserted notes that they both have some of the highest peaks in the Americas. So the two sentences go together.

10

Fill in a Table Question

*Partial-Credit Item

5 key items
3 correct answers: 1 point
4 correct answers: 2 points
5 correct answers: 3 points

7 key items
4 correct answers: 1 point
5 correct answers: 2 points
6 correct answers: 3 points
7 correct answers: 4 points

Himalayas: 2, 6, 7
Appalachians: 1, 3
According to the passage, the Himalayas have some of the world's highest peaks, are fairly young, and were formed by an Indian tectonic plate. As for the Appalachians, they have rounded tops due to erosion, and they were created half a billion years ago.

11 *Directions:* An introductory sentence for a brief summary of the passage is provided below. Complete the summary by selecting the THREE answer choices that express the most important ideas of the passage. Some sentences do not belong because they express ideas that are not presented in the passage or are minor ideas in the passage. *This question is worth 2 points.*

Drag your answer choices to the spaces where they belong.
To remove an answer choice, click on it. To review the passage, click **View Text.**

Forces of nature are constantly changing the heights of mountains, including causing them to rise high and eroding them until they become smaller.

-
-
-

Answer Choices

1. The Appalachian Mountains were formed hundreds of millions of years ago while the Himalayas are much younger.

2. Wind, rain, ice, and other forces, such as glaciers, can wear down mountains and make them smaller than they once were.

3. Areas such as the Andes and Rocky mountains that have active tectonic plates are susceptible to powerful earthquakes.

4. Plate tectonics, in which two plates collide with each other, is a major factor in the creation of mountain ranges.

5. The Appalachian Mountains were likely once higher than they are now, but time has seen them get eroded to lower heights.

6. Most geologists believe that Mount Everest will not always remain the highest mountain in the world.

Part B

Building Background Knowledge of TOEFL Topics

History is the study of the past. Historians learn facts about the past and also try to interpret the events that happened. Thus they seek to explain why certain actions or events happened. Historians often disagree with one another about why historical events occurred. This has caused history to be filled with different theories. All of these theories try to explain past events. Historians practice historiography, which consists of different approaches to the field they can take. There are many kinds of history. Some examples are political, military, economic, social, women's, and cultural history.

Mastering **the Question Types**

☑ Vocabulary ☐ Fill in a Table ☐ Factual Information ☐ Negative Factual Information ☑ Prose Summary
☐ Insert Text ☐ Reference ☑ Rhetorical Purpose ☐ Sentence Simplification ☐ Inference

Feudalism

¹➔ After the fall of the Roman Empire in Western Europe in 476 A.D. a long period of decline began. Trade became less frequent, and most people survived through self-sufficient farming. There was little central leadership until Charlemagne founded the Holy Roman Empire in 800 A.D. As Charlemagne and other rulers following him began to establish order, a new system of land ownership, which historians called feudalism, was developed. Feudalism depended primarily upon land ownership and **bonds** of loyalty.

Before modern times, most economic wealth came from land ownership. In Western Europe after Rome fell, most land was seized by the strong. Thereafter, its ownership was determined by hereditary rights. The noblemen who ruled the land required loyal subjects who would help them remain in power and also fight their wars. So they got men—their vassals—to swear oaths of loyalty to them. The lords then bestowed a fief—the land and the labor of the peasants living on it—upon each of their vassals.

In Western European feudalism, there were many levels of **vassalage**. The king stood at the top. His vassals were all of the high nobility, such as dukes and earls, who had huge landholdings. Below the high nobles were lower-ranking ones with less land. Further below them were the knights who only owned small plots of land. Some medieval kings had so many vassals that they could call on tens of thousands of men when war was looming.

Feudalism was not practiced identically throughout Europe. However, its essentials were similar. It was also more prominent in northern European locales, including Britain and France, than it was in Italy and other southern European locations. For several centuries, feudalism dominated the political structure in Europe. Yet it gradually disappeared during the late medieval period due to the rise of the nation-state.

Glossary
bond: a link; a connection
vassalage: the condition of subordination to a feudal lord

1 The author discusses "Charlemagne" in paragraph 1 in order to

    (A) mention his connection with the Roman Empire

    (B) note that he was the first Holy Roman Emperor

    (C) suggest that he was the person who began feudalism

    (D) say that he started to provide leadership in Europe

2 The word "essentials" in the passage is closest in meaning to

    (A) relationships

    (B) fundamentals

    (C) coordinates

    (D) rulers

3 ***Directions:*** An introductory sentence for a brief summary of the passage is provided below. Complete the summary by selecting the THREE answer choices that express the most important ideas of the passage. Some sentences do not belong because they express ideas that are not presented in the passage or are minor ideas in the passage. ***This question is worth 2 points.***

Feudalism in Western Europe developed based on a system that focused on the ownership of land as well as the loyalty of those involved in the system.

Answer Choices

1 Most land ownership in Western Europe was passed on from generation to generation by hereditary rights.

2 There were descending levels of land ownership involved in the ranking of a king's vassals.

3 The vassals of a lord received fiefs in return for pledging to be loyal to the lord and to fight for him.

4 From the fall of Rome to the time of Charlemagne, there was little centralized government in Western Europe.

5 People in the southern and northern regions of Europe practiced feudalism in ways different from one another.

6 A vassal was expected to help his lord in battle if there were ever any wars that had to be fought.

Summarizing Complete the summary by using the words or phrases given in the box.

centralized leadership	subjects	the nation-state	loyalty bonds

After Rome fell, there was little _____ in Western Europe for centuries. Following Charlemagne though, the system of feudalism was formed. It focused on land ownership and _____ . Nobles owned the land, but they needed _____ to help them. So they gave their vassals fiefs of land and peasants. In return, the vassals fought for their lords. In the feudal system, the king ruled while peasants were at the bottom. Feudalism eventually disappeared and gave way to _____ .

Mastering **the Question Types**

B

☑ Vocabulary   ☑ Fill in a Table   ☐ Factual Information   ☑ Negative Factual Information   ☐ Prose Summary
☐ Insert Text   ☐ Reference   ☐ Rhetorical Purpose   ☐ Sentence Simplification   ☑ Inference

The Great Fire of London

For centuries, most people constructed their homes with nearby inexpensive materials. Throughout Europe, this meant that many houses were built with wood, making them **fire hazards**. At various times in the past, devastating fires swept through cities.

This happened in London, England, in the year 1666. On September 2, a fire started in a bakery located on Pudding Lane near London Bridge. Fires were commonplace in London, but the city had not gotten any rain for several weeks, and summer had been unusually hot. The fire spread quickly, and hundreds of houses burned to the ground. The wind picked up and spread the flames farther. Firefighting efforts failed dramatically, and people were forced to grab their valuables and then swiftly evacuated.

³→ The fire rapidly spread out of control. **Firebreaks** were created by pulling down houses in the fire's path, yet those efforts failed. Buildings were destroyed with gunpowder to slow the spread, but those efforts frightened Londoners into believing the French were attacking the city, causing tremendous panic. By September 4, more than half of London was burning. King Charles II himself joined a bucket brigade to help quench the flames. By September 6, the fire was finally extinguished, but an enormous amount of damage had occurred. Approximately one-fifth of London had been untouched by the fire. Elsewhere in the city, thousands of homes, businesses, churches, and other establishments were completely destroyed. Hundreds of thousands of people were homeless, yet oddly, only six people were killed by the conflagration.

⁴→ The reconstruction effort took years. For instance, St. Paul's Cathedral was rebuilt. Work on it started in 1675 and concluded in 1711. Other smaller buildings were repaired or built much more rapidly. Overall, London was greatly improved after it was rebuilt, and the conditions in the city improved in the decades after the great fire.

Glossary

fire hazard: something that may either start a fire or may provide fuel for a fire to spread
firebreak: a strip of cleared land created to halt the spread of a fire

1 In paragraph 3, all of the following questions are answered EXCEPT:

(A) How much of the city of London was damaged by the great fire?

(B) What enabled the people of London finally to put out the great fire?

(C) What was the reason that Londoners thought the city was under attack?

(D) How did the king provide assistance during the great fire?

2 In paragraph 4, the author implies that St. Paul's Cathedral

(A) was the largest building in London in the seventeenth century

(B) was destroyed by the fire in London in the year 1666

(C) was located near the place where the great fire started

(D) was the site where six people lost their lives in the fire

3 *Directions:* Select the appropriate sentences from the answer choices and match them to the cause and effect of the Great Fire of London to which they relate. TWO of the answer choices will NOT be used. **This question is worth 3 points.**

Answer Choices

1. The French were believed to be attacking the city.
2. The weather in London had been very hot and dry.
3. The majority of the city burned to the ground.
4. It required decades to reconstruct some buildings.
5. A large number of homes in London were constructed of wood.
6. The city of London was made better overall.
7. Many people lost their homes and valuables.

THE GREAT FIRE OF LONDON

Cause

•

•

Effect

•

•

•

Summarizing Complete the summary by using the words or phrases given in the box.

| firebreaks and gunpowder | made of wood | rebuilding London | thousands of buildings |

Large fires were problems in the past because many homes were _____. On September 2, 1666, a fire broke out in London. It spread out of control due to the wind and hot, dry weather. _____ failed to stop the fire, and even the king helped try to extinguish it. The fire was finally put out on September 6, but _____ were destroyed, and hundreds of thousands of people lost their lives. _____ took a long time, but the city was improved afterward.

Mastering **the Question Types**

C

☐ Vocabulary   ☐ Fill in a Table   ☑ Factual Information   ☐ Negative Factual Information   ☐ Prose Summary
☑ Insert Text   ☑ Reference   ☐ Rhetorical Purpose   ☑ Sentence Simplification   ☐ Inference

Alexander the Great

Alexander the Great was one of the greatest military commanders not only in ancient times but also in recorded history. He was born in Macedonia, north of Greece, in 356 B.C. His father, Phillip II, was also a great military commander who taught Alexander everything he knew. In 338 B.C., Phillip led his army against the Greeks and defeated them. After Phillip was assassinated in 336 B.C., Alexander became the leader of the Macedonians. He believed his destiny was to **vanquish** the great Persian Empire, which was located in western Asia. Starting in 334 B.C., Alexander led the Macedonian army on a ten-year campaign against Persia in which his army won almost every battle it fought and marched as far as India. On the return journey, Alexander fell ill in Babylon and died in 323 B.C.

Alexander and Phillip, despite being Macedonians, both embraced many Greek ideas. **1** Phillip had made the Athenian **dialect** of Greek the official language of Macedonia. **2** One of Alexander's teachers had been Aristotle, the great Greek philosopher. **3** Alexander had also spent time in the Greek city of Thebes during his youth. **4** As the Macedonian army moved eastward, the language, customs, and ideals of Greece were brought along with it. These spread far and wide across the empire Alexander conquered as many of the defeated people adopted Greek notions. This was called Hellenism.

3→ Alexander's successors continued to spread both Greek ideas and the Greek language as they maintained power in the old Persian Empire for hundreds of years. In addition, the newly founded city of Alexandria in Egypt became the center of Hellenism. Scholars from all over the region moved there to study. This influence continued after Greece was conquered by the Romans and others. Even today, many signs of Hellenism are evident in the Middle East.

Glossary
vanquish: to defeat
dialect: a local or irregular version of a language

1 Which of the sentences below best expresses the essential information in the highlighted sentence in the passage? *Incorrect* answer choices change the meaning in important ways or leave out essential information.

   Ⓐ While almost never being defeated by the Persians, Alexander not only conquered them in 334 B.C. but also traveled to India.

   Ⓑ In the decade of fighting that began in 334 B.C., Alexander's army rarely lost any fights against the Persians while on its way to India.

   Ⓒ By 334 B.C., Alexander's army had conquered the Persian Empire, won every time it engaged the enemy, and gone to India.

   Ⓓ Alexander's ultimate goal was to get to India, which he did after ten years of fighting against the Persians beginning in 334 B.C.

2 The word "it" in the passage refers to

   Ⓐ the Macedonian army

   Ⓑ eastward

   Ⓒ the language

   Ⓓ Greece

3 According to paragraph 3, which of the following is true of Hellenism?

   Ⓐ It has persisted in the Middle East until modern times.

   Ⓑ It was responsible for the defeat of the Persian Empire.

   Ⓒ It made Greek the dominant language throughout the Middle East.

   Ⓓ It was responsible for the founding of Alexandria.

4 Look at the four squares [■] that indicate where the following sentence could be added to the passage.

These facts all combined to give Alexander an appreciation of Greece and its culture.

Where would the sentence best fit?

Summarizing   Complete the summary by using the words or phrases given in the box.

customs, and ideals	greatly influenced	influence	killed

Philip of Macedonia conquered Greece in 338 B.C. but was _____ two years later. His son Alexander then took over the Macedonians. His goal was to defeat the Persian Empire. It took him ten years, but he was successful. Then, Alexander died in 323 B.C. Alexander was _____ by Greek culture. His army spread the Greek language, _____ throughout the lands it conquered. This was called Hellenism. Even after Alexander died, Hellenism remained _____ in the Middle East.

Geography and the Early American Economy

Virtually all early American colonists farmed and fished. But by the late 1700s, two separate economic <u>paradigms</u> had emerged. The northern colonies were more industrial in nature while the southern colonies survived primarily by farming. Geography was a major reason for these differing economies. The hilly, rocky northern colonies were not conducive to farming. So people simply abandoned it for other pursuits. Meanwhile, the more open, wider southern colonies were perfect for agriculture.

The first thirteen American colonies ran down the Atlantic coast from New Hampshire in the north to Georgia in the south. Much of the coastline of Massachusetts, Rhode Island, Connecticut, and New York—all northern colonies—was rocky but had many harbors. Thus fishing, as well as shipbuilding, became a major industry there. The land inland was both rocky and hilly. **1** This made it less than ideal for large farms. **2** While people in the North, like most settlers, still farmed, their farms were small. **3** Northern farmers customarily grew enough food to support their families and then sold the surplus. **4** But the land changed starting around Maryland and Virginia as it moved southward. It became more level and less rocky. Enormous farms—called plantations— soon covered the land there.

[3]→ By 1775, when the American Revolution began, the two economic systems were well established. Southern farms were much larger than northern ones. Southern farms were also supported by slave labor. This had been a fact of life since 1619, when the first black African slaves were imported. The plantations relied upon tobacco and cotton as their major cash crops. The North, meanwhile, was developing an industrial economy. The hilly land there provided many sources of falling water. In the days prior to steam and electric power, waterfalls ran machinery in mills and textile factories. Then, in the late 1700s, the steam engine was perfected in England. It was soon imported to America. The North was equipped with the infrastructure to use this new technology. By the mid-1800s, the northern American states were second only to England in industrial strength.

As the years progressed, the northern and southern economies became more <u>divergent</u>. This was a major factor in the Civil War in the 1860s. The North relied upon its heavy industry to produce weapons and other war materials. The South could not do the same. Its dependence on farming and reliance on imports of finished goods hurt its war effort. When the North blockaded its ports, the South could not export cotton, tobacco, and other raw materials. So its economy collapsed. This was a contributing factor to the North's victory.

Glossary

paradigm: a standard; a model
divergent: differing; varying; opposing

NOTE

Jamestown was the first permanent colony in America to be founded by the British. Jamestown was located in Virginia. It was founded in 1607. Later, in 1620, the Pilgrims arrived in Plymouth, Massachusetts. They sailed across the Atlantic Ocean on the *Mayflower*.

Because there was less farming in the North, people tended to live in larger cities. Most of the American colonies' biggest cities were in the North. They included Boston, New York, and Philadelphia.

Some plantations covered hundreds of acres. They required an enormous number of people to operate.

Most African slaves were in the South. However, many people also kept slaves in the North. Over time, several states in the North outlawed slavery. In the 1800s, this led to tension with many of the people living in the South.

After starting in England, the Industrial Revolution quickly moved to America. Many Americans made new inventions that helped the Industrial Revolution continue throughout the 1800s.

1 The word "it" in the passage refers to

(A) nature

(B) farming

(C) geography

(D) a major reason

2 The author's description of plantations in paragraph 3 mentions which of the following?

(A) How the majority of the workers on them were slaves

(B) Which crops were primarily grown to make money

(C) The fact that some of them covered thousands of acres

(D) The number of them with mills or textile factories located nearby

3 Look at the four squares [■] that indicate where the following sentence could be added to the passage.

Farmers thus frequently had to clear the land of stones and rocks while they were tilling their fields.

Where would the sentence best fit?

4 *Directions:* Select the appropriate sentences from the answer choices and match them to the location to which they relate. TWO of the answer choices will NOT be used. ***This question is worth 3 points.***

Answer Choices	**LOCATION**
① Their farmers mostly provided only for their families.	**Northern Colonies**
② More of their people worked in the agricultural sector.	•
③ People other than the British founded them.	•
④ They were responsible for starting the Civil War.	•
⑤ They had a geography that was fairly level.	**Southern Colonies**
⑥ They imported machinery from Great Britain.	•
⑦ Many of their shores had excellent harbors.	•

Summarizing **Complete the summary by filling in the blanks.**

Almost all early Americans farmed and fished, but the American colonies developed different types of economies. _____ was a primary reason for this. The northern colonies were into _____ because of their good harbors. But their rocky, hilly land made farming difficult. Thus, the North developed more industries. The South, however, had good land for farming, so _____ arose there. When the Civil War began, the two regions were very different. The North used its _____ to defeat the agrarian South.

Ancient Greek City-States

City-states dominated ancient Greece. These included such places as Athens, Sparta, Thebes, and Corinth. City-states were similar to modern countries, albeit small ones. They included the actual city they were named for and the surrounding villages and farms. Despite their people all being Greek and sharing the same language and heritage, each place had its own ways that set it apart from the others. For instance, every city-state had its own laws, customs, economy, and culture. In addition, while the city-states sometimes united against external threats, such as the Persians, in other instances, they battled one another for power in Greece.

2→ City-states in Greece originated at the end of the period called the Greek dark ages. They lasted from around 1200 B.C. to 800 B.C. There was no writing in Greece then, so little of what happened is known. As the dark ages ended, city-states began emerging. They started as villages that developed around a larger town. They were often formed for protection and trading purposes. Many had kings, but most turned to political systems involving their citizens. Discussions were held, and citizens voted on what to do. This marked the beginning of democracy.

Citizens were frequently involved in Greek city-state politics. Yet the definition of a citizen varied everywhere. In some places, every free man was a citizen. In others, citizens were only property-owning men. In virtually no cases were women or slaves considered citizens. The government in each city-state also differed. It was not always democracy. An **oligarchy** of leading citizens was one common form.

Economically, most city-states depended on farming for **sustenance**. Some, such as Athens, amassed wealth by trading and maintained large merchant fleets and navies. Others, such as Sparta, were land powers. Being relatively close to one another, the city-states typically had good relations. However, warfare occasionally flared up between city-states. One such example of this was the Peloponnesian War between Sparta and Athens in the fifth century B.C.

The concept of the city-state did not remain only on the Balkan Peninsula. Instead, the Greeks exported their ideas. They colonized islands in the Aegean Sea and as far west as Sicily. There, they introduced city-states. Even Rome's government was influenced by the Greeks. Eventually, though, the system declined in Greece. In 338 B.C., Alexander the Great conquered the entire peninsula. For the first time, every Greek city-state was united under one ruler. Later, in the middle of the second century B.C., the Roman Empire defeated Greece. Thereafter, city-states would emerge in other places—such as in medieval and Renaissance Italy—but they no longer existed in Greece.

NOTE

Greek city-states typically dominated their geographical regions. Still, some became more powerful than others. For much of ancient Greek history, Athens and Sparta were the two most powerful city-states.

Athens is famous as the birthplace of democracy. In addition, many notable historical individuals were from Athens. They include Socrates, Plato, Pericles, Alcibiades, and Solon.

For most of history, women in all societies had little power. For instance, it was only in the 1900s that women were allowed to vote in most countries.

The Peloponnesian War lasted from 431 to 404 B.C. It was primarily between Sparta and Athens. Other city-states, however, were sometimes involved. Sparta eventually won the war and defeated Athens.

The ancient Greeks were responsible for much of Western culture. However, after Alexander the Great, Greece itself was frequently ruled by empires. These included the Roman Empire, the Byzantine Empire, and the Ottoman Empire. Greece finally regained its freedom in the 1820s.

Glossary

oligarchy: a form of government in which a small number of people or families rule
sustenance: food; nourishment; survival

1   Which of the sentences below best expresses the essential information in the highlighted sentence in the passage? *Incorrect* answer choices change the meaning in important ways or leave out essential information.

- Ⓐ The Persians sometimes convinced the city-states of Greece to battle one another instead of uniting as allies.
- Ⓑ When they were united to fight enemies such as the Persians, the city-states had no time to fight one another.
- Ⓒ Since they were all rivals, the Greek city-states rarely united, even to fight enemies such as the Persians.
- Ⓓ Greek city-states were known to clash with one another domestically but could ally to fight foreign enemies.

2   The author discusses "the Greek dark ages" in paragraph 2 in order to

- Ⓐ compare the political situation in them with the age of the city-state
- Ⓑ explain why it was not possible for city-states to have existed then
- Ⓒ make note of the time period during which city-states were founded
- Ⓓ counter a theory about the origins of the first Greek city-states

3   In stating that warfare occasionally "flared up," the author means that warfare sometimes

- Ⓐ ceased
- Ⓒ occurred
- Ⓑ threatened
- Ⓓ persisted

4   *Directions:* An introductory sentence for a brief summary of the passage is provided below. Complete the summary by selecting the THREE answer choices that express the most important ideas of the passage. Some sentences do not belong because they express ideas that are not presented in the passage or are minor ideas in the passage. *This question is worth 2 points.*

The city-state played an integral role in many aspects of people's lives in ancient Greece.

Answer Choices

- ① City-states are believed to have been founded to protect the lives of the people who lived in them.
- ② City-states were established in the Middle Ages thanks to the influence of the ancient Greeks.
- ③ Some city-states became rich by using ships to engage in maritime trade throughout the region.
- ④ Alexander the Great managed to defeat all of the Greek city-states and united them by 338 B.C.
- ⑤ Individual city-states, despite being close to one another, had their own distinct customs and practices.
- ⑥ Democracy, which is said to have been first practiced in Athens, was the form of government in most city-states.

Summarizing   Complete the summary by filling in the blanks.

City-states dominated ancient Greece. Each city-state had its own laws, customs, economy, and culture. The first ones arose when the _____ ended. Most were founded to _____ . The governments of city-states were often _____ . Some, such as Athens, became wealthy through trade. Others, such as Sparta, became powerful thanks to _____ . City-states sometimes battled each other in wars. After Alexander the Great conquered them, city-states disappeared in Greece. Yet they later appeared in medieval and Renaissance Italy.

Mastering **the Subject**

Heian Japan

The Heian period in Japan lasted from 794 to 1185. It is noteworthy for several reasons. It saw powerful families influencing the emperor and his court. Warriors gained importance, and the samurai class began during it. Buddhism began shaping the Japanese way of life. Finally, both art and literature developed then. In fact, many Japanese regard this age as the peak of their cultural achievements.

²➜ The Heian period is named after the city of Heian, which is modern-day Kyoto. Nagaoka had previously been the Japanese capital. But Emperor Kammu moved it to Heian in 794. It remained the capital until 1868. This was the year when Emperor Meiji moved the imperial seat of power to Tokyo. During the Heian period, land-owning families controlled Japan. The strongest was the Fujiwara family. Starting around 850 A.D., it held great **sway** over the emperor and his court. It achieved its power by becoming interrelated to the imperial family through marriage. Many emperors had Fujiwara mothers. Often, the emperor was too young to rule. So a Fujiwara member served as the **regent**. Members of the Fujiwara also held critical positions in the imperial court and government. This let them make many imperial decisions for over 200 years.

³➜ To stay in control, the Fujiwara relied upon strong military forces. This led to the rise of the samurai class of warriors. The samurais were at first akin to local law enforcers in the provinces. They were loyal to the emperor. So they were also loyal to the Fujiwara. Gradually, they shifted their loyalties to families in the provinces. By the end of the Heian period, these families used the samurais to rebel against the Fujiwara.

⁴➜ Before the families revolted, the dominance of the Fujiwara resulted in a long period of peace. The absence of constant warfare let Japanese culture develop. At that time, Chinese characters were used in Japan. But the Japanese developed the *kana* writing system during the Heian period. This resulted in an outpouring of high-quality Japanese literature. Buddhism also gained more significance during this time. More people turned to it as a religious faith. It also deeply affected the artwork created then.

The decline of the Heian period began in 1068. That year, a new emperor—one without a Fujiwara mother—ascended the throne. The Fujiwara tried to retain power yet failed. Other families throughout the country gathered military forces. There was a struggle for power. Over the next century, there were numerous rebellions. Finally, the Heian period ended in 1185. For the next 700 years, military strongmen—called daimyos—would dominate Japan.

NOTE

Many historians consider the Heian period to have been a part of Japan's golden age. They often include it and Nara Japan, which lasted from 710 to 794, in a period called Classical Japan.

Modern-day Kyoto is an important city for the study of Japanese history. Many buildings—including palaces and castles—from the past remain. There are also numerous imperial tombs there. Today, Kyoto is a center of Buddhism in Japan.

One of the most powerful members of the Fujiwara family was Michinaga, who lived from 966 to 1028. After he died, the family began to lose power.

The samurai had a low status in Japan at first. However, as warfare became more common in the country, the status of the samurai began to increase.

After the Heian period ended, the country was not as united as it once was. The result was that warfare became much more common than it was during the Heian period.

Glossary

sway: power or influence, often in a political situation
regent: a person who temporarily wields power in the place of another, such as a king or emperor

1 According to paragraph 2, which of the following is NOT true of the Fujiwara family?

    Ⓐ Its members served as emperors for two centuries.

    Ⓑ Some of the women in it gave birth to future emperors.

    Ⓒ It was the preeminent family during the Heian period.

    Ⓓ Its members were often related to the emperor.

2 According to paragraph 3, which of the following is true of the samurai?

    Ⓐ They eventually became the emperor's police force.

    Ⓑ They were established by the Fujiwara family.

    Ⓒ They had a role in rebellions against the emperor.

    Ⓓ They were the best-trained warriors in Japan.

3 In paragraph 4, the author implies that Japanese literature during the Heian period

    Ⓐ often had a religious nature to it

    Ⓑ was written mostly in Chinese characters

    Ⓒ was more abundant than in previous times

    Ⓓ is better than much modern literature

4 *Directions:* An introductory sentence for a brief summary of the passage is provided below. Complete the summary by selecting the THREE answer choices that express the most important ideas of the passage. Some sentences do not belong because they express ideas that are not presented in the passage or are minor ideas in the passage. ***This question is worth 2 points.***

The Heian period in Japan was dominated by the Fujiwara family, which exerted control over the imperial family and helped establish a time of peace during which culture flourished.

Answer Choices

1. Rebellious families employed samurais to fight the Fujiwara all throughout the Japanese countryside.

2. Many Fujiwara women's sons became emperors, which enabled them to have influence in the government.

3. Both Japanese literature and art were focused on during this time since there was little fighting during it.

4. Once the capital was moved to Tokyo, it was no longer possible for the Fujiwara family to exert control over the emperor.

5. It was necessary for the Fujiwara family to raise armies of samurais in order to keep wars from breaking out.

6. While the Chinese language declined in influence, the Buddhist religion became important to many Japanese then.

Summarizing Complete the summary by filling in the blanks.

The Heian period in Japan lasted from 794 to 1185. Heian became the capital of Japan in 794. The Fujiwara were the strongest of many _____ during this age. They became interrelated with the _____, which increased their power. Members of the Fujiwara often made imperial decisions. They maintained _____ to help prevent wars. During this peaceful age, literature and art in Japan developed. The Fujiwara eventually lost influence, there were many rebellions, and Japan became controlled by _____.

The Spanish Invasion of the New World

A meeting between Herman Cortez and an Aztec chief

1 → Christopher Columbus sailed across the Atlantic Ocean and discovered the New World in 1492. An Italian who sailed for Spain, Columbus made four trips to the islands in the Caribbean Sea. Columbus himself never set foot on mainland Central or South America, but his successors did. There, they discovered two prosperous empires: the Aztecs in central Mexico and the Incas in the Peruvian highlands. The Spanish considered them threats. So they went to war against both empires to become the reigning power in the New World.

2 → The Spanish explorers in the fifteenth and sixteenth centuries were called conquistadors. The two most famous were Hernan Cortez and Francisco Pizarro. Cortez conquered the Aztecs while Pizarro defeated the Incas. Both went to the New World as colonists, Pizarro arrived in 1502, and Cortez landed in 1504. Cortez was the first to reap glory. **1** In July 1519, he landed an expedition at Veracruz. **2** There, he ordered his ships burned to prevent his men from retreating. **3** With only 600 men, a few horses, and some cannons, his tiny army marched inland. **4** As they traveled, they fought some minor battles. The Spanish also found many natives willing to fight alongside them. These natives' tribes had often been defeated by the ruthless Aztecs. Thus, they were eager for revenge. For almost two years, the Spanish experienced some setbacks and lost a few men. However, against great numerical odds, they managed to crush the Aztecs. Almost all aspects of the Aztecs—their history, culture, and customs—were eliminated.

3 → Pizarro's conquest of the Incas, who lived in modern-day Peru, followed a similar pattern: A small band of men bested a numerically superior force. Starting in 1522, the Spanish heard rumors of a wealthy empire in South America. This was the Inca Empire. Pizarro was chosen to find it. Two early expeditions in 1524 and

1526 failed. Finally, in 1532, he found the Incas. While he had fewer than 200 soldiers, Pizarro still defeated an **exponentially** larger Incan force. His men even captured the Incan emperor, whom they ransomed for treasure and then later executed. By 1535, the Inca Empire had been defeated. Like the Aztecs, the Incas soon vanished.

4➜ Both Cortez and Pizarro had several advantages over their foes. The Spanish had metal weapons and armor, gunpowder weapons, and horses. These were all unknown to the natives. But the Spaniards' greatest ally was disease. The natives lacked **immunity** to European diseases such as smallpox and influenza. These diseases ravaged native populations. Some historians believe they killed millions. A few estimates claim that around ninety percent of some tribes were killed by imported diseases.

5➜ Those natives not killed were weakened by the diseases. This made it simpler for rather small bands of Spaniards to conquer the Aztecs and the Incas, which had enormous populations. Still, even without the advantage of fighting an enemy weakened by diseases, the Spanish would likely have triumphed. But they definitely would have lost many more men. And they would have had to struggle for a longer period of time.

Glossary
exponentially: incredibly; tremendously
immunity: protection from something; the ability not to be harmed by something

1   According to paragraph 1, which of the following is true of Christopher Columbus?

ⓐ He was interested in increasing the holdings of Spain.

ⓑ He made multiple journeys across the Atlantic Ocean.

ⓒ He founded colonies on islands in the Caribbean Sea.

ⓓ He sailed to the New World under the Italian flag.

2   The word "reap" in the passage is closest in meaning to

ⓐ attain

ⓑ seek

ⓒ refuse

ⓓ consider

3   According to paragraph 2, Hernan Cortez recruited allies to fight the Aztecs because

ⓐ he promised them treasure if they would help defeat the Aztecs

ⓑ they wanted to sacrifice all of the Aztec warriors they captured

ⓒ they sought revenge because of how the Aztecs had treated them

ⓓ they believed Cortez would kill them if they did not help him

4   In paragraph 2, the author implies that Cortez's military force

ⓐ rarely took prisoners in their war against the Aztecs

ⓑ had the most advanced weapons of the age

ⓒ made attempts to understand the natives' cultures

ⓓ was much smaller than that of the Aztecs

5   The word "it" in the passage refers to

ⓐ modern-day Peru

ⓑ a numerically superior force

ⓒ South America

ⓓ the Inca Empire

6   According to paragraph 3, which of the following is NOT true of the Inca Empire?

ⓐ It had an army much larger than Pizarro's force.

ⓑ It was initially hard for the Spanish to locate.

ⓒ It fell because its emperor was killed in battle.

ⓓ It did not successfully resist the Spanish attacks.

7   According to paragraph 4, many Native Americans were killed because

ⓐ they were captured and then executed while prisoners

ⓑ the Spanish were efficient at killing many of them in battle

ⓒ they died when famines struck many of their lands

ⓓ they could not resist the diseases the Spanish brought with them

8 Which of the following can be inferred from paragraph 5 about the Spanish?

    Ⓐ They were not prepared to lose large numbers of men in the New World.

    Ⓑ They had an easy time in the New World because of the effects of diseases.

    Ⓒ They intentionally infected many of the natives with fatal diseases.

    Ⓓ The populations of the Aztec and Inca empires were greater than Spain's population.

9 Look at the four squares [■] that indicate where the following sentence could be added to the passage.

This act proved to be a highly motivating factor for Cortez's men.

Where would the sentence best fit?

    Click on a square [■] to add the sentence to the passage.

10 *Directions:* Select the appropriate phrases from the answer choices and match them to the conquistador to whom they relate. TWO of the answer choices will NOT be used. *This question is worth 3 points.*

    Drag your answer choices to the spaces where they belong.
    To remove an answer choice, click on it. To review the passage, click on **View Text**.

Answer Choices

1. Had only a small number of his men killed in battle

2. Did not succeed in his first two attempts against the natives

3. Recruited forces that already lived on the continent

4. Was responsible for the discovery of the New World

5. Fought against the natives living in South America

6. Destroyed his own ships to stop his men from leaving

7. Personally introduced foreign diseases that killed the natives

CONQUISTADOR

Hernan Cortez

- •
- •
- •

Francisco Pizarro

- •
- •

1 The Silk Road

China and the Roman Empire were thousands of miles apart, yet there was trade between the two. It was done on the Silk Road, a network of trade routes that ran from the Mediterranean Sea all the way to China. Merchants transported goods on it. Travelers also used it to go from Rome to China and to places in between. The Italian Marco Polo followed the Silk Road on his famous journey east in the thirteenth century. The Silk Road fell out of use after the Byzantine Empire was defeated in 1453 since it became too dangerous to travel on.

2 The Industrial Revolution

Generations of men used human and animal power to do work. They also had access to simple machines such as the wheel and the lever. Yet these were all fairly inefficient. So work was done slowly. In the 1700s though, people began to invent more complex machines. This began the Industrial Revolution. One of the most important inventions was the steam engine. It enabled work to be done much more swiftly. Soon, this led to further developments, particularly in the textile, manufacturing, shipping, and transportation industries. The Industrial Revolution ultimately helped create the modern civilization that exists today.

3 The Roman Empire

For centuries, Rome thrived as a republic. However, it was eventually transformed into an empire by Augustus, who ruled from 27 B.C. until 14 A.D. The empire would last until 476, when Gothic barbarians took over the city. At its peak, Rome dominated the European continent and even reached all the way into northern England. Long after it fell, Rome had an effect on the areas it had conquered. Its language—Latin—became the basis for the Italian, French, and Spanish languages. Its infrastructure—especially its roads—helped unite many areas. And it enabled Christianity to spread throughout all of Europe.

4 Industrialization in the United States

When colonists first moved to America, they farmed and fished. Slowly, a few industries began to develop. But starting around 1860, the process of industrialization in the United States began. Many factors caused this. First, transportation methods got better. Railroads were built all across the country. Waterways were improved, too. These let finished goods be transported more easily. In addition, mass-production methods such as the assembly line began to be used around the turn of the century. Finally, the large numbers of immigrants arriving in the U.S. provided a large labor force to work in the factories.

5 Renaissance Italy

From the late fourteenth century to around 1600, the Renaissance took place in Italy. This was a period when there was a rebirth of learning in Europe. From Italy, the Renaissance quickly spread to almost every country in Europe. But it began in Italy. The Italian Renaissance was most noteworthy for its cultural achievements. It was prominent in city-states such as Venice, Rome, and Florence. There were great advances in many fields. Among them were art, science, engineering, mathematics, and languages. Men such as Petrarch, Leonardo da Vinci, and Michelangelo were notable figures during this time.

6 Improvements in Communication Methods

For most of human history, news traveled slowly through word of mouth or by print. Even going from one town to another could take a day. In the 1800s, two inventions—the telegraph and the telephone—accelerated the speed of communication. When Morse code was invented in the 1840s, messages could be sent electronically. Telegraph wires were quickly put up—even across the Atlantic Ocean. The speed of unspoken communications became much faster. In 1876, the telephone was invented. This let people speak with one another electronically. Thus communication between people far from one another became much faster than before.

7 ▶ European Colonization

In the 1400s, the Age of Discovery began in Europe. Europeans traveled by ship to places in Africa, Asia, and North and South America. One primary result was that they colonized many of the lands they visited. The Europeans basically took over the lands and used them and the people living in them for their own purposes. They sent colonists to these places to help oversee things or to start new settlements. Life was often brutal for the colonized people. The Spanish in particular plundered their colonies. In the 1700s and 1800s, many colonies rebelled and gained their freedom.

8 ▶ Great Britain as a Global Power

Despite being a small island nation, Great Britain was once the world's most powerful country. A popular saying in the 1800s was "the sun never sets on the British empire" since Britain had colonies all over the world. Britain became powerful for several reasons. One was that its navy was the preeminent naval force on the planet. It protected shipping lanes and defeated other challengers to Britain's power. The Industrial Revolution also started in Britain. This gave Britain a great advantage over other countries. Its industrial might granted the country more wealth and a technological lead over its rivals.

9 ▶ The Effects of Population Growth

Around 10,000 B.C., the Earth's human population was around four million. Around 500 B.C., it reached 100 million. It did not get to one billion until sometime between 1800 and 1850. Today, there are more than seven billion people. Historically, as the human population grows, technology improves. When people have enough food to eat, the population tends to increase. Then, the people who do not need to be involved in agriculture can spend their time on other endeavors. These often improve the overall state of civilization. During times when the population declines—such as from famine or plague—human society traditionally regresses to more primitive levels.

10 ▶ Early American Colonists

The British settled most of the areas that became the thirteen American colonies. These colonists had various motives for leaving Britain. Some— the Pilgrims and Puritans of Massachusetts— left for religious reasons. Others, such as those in Virginia, wanted to benefit financially by farming. Yet not all of the settlers in these areas came from Britain. In the northern areas, there were French settlers. Many Dutch settlers lived in New York and Pennsylvania. And the Spanish settled in the southern areas around Florida. This helped increase the cultural diversity of the colonies.

11 ▶ The Middle Ages

In 476, the Roman Empire fell. In 1453, Constantinople, the capital of the Byzantine Empire, fell. The period in between was the Middle Ages. At first, there was a period of decline. There were few centralized powers, and there was a lack of learning and knowledge. This changed around the year 800 as various kingdoms were established in the areas today known as England, France, Germany, and Spain. Eventually, they became the basis for modern-day nation-states. One constant during the Middle Ages was the Church. It dominated religious as well as scholastic life for those living during medieval times.

12 ▶ Latin American Independence Movements

In the 1800s, the Europeans had many colonies. Yet most people in these places yearned for freedom. In the late 1700s, there were revolutions in America and France. These inspired people in other places to rebel, too. In Latin America, which includes Central and South America, there were several independence movements in the late 1700s and 1800s. They happened in Haiti, Argentina, Peru, Venezuela, Mexico, Brazil, and other places. Two famous leaders from this period were Simon Bolivar and Miguel Hidalgo. Many revolutions were successful. As a result, lots of people gained their freedom.

- **abandon** (v) to give up; to stop
- **adopt** (v) to take on; to assume
- **akin** (adj) similar; resembling something else
- **amass** (v) to collect; to accrue
- **ascend** (v) to take over; to rise to a certain position
- **assassinate** (v) to kill a person of importance, such as a political leader or general
- **blockade** (v) to prevent others from leaving or entering a place
- **coast** (n) the shoreline of an area
- **collapse** (v) to crumble; to fail; to fall to pieces
- **colonist** (n) a settler; a person who goes to settle in another, often uncivilized, land
- **commander** (n) a leader, typically in a military organization
- **conducive** (adj) beneficial; advantageous; helpful
- **conflagration** (n) a fire, typically a large one
- **conquer** (v) to defeat, usually in battle
- **democracy** (n) a system of government in which the people take great part
- **dependence** (n) reliance
- **destiny** (n) fate
- **dominate** (v) to rule over others
- **eliminate** (v) to wipe out; to kill; to destroy
- **embrace** (v) to accept
- **execute** (v) to kill
- **export** (v) to send out of one country and to another
- **feudalism** (n) a system of government used in medieval Europe
- **fief** (n) a landholding given to a vassal in the feudal system
- **gunpowder** (n) an explosive material used for weapons and for blasting
- **harbor** (n) a port
- **hereditary** (adj) passed on from one ancestor to the next
- **heritage** (n) a tradition; an inheritance
- **imperial** (adj) relating to an empire
- **import** (v) to bring into one country from another
- **infrastructure** (n) the facilities and systems in a certain place
- **interrelated** (adj) connected
- **knight** (n) a medieval warrior who fought with a sword while wearing armor
- **landholding** (n) the land that is owned by a person or group
- **leadership** (n) the people in control of a group, organization, or country

- **loom** (v) to threaten; to impend
- **loyalty** (n) devotion; faithfulness
- **medieval** (adj) relating to the Middle Ages
- **navy** (n) seaborne military forces
- **noteworthy** (adj) important; worth mentioning
- **oath** (n) a promise; a vow
- **outpouring** (n) an outburst
- **ownership** (n) legal possession of something
- **peak** (n) the highest point of something
- **peasant** (n) a serf; a poor person who typically farms the land
- **peninsula** (n) an area of land surrounded by water on three sides
- **politics** (n) government; affairs of state
- **port** (n) a place where ships can dock close to land
- **prominent** (adj) important; influential
- **pursuit** (n) an activity that one engages in
- **ransom** (v) to refuse to give up something that has been seized until money is paid
- **ravage** (v) to destroy; to harm someone or something very much
- **reigning** (adj) ruling; in power, usually referring to a king or member of the nobility
- **retain** (v) to keep; to maintain
- **retreat** (v) to move back or away from; to run away, especially in battle
- **revolt** (v) to rebel; to fight against political authority
- **ruthless** (adj) vicious; cruel
- **quench** (v) to put out, as in a fire
- **seize** (v) to take; to grab
- **slave** (n) a person who is owned by another
- **subject** (n) a person who lives in a land ruled by a king or queen
- **surplus** (n) extra; excess; a supply of more than what is needed
- **surrounding** (adj) neighboring; nearby
- **survive** (v) to live; to manage to remain alive
- **textile** (n) cloth or clothing produced by weaving or sewing
- **throne** (n) the seat upon which a king or queen sits
- **triumph** (v) to win; to be victorious; to defeat one's enemies
- **vanish** (v) to disappear
- **vassal** (n) an underling in the feudal system
- **warrior** (n) a person skilled at fighting, often in hand-to-hand combat

⚓ **Choose the word or phrase closest in meaning to the highlighted part of the sentence.**

1 Firefighting efforts failed dramatically, and people were forced to grab their valuables and then swiftly evacuated.

   Ⓐ hid
   Ⓑ fled
   Ⓒ buried
   Ⓓ observed

2 When the North blockaded its ports, the South could not export cotton, tobacco, and other raw materials.

   Ⓐ coarse
   Ⓑ valuable
   Ⓒ unfinished
   Ⓓ rare

3 Both Cortez and Pizarro had several advantages over their foes.

   Ⓐ conquerors
   Ⓑ allies
   Ⓒ opponents
   Ⓓ inferiors

4 Yet it gradually disappeared during the late medieval period due to the rise of the nation-state.

   Ⓐ progressively
   Ⓑ slowly
   Ⓒ fortunately
   Ⓓ completely

5 He believed his destiny was to vanquish the great Persian Empire, which was located in western Asia.

   Ⓐ mission
   Ⓑ potential
   Ⓒ fate
   Ⓓ duty

6 Before the families revolted, the dominance of the Fujiwara resulted in a long period of peace.

   Ⓐ power
   Ⓑ wishes
   Ⓒ leaders
   Ⓓ appearance

7 The plantations relied upon tobacco and cotton as their major cash crops.

   Ⓐ grains
   Ⓑ sources
   Ⓒ supplies
   Ⓓ plants

8 In Western Europe after Rome fell, most land was seized by the strong.

   Ⓐ snatched
   Ⓑ purchased
   Ⓒ acquired
   Ⓓ reserved

9 This marked the beginning of democracy.

   Ⓐ denoted
   Ⓑ resembled
   Ⓒ foretold
   Ⓓ portrayed

10 The hilly, rocky northern colonies were not conducive to farming.

   Ⓐ given to
   Ⓑ interested in
   Ⓒ favorable to
   Ⓓ instructed in

11 His men even captured the Incan emperor, whom they ransomed for treasure and then later executed.

(A) imprisoned
(B) demoted
(C) exiled
(D) killed

12 By September 6, the fire was finally extinguished, but an enormous amount of damage had occurred.

(A) put out
(B) under control
(C) spreading
(D) made smaller

13 Some, such as Athens, amassed wealth by trading and maintained large merchant fleets and navies.

(A) constructed
(B) purchased
(C) kept
(D) leased

14 The absence of constant warfare enabled Japanese culture to develop.

(A) threat
(B) lack
(C) possibility
(D) image

15 So they got men—their vassals—to swear oaths of loyalty to them.

(A) contracts
(B) vows
(C) speeches
(D) warnings

16 Almost all aspects of the Aztecs—their history, culture, and customs—were eliminated.

(A) theories
(B) remnants
(C) ruins
(D) features

17 Even today, many signs of Hellenism are evident in the Middle East.

(A) apparent
(B) resurfacing
(C) looming
(D) hidden

18 Nagaoka had previously been the Japanese capital.

(A) reliably
(B) formerly
(C) traditionally
(D) consistently

19 In addition, while the city-states sometimes united against external threats, such as the Persians, in other instances, they battled one another for power in Greece.

(A) barbarian
(B) hostile
(C) foreign
(D) dangerous

20 Alexander and Phillip, despite being Macedonians, both embraced many Greek ideas.

(A) established
(B) accepted
(C) studied
(D) reformed

Part **B**

Chapter 02 The Arts

There are many fields in the arts. All of them focus on creating works that are pleasing to the eye and the ear. The arts include art, music, literature, and architecture. Art has many genres, such as painting, drawing, etching, sculpting, and photography. Music has a number of genres itself, and it may include both instrumental and choral works. Literature has a multitude of forms. Some of them are poetry, novels, and dramatic productions such as comedies and tragedies. Architecture involves the designing of buildings that are both pleasing to look at and practical. Artists are typically creative people, yet they also look to the past to seek inspiration from those who came before them

Mastering **the Question Types**

☑ Vocabulary   ☐ Fill in a Table   ☐ Factual Information   ☐ Negative Factual Information   ☑ Prose Summary

☐ Insert Text   ☐ Reference   ☑ Rhetorical Purpose   ☐ Sentence Simplification   ☐ Inference

Medieval Musical Instruments

Gregorian chants are arguably the best-known music from the Middle Ages. This music relies only on singers' voices and has no accompanying instruments. This has caused some people mistakenly to believe that there were few musical instruments during the medieval period. On the contrary, a wide variety of them were used during the Middle Ages. They include string, percussion, brass, keyboard, and wind instruments.

The most influential of all medieval musical instruments was the lute. This is a string instrument that is the ancestor of the modern guitar. The lute was introduced to Europe by the Islamic world during its invasion of Spain in the eighth century. During the Crusades, the lute became more widespread. Typically, a lute had four or five pairs of strings that were plucked. It was easy to play, and many **wandering minstrels** used it as they could easily carry it with them from place to place. Minstrels also played the harp. The rebec, the viol, and the hurdy gurdy were other string instruments from that time.

³→ Another instrument from the Middle Ages was the harpsichord. It was created during the late medieval period, but this keyboard instrument quickly gained popularity. The harpsichord would maintain its popularity even after medieval times as there were numerous works written for it during the Renaissance and the **Baroque Period**. It would later be replaced by the piano, but it was one of the most important of all musical instruments.

The shawm was a woodwind instrument that many people enjoyed playing. The oboe later evolved from it and caused people to lose interest in the shawm during the Renaissance. Other woodwinds included the flute and the pipe. As for brass instruments, both the trumpet and the sackbut, an early version of the trombone, were played by medieval musicians.

Glossary

wandering minstrel: a medieval poet and musician that traveled from town to town to put on performances
Baroque Period: a musical period in Europe that lasted from roughly 1600 to 1750

1 The word "accompanying" in the passage is closest in meaning to

- (A) contributing
- (B) leading
- (C) loud
- (D) harmonious

2 The author discusses "the harpsichord" in paragraph 3 in order to

- (A) explain how it later evolved into the modern piano
- (B) describe the types of sounds that it was able to make
- (C) discuss what types of music were commonly played on it
- (D) focus on how popular it was during different periods

3 *Directions:* An introductory sentence for a brief summary of the passage is provided below. Complete the summary by selecting the THREE answer choices that express the most important ideas of the passage. Some sentences do not belong because they express ideas that are not presented in the passage or are minor ideas in the passage. *This question is worth 2 points.*

People in medieval times played many different musical instruments.

Answer Choices

1. A large number of modern instruments, such as the oboe and the piano, were first developed by musicians in the Middle Ages.

2. Instruments such as the shawm, the harp, and the sackbut were among those that were played by medieval musicians.

3. The lute was a type of string instrument that ranked among the most influential of all medieval musical instruments.

4. Because Gregorian chants were so common, many people think that there were no musical instruments during medieval times.

5. A wide variety of musical instruments, including woodwinds, brass, keyboards, and strings, were popular during the Middle Ages.

6. The harpsichord achieved a great amount of popularity with musicians during both the Renaissance and the Baroque Period.

Summarizing Complete the summary by using the words or phrases given in the box.

| the harpsichord | influential medieval instrument | four of five pairs | few musical instruments |

It is not true that there were _____ in the Middle Ages. There were many, including string, percussion, brass, keyboard, and wind instruments. The lute was the most _____ . It— along with the harp—was popular with wandering minstrels. They would pluck the _____ of strings that the lute had. _____ was another instrument that became very popular during the Middle Ages. There were other instruments, such as the shawm, the flute, the pipe, the trumpet, and the sackbut, that medieval musicians played.

Mastering **the Question Types**

☐ Vocabulary ☑ Fill in a Table ☐ Factual Information ☑ Negative Factual Information ☐ Prose Summary
☐ Insert Text ☐ Reference ☐ Rhetorical Purpose ☐ Sentence Simplification ☑ Inference

Impressionism

1 ➜ During the 1800s, most artists painted in a similar manner. They preferred the realist style and painted indoor scenes. But a new type of art arose in France in the late 1800s. It came to be known as Impressionism. It differed from the prevailing school of art in several ways. Despite being new, it rapidly attracted many followers. Painters began experimenting with this innovative style. A few excelled at it so much that they became some of the most famous artists in history.

One way the Impressionists differed from the past concerned the colors they used. Impressionists preferred vivid colors and shunned the dark and drab ones used by realists. In addition, they made short brushstrokes. This made lines much less important to them. Accordingly, many of the images they painted on their canvases were abstract, not realistic. This would become a primary feature of Impressionist art. The artists frequently painted outdoor scenes. They painted **landscapes** and people in nature. As a result, their paintings were bright, airy outdoor works.

3 ➜ The movement got its name from a painting by Claude Monet entitled *Impression, soleil levant*. He displayed it in 1874 at an art exhibition in France. Among the other earlier practitioners of Impressionism were Edouard Manet, Edgar Degas, and Pierre Auguste Renoir. Yet a mere **glance** at their works shows that they often differ. In fact, many Impressionist paintings had only a few basic similarities. The movement itself was incredibly diverse. The artists often argued amongst themselves as to what constituted Impressionist art. Ultimately, while there was some disagreement, it was generally agreed that the use of bright colors, short brushstrokes, and light in outdoor scenes constituted the main ideals of the movement.

Glossary

landscape: a kind of painting that depicts the outdoors and features such as trees, mountains, and rivers
glance: to look at quickly

1   In paragraph 1, all of the following questions are answered EXCEPT:

       Ⓐ How did the newness of Impressionism affect its ability to get followers?

       Ⓑ How did Impressionist artists use realism in their works?

       Ⓒ What happened to some of the best Impressionist artists?

       Ⓓ When did Impressionism start to become an art movement?

2   Which of the following can be inferred from paragraph 3 about Impressionism?

       Ⓐ Its practitioners followed few set standards.

       Ⓑ It was rejected by the public until 1874.

       Ⓒ Claude Monet was the movement's leader.

       Ⓓ Art exhibitions were responsible for popularizing it.

3   ***Directions:*** Select the appropriate phrases from the answer choices and match them to the painting style to which they relate. TWO of the answer choices will NOT be used. ***This question is worth 3 points.***

Answer Choices	PAINTING STYLE
① Was created by the artist Claude Monet	**Pre-Impressionist**
② Utilized an abstract form of art	•
③ Used long brushstrokes on paintings	•
④ Had a diverse number of styles	**Impressionist**
⑤ Preferred colors that were dark	•
⑥ Often painted items found in nature	•
⑦ Painted pictures that looked realistic	•

Summarizing Complete the summary by using the words or phrases given in the box.

never agree on	short brushstrokes	a few similarities	vivid colors

Most traditional art was realistic. But in France in the late 1800s, the Impressionist school of art began. Impressionists preferred _____, not dark ones. They also used _____, so their paintings were usually abstract. And they painted landscapes and other outdoor scenes. The movement's name came from a painting by Claude Monet. The works of the Impressionists often have only _____. The Impressionists themselves could _____ what exactly Impressionist art was. This makes the works of these artists quite diverse.

Theatrical Makeup

In most theatrical productions, which include plays, operas, ballets, and musicals, the performers wear makeup. The main reason is that it enables the audience more clearly to see the features of each performer's face. Most theaters have seats far from the stage, so many viewers would not be able to see the performers' faces well if they were not wearing makeup. Additionally, the stage lighting used in modern-day productions can affect how the performers look. It can give an actor's face a flat, expressionless appearance. The use of makeup, however, can **mitigate** this problem.

²➡ There are several types of makeup that performers use. The most common is foundation, or base, makeup. This is used to highlight the jaw line and other contours of an actor's face. It gives a person's skin tone a darker color, so it does not appear washed out when seen under bright stage lighting. Many actors apply makeup around their eyes to make them stand out. Since the eyes can convey emotions, it is important for the audience to see them clearly. The same is true for the mouth. Most actors apply lipstick so that their lips and mouths can be viewed with no problem.

Aside from the basic types of makeup utilized by virtually all performers, there are other special instances when cosmetics are used. For instance, clowns are characters known for their exaggerated facial expressions. These are attained through the application of excessive amounts of makeup. **1** Similarly, a person playing a **vampire** would apply more makeup to give that individual a paler face. **2** Finally, actors may use makeup to give themselves scars and bruises. **3** And some might even utilize it to create the semblance of blood on their bodies. **4** This helps make a performance more realistic, which is the ultimate goal of every performer.

Glossary
mitigate: to lessen; to moderate
vampire: an undead monster that avoids sunlight and sucks the blood of its victims

1 Which of the sentences below best expresses the essential information in the highlighted sentence in the passage? *Incorrect* answer choices change the meaning in important ways or leave out essential information.

    (A) When viewers in the audience are sitting far away from the stage, they cannot see the makeup the actors are wearing.

    (B) The usage of makeup enables people watching from a distance to see the actors' faces more clearly.

    (C) If the actors wear makeup, then their facial expressions become much easier for people to understand.

    (D) A person sitting far away from the stage has to pay close attention to see the faces of all of the performers.

2 The word "them" in the passage refers to

    (A) many actors

    (B) the eyes

    (C) emotions

    (D) the audience

3 According to paragraph 2, which of the following is true of the makeup that actors wear?

    (A) They wear eye makeup to prevent themselves from looking tired.

    (B) The most important makeup they use highlights their eyes.

    (C) Some of the cosmetics they use give their skin a lighter color.

    (D) They utilize a variety of cosmetics to make viewing them easier.

4 Look at the four squares [■] that indicate where the following sentence could be added to the passage.

While somewhat gory, the appearance of an open wound may be necessary for performers at times.

Where would the sentence best fit?

Summarizing Complete the summary by using the words or phrases given in the box.

convey their emotions	at their faces	clowns and vampires	darkens the skin

Most actors in dramatic productions wear makeup. This lets the audience get a better look _____. Actors use different kinds of cosmetics. Foundation makeup highlights the jaw and facial contours and _____. Eye makeup and lipstick help actors _____ to the audience. Some actors wear makeup for special reasons. _____ need to wear lots of makeup. Actors may need to put scars, bruises, or blood on their bodies, too. These all require the usage of makeup.

Mastering **the Subject**

Sound in Film

A completed motion picture consists of several elements. One of them is sound. Movies have three main types of sound: spoken dialogue, music, and sound effects. Most of the time, the spoken dialogue is recorded as the movie is being shot. The music and the sound effects are added in post-production after everything has been filmed. Thanks to the use of sound, directors can make movies that are more believable, exciting, and entertaining.

2→ The main purpose of spoken dialogue is to convey information. The audience is able to understand the story from the dialogue as well as from the film's visuals. The pitch of the actors' voices, the pacing of the words, and the tones of the conversations tell the audience which emotions the characters are feeling. Human and animal voices can also be included to shock or frighten an audience. These might include screams of distress or the growls of wild animals.

Music is typically used by directors to establish the mood of the film. If the music is **sinister** or somber, the audience may experience a sense of dread. If the music is more upbeat and lively, the audience will likely feel more lighthearted. Songs may also be used in movies to help set the tone. Music—with and without lyrics—can often build tension. For instance, as the hero of the film approaches a dangerous situation, the director might employ music to keep the viewers in the audience on the edges of their seats as they await the outcome. The genre of the film often determines the type of music used. Darker, more serious music may be heard in dramas, thrillers, histories, and horror movies. Comedies and musicals have lighter scores and often include one or more songs.

Sound effects are employed to give a film a more realistic feel. These may include everyday sounds such as driving cars, operating machinery, walking people, and tapping keyboards. Other sounds may be more atypical. Gunshots and explosions are two sound effects common in action movies but which people rarely hear in real life. Science-fiction movies also have uncommon sound effects. These may be rockets blasting off, laser guns firing, and robots functioning. Technicians employ a variety of **ingenious** methods to create these sounds. Thanks to computers, making sound effects is much easier today than it was in the past. Modern sound effects are also quite realistic, which was not always the case in movies filmed in past decades.

NOTE

The first movies ever made lacked sound. However, in 1927, *The Jazz Singer* became the first full-length movie to include sound. After it, silent movies disappeared, and "talkies" started to be produced.

Nowadays, computers are often used to create the more extreme or strange sounds that some films require.

In modern times, some composers have become famous for the soundtracks they write for movies. John Williams, Jerry Goldsmith, and Basil Poledouris are three of the most famous movie soundtrack composers.

As computer technology has improved, so too has sound effects technology. Sound effects in the past were much more primitive than those used nowadays.

Glossary
sinister: evil; threatening
ingenious: creative; brilliant

1 According to paragraph 2, movie directors use spoken dialogue because

  (A) it makes their films more believable

  (B) it helps tell the story for the viewers

  (C) they want all of the actors to talk

  (D) the audience needs to experience emotions

2 Which of the sentences below best expresses the essential information in the highlighted sentence in the passage? *Incorrect* answer choices change the meaning in important ways or leave out essential information.

  (A) Music played during a scene in a film can make the audience nervously anticipate what will happen.

  (B) When directors film scenes with heroic individuals, they use music that fills the audience with anticipation.

  (C) Film viewers may become concerned when the music starts to play during a particularly dangerous situation.

  (D) Some directors choose to use music so that the people in the audience will eagerly await the next scene.

3 The word "atypical" in the passage is closest in meaning to

  (A) uncommon   (B) annoying

  (C) extraordinary   (D) peaceful

4 *Directions:* An introductory sentence for a brief summary of the passage is provided below. Complete the summary by selecting the THREE answer choices that express the most important ideas of the passage. Some sentences do not belong because they express ideas that are not presented in the passage or are minor ideas in the passage. *This question is worth 2 points.*

Movie directors utilize sound in a number of ways in order to create better and more entertaining films.

Answer Choices

  1 Some directors use animal voices in their films in order to create different emotions in the viewing audience.

  2 The type of music used is often determined by the emotions in the audience that the director wants to appeal to.

  3 By including sound effects in their films, the movies become much more realistic than those without sound effects.

  4 The use of spoken dialogue permits the audience to know exactly what is happening in the film.

  5 Thanks to computers, sound effects today are more realistic than those that were utilized in the past.

  6 Horror films have music that increases the level of suspense in a scene in the film until a crucial moment.

Summarizing   **Complete the summary by filling in the blanks.**

One important element in movies is sound. The three _____ are spoken dialogue, music, and sound effects. _____ expresses information to the audience. It lets the viewers know exactly what is happening in the film. Music can _____ in the film. Different kinds of music are used to create various feelings or emotions. Sound effects make films _____ . Some are everyday sounds while others are more unusual sounds. Sound effects today are more believable than ones from the past.

Mastering **the Subject**

The Changing Status of Artists

In the centuries prior to the Renaissance, few artists achieved any fame. They were merely considered craftsmen hired to do various jobs. This changed during the Renaissance. Ever since then, artists have acquired a level of respect and fame that they had rarely previously received. Sometimes, this fame has only come after the artist's death. At other times, artists have received some measure of recognition during their lifetimes. This has led to increased prices for their art. Works that were originally **commissioned** for little money have suddenly become worth small fortunes as people have strived to collect art both for its beauty and its monetary value.

2→ Several events occurred during the Renaissance that increased the status of artists. First of all, the quality of the art itself improved. There were some brilliant artists in the Middle Ages. Yet most were not especially talented. Around 1400, when the Renaissance began, this changed. At that time, artists began receiving better training. They rediscovered the lost methods classical Greek and Roman masters had used to make their art appear more realistic. For instance, in medieval times, many works of art were flat and two dimensional. They lacked depth. Renaissance art, on the other hand, used perspective, depth, and brighter colors. These features improved the quality of artists' works. Thus masters such as Leonardo da Vinci, Michelangelo, and Raphael became well known during their lifetimes. When other artists copied their styles, this also increased their fame.

During the Renaissance, the upper classes became art patrons. The Medici family in Florence, Italy, sponsored many artists. Florence accordingly became a center of art. Collecting art also became fashionable. Many wealthy families became **avid** art collectors. But sometimes they got rid of certain works by selling them at auctions. During the 1600s, art auctions began attracting wealthy buyers. England, among other countries, became a center of art sales. This was mainly on account of the relative lack of warfare in England, which meant that art could be safely stored there.

4→ As time passed, the fame of artists from the Renaissance grew. Paintings that sold for a few hundred pounds or francs in the 1700s garnered tens of thousands of pounds or francs in the 1800s. By the end of the 1900s, some paintings were selling for millions of pounds, francs, and dollars. Having a masterpiece in one's collection became a status symbol. And modern-day artists, such as Pablo Picasso, Salvador Dali, and Andy Warhol, became world famous during their lives. Today, artists are no longer mere craftsmen. They can become living icons in the world of art.

NOTE

Many of the most beautiful paintings from the Middle Ages are found in illuminated manuscripts such as the *Book of Kells*. The artists who painted the pictures in these manuscripts are almost all unknown.

The knowledge that artists learned from ancient Greece and Rome tremendously improved the quality of their work. It also influenced the artists so much that a lot of their subject matter came from Greece and Rome.

Prior to the Renaissance, the Church had commissioned the majority of paintings. During the Renaissance, it still commissioned paintings, but the number of private individuals who ordered paintings increased dramatically.

Artwork by Picasso commonly sells for millions of dollars. The works of many Impressionist artists, especially Vincent van Gogh, regularly sell for tens—or hundreds—of millions of dollars.

Glossary
commission: to order an artistic production from a person
avid: enthusiastic

1 The word "their" in the passage refers to

    Ⓐ these features

    Ⓑ the artists' work

    Ⓒ masters

    Ⓓ other artists

2 According to paragraph 2, which of the following is NOT true of art during the Middle Ages?

    Ⓐ The paintings did not have any depth.

    Ⓑ Artists rarely became famous during it.

    Ⓒ The majority of its artists were brilliant.

    Ⓓ Most works had a flat look to them.

3 Which of the following can be inferred from paragraph 4 about art?

    Ⓐ It always increases in value over time.

    Ⓑ Many paintings are worth millions of dollars.

    Ⓒ Art is made because its creators want to become wealthy.

    Ⓓ Purchasing it can be a good investment.

4 ***Directions:*** An introductory sentence for a brief summary of the passage is provided below. Complete the summary by selecting the THREE answer choices that express the most important ideas of the passage. Some sentences do not belong because they express ideas that are not presented in the passage or are minor ideas in the passage. ***This question is worth 2 points.***

As the quality of art increased during and after the Renaissance, so too did the fame of artists increase.

Answer Choices

① Since many artists imitated the styles of great masters in the Renaissance, those painters achieved more fame than they had before.

② Nowadays, it is possible for a person to spend millions of dollars on a painting made by a famous artist.

③ Renaissance artists began to learn more about painting, so they started to use perspective when making pictures.

④ Some artists living in modern times are no longer anonymous but have managed to become famous while they are still alive.

⑤ Leonardo da Vinci, Michelangelo, and Raphael were three of the greatest artists the world has even seen.

⑥ Medieval artists tended to lack talent, which caused many of them to make flat, two-dimensional paintings.

Summarizing   Complete the summary by filling in the blanks.

During the Middle Ages, most artists had little skill. They were _____ and were almost never famous. But during the Renaissance, this changed. Artists began to learn skills such as using _____. This improved the quality of their work. This brought some artists more fame. Over time, people began _____, which caused the prices of some works of art to increase. Today, many artists have achieved _____, and some paintings sell for millions of dollars.

Mastering **the Subject**

The Uses of Music and Songs

Most people listen to music and songs for enjoyment. That has been the case ever since the first person sang a song or played a musical instrument. Entertainment is one of the main objectives of all kinds of music. Yet it serves other purposes as well. It can also be used to inspire people. In these cases, the music is often different from that which is meant to entertain.

2➡ Still, music is above all intended to entertain. Today, people have a variety of options when they want to listen to music. They can listen to it on their stereos or portable electronic devices, the radio, or the Internet. They can watch music videos on television, computers, and mobile phones, or they can attend live concerts. In the past, however, people's options were more limited. They played their own music, sang their own songs, or else listened to others. There were simply no other choices available.

3➡ This made musicians such as wandering minstrels popular with most people. Minstrels were musicians who traveled the countryside to play their music. They frequently sang songs that were well known to the villagers. Their songs could be short. **1** They could also be long epic poems, chansons, or other tales that told the deeds of great heroes from the past. **2** When a minstrel visited most villages, he instantly became the most popular person there. **3** While the people knew a majority of the songs in his **repertoire**, they were still eager for any kind of entertainment to help brighten their often dreary lives. **4**

Music does not only entertain; it also inspires. In past centuries, there were two main forums for inspirational music: churches and battlefields. While they may seem an unlikely combination, both sacred and battle music served to inspire the people hearing it. In the Western world in the past, religion—particularly Christianity—was an integral part of people's lives. When services were held in a church or cathedral, religious music was played. Its purposes were to **uplift** people and to instill in them a sense of the divine.

Meanwhile, soldiers too were exposed to songs of an inspiring nature. Prior to engaging in battle, many soldiers sang fight songs that would lift their spirits and provide encouragement. Some of the songs were even meant to frighten the enemy, which would give the singers the advantage in battle. And for centuries, armies going to battle marched to the beat of a drum and the sounds of pipes and horns. Although different from church music, battle music accomplished the same basic purpose.

NOTE

There are many genres of music. During modern times, the number of musical genres has increased very much. People listen to these genres depending on their tastes in music.

Minstrels were often called bards. They were frequently able to recall hundreds or even thousands of lines of poetry, which they would sing while playing some sort of musical instrument at the same time.

Chants are one type of sacred music. They are often sung without any accompanying music. Typically, the words in chants are sung in monotonous voices.

Military music is popular in many cultures. In addition, the national anthems of many countries are songs that were written during times of war or are about military feats.

Glossary

repertoire: the entire list of songs, plays, or other forms of entertainment that a performer is able to do

uplift: to inspire; to encourage

1 In paragraph 2, the author's description of how people currently listen to music mentions all of the following EXCEPT:

- Ⓐ By listening to it while they are moving
- Ⓑ By using the Internet to hear it
- Ⓒ By watching it being performed live
- Ⓓ By listening to it on cassettes

2 The author discusses "wandering minstrels" in paragraph 3 in order to

- Ⓐ show how they entertained many people
- Ⓑ describe the songs in their repertoires
- Ⓒ discuss the reasons behind their popularity
- Ⓓ compare their music with religious songs

3 Look at the four squares [■] that indicate where the following sentence could be added to the passage.

During medieval times, stories about King Arthur and his knights were popular as well.

Where would the sentence best fit?

4 *Directions:* Select the appropriate statements from the answer choices and match them to the purpose of music in the past to which they relate. TWO of the answer choices will NOT be used. ***This question is worth 3 points.***

Answer Choices	**PURPOSE OF MUSIC**
① Involved the singing of epic poems	**Entertainment**
② Utilized the playing of violins and pianos	•
③ Had to be listened to on the Internet	•
④ Was meant to help people experience the divine	**Inspiration**
⑤ Was played for the benefit of soldiers	•
⑥ Was sung by wandering minstrels	•
⑦ Could improve people's spirits	•

Summarizing   Complete the summary by filling in the blanks.

People usually listen to music because it entertains them. Nowadays, people can listen to music through _____ mediums. This was not true in the past. Centuries ago, wandering minstrels often _____ and played music for the people. But music did not just entertain. _____ and battle music inspired people. Religious music was played in churches and cathedrals. And soldiers often listened to battle music before they fought. Sometimes the music was even played as they _____ .

TOEFL **Practice Test**

Cave Paintings

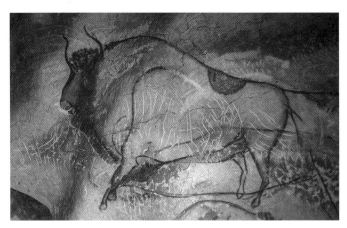

Cave art of a bison in Chauvet, France

1 ➙ In the late 1800s, people exploring caves throughout Europe began making startling discoveries: The caves often had paintings on their walls. Since the first example of cave art was spotted, more than 350 caves in France and Spain have been found to have cave art. There are many more instances of cave paintings in Europe and around the world. These pictures have been determined to be thousands of years old. A cave in Chauvet, France, has paintings estimated to be 32,000 years old. This makes them among the world's oldest-known cave paintings. Cave paintings **depict** a variety of images. Most are animals, yet there are other images. They include shapes, tracings of hands, and abstract images. Art historians and archaeologists have learned much about the past from cave paintings. But one thing has eluded them: what the purpose of the cave paintings was.

2 ➙ ❶ Experts have come up with three main theories as to why prehistoric humans made cave paintings. **❷** All of them, however, have weak points. **❸** The first theory is that the paintings were made for decoration. **❹** It, however, seems the most unlikely. It is indisputable that early humans led bleak lives. They surely would have enjoyed anything that would have brightened their days. Thus some experts believe prehistoric humans made cave art to beautify their surroundings. Yet many paintings are found deep in caves in hard-to-reach places. They are well away from the places people would have inhabited. In addition, some scholars argue that humans did not actually live in caves. Instead, they lived near them. They only used the caves for shelter in bad weather or to make cooking fires in the cave mouths. These scholars argue that people would not have decorated places in which they did not live.

3 ➙ The second idea is that the cave paintings had some sort of religious significance. Perhaps, some say, religious leaders—called shamans—went deep into the caves away from the rest of the clan. They then performed rituals as they drew the paintings on the walls. While this seems like a **valid** theory, there is little evidence to support it. Since prehistoric people were illiterate, they have left no writings concerning their beliefs. This makes it impossible to determine what their religious beliefs or practices were. Accordingly, the idea that the paintings were for religious purposes cannot be verified.

The third notion is that the paintings were meant to teach people about the animals that lived in the region as well as the best ways to hunt them. Many cave paintings portray animals such as deer, bison, horses, and various now-extinct beasts. There are also paintings of predators, including lions. Some paintings appear to show humans with spears and other weapons. Perhaps these are depictions made by tribal elders to instruct the younger members in how to hunt. Again, much like the second idea, while this theory shows some promise, it is virtually impossible to determine whether or not it is the actual reason why prehistoric humans made cave paintings. Without any more evidence, this idea too will remain merely a theory, and the reasoning behind the making of cave paintings will stay a mystery.

Glossary
depict: to show; to portray
valid: legitimate; truthful

1   In paragraph 1, why does the author mention "Chauvet, France"?

    (A) To state that it was the first place that cave paintings were found

    (B) To claim it has some of the oldest cave paintings in the world

    (C) To note that the paintings in the caves there are well done

    (D) To describe a variety of images painted on the caves there

2   According to paragraph 1, which of the following is true of cave paintings?

    (A) They have only been found in Europe.

    (B) The majority of them are located in Spain and France.

    (C) Archaeologists have found more than 32,000 of them.

    (D) The paintings show a number of different images.

3   In paragraph 2, which of the following can be inferred about the first theory on why prehistoric people made cave paintings?

    (A) It shows why people thought decorating caves was crucial.

    (B) It explains why prehistoric men avoided living in caves.

    (C) The least number of scholars believe it is accurate.

    (D) There are many people who are willing to defend it.

4   According to paragraph 2, which of the following is NOT true of why the first theory on cave paintings is doubted?

    (A) The art made people feel better about their lives.

    (B) People did not usually live in caves.

    (C) Many paintings are located far from where people resided.

    (D) The caves were typically only used for cooking.

5   In stating that prehistoric people were "illiterate," the author means that these people

    (A) had primitive technology

    (B) were intolerant

    (C) lacked an organized religion

    (D) could not read

6   In paragraph 3, the author implies that shamans

    (A) taught their tribe members about religion

    (B) recorded some of their religious beliefs

    (C) conducted rituals in front of other people

    (D) were important people in prehistoric tribes

7 According to paragraph 3, the second theory cannot be verified because

    (A) prehistoric people left no written explanations

    (B) prehistoric people rarely had shamans

    (C) prehistoric shamans were likely not artists

    (D) not enough paintings have been found

8 Which of the sentences below best expresses the essential information in the highlighted sentence in the passage? *Incorrect* answer choices change the meaning in important ways or leave out essential information.

    (A) Despite having come up with some attractive theories, historians fear they will never be able to prove why early humans made cave paintings.

    (B) Prehistoric humans never explained why they made paintings in caves, so the second or third explanation concerning them could be true.

    (C) This theory is like the second one in that it could be true, but no one can verify that it explains the reasoning behind making the cave paintings.

    (D) Because so many cave paintings have been discovered, experts have come up with theories on why people actually made them.

9 Look at the four squares [■] that indicate where the following sentence could be added to the passage.

Each theory has strong supporters who believe their interpretation is correct.

Where would the sentence best fit?

> Click on a square [■] to add the sentence to the passage.

10 *Directions:* Select the appropriate statements from the answer choices and match them to the theory on cave paintings to which they relate. TWO of the answer choices will NOT be used. ***This question is worth 4 points.***

> Drag your answer choices to the spaces where they belong.
> To remove an answer choice, click on it. To review the passage, click on **View Text**.

Answer Choices	THEORY ON CAVE PAINTINGS
1 Provides a religious explanation	**First Theory**
2 Has been shown to be correct	•
3 Considers people's need for decorations	•
4 Accounts for the oldest cave paintings discovered	**Second Theory**
5 Notes why there are paintings of animals	•
6 Shows they could have been providing instructions	•
7 Is the least likely of the three	**Third Theory**
8 May have been done by a shaman	•
9 Were messages from older people to younger ones	•
	•

1 Opera

An opera is a kind of dramatic stage performance in which most of the dialogue is sung. Operas are typically tragedies, but they may also be of a comedic nature. The types of songs in them vary. They may be arias, which are solos, duets, or choruses with a number of singers. Opera was first created in Italy during the sixteenth century. It quickly became popular and spread throughout Europe. Many famous composers have written operas. Among the more famous operas are *The Marriage of Figaro* by Mozart and *Aida* by Verdi.

2 Photography

The art of taking pictures with a camera is photography. Cameras were invented in the nineteenth century, and they were rapidly improved upon. Initially, cameras could only take pictures in black and white. But color film was eventually developed. At first, photography was not considered art. However, Ansel Adams and others helped convince the public that it was. Adams became famous for the many outdoor photographs that he took. Aside from Adams, many other photographers took beautiful and inspirational photographs that people today still recognize.

3 Film Studios

Making a film is a laborious process. Large numbers of people with many specialties are required. This was even truer in the past when moviemaking technology was less advanced than it is today. Thus, film studios have often dominated the movie industry. Film studios, also called movie studios, are companies that make and distribute movies. In the early years of movies, film studios signed actors and actresses to contracts and assigned them roles in movies. In the past, film studios were extremely influential. There are still many studios today, but other, independent, moviemakers are able to get their films distributed as well.

4 Sculptures

Some artists do not paint or draw. Instead, they create sculptures or statues. These are figures often created from stone, clay, or metal. Sculptors who work with stone typically prefer marble, which they appreciate for its beauty. Sculptures may be tiny enough to be held in a person's hand or incredibly large. Some of the world's most famous works of art are sculptures. They include Michelangelo's *David* and *Pieta*. The *Venus de Milo* and Rodin's *The Thinker* are well known, too. Sculpting is a difficult field as sculptors must meticulously chip away at the stone or other material in order to complete their work.

5 Architecture

The art of designing and constructing buildings is architecture. Architects are those who design buildings. They must create buildings that are both practical and aesthetically pleasing. They often consider aspects such as the location of the building and others around it, the building's function, and the material that will be used to make it. Architects must be knowledgeable in many different fields, including mathematics, art, and engineering. Some architects become famous for their work. Frank Lloyd Wright was a famous architect, and I.M. Pei was another well-known designer.

6 Pottery Making

Humans have been making pottery, or ceramics, for thousands of years. Pottery is made from clay and is formed into various shapes, including bowls, plates, vases, and pots. The pottery-making process is somewhat involved. First, the potter must shape wet clay into the design that is desired. This may be done by hand or with a potter's wheel. The clay must then be heated so that it dries. Next, designs are added and the pot glazed. Once this is done, the pot is put in a kiln, which is a special oven. It must be cooked for hours, after which the pot is essentially complete.

7 ▶ Landscape Art

Some artists paint images of nature. These may include mountains, forests, lakes, rivers, the sky, and other scenes that are found outdoors. These works of art are called landscapes. Artists have been painting landscapes for centuries. However, in the nineteenth century, landscapes began to take on more importance. Many Impressionist artists in Europe began painting outdoor scenes, so landscapes became popular with them. In the United States, many artists belonging to the Hudson River School painted landscapes, too. They were mostly abstract paintings, but there were other artists who painted more realistic landscapes.

8 ▶ Epic Poems

One form of literature is the epic poem. This is among the oldest types of literature. Epic poems tell stories of heroes performing great deeds. The poems are typically long; some can be thousands of lines in length. They may involve magic, gods and goddesses, monsters, and other beings from mythology. They usually start *in medias res*—in the middle of the story—and then go back in time to describe prior events. The *Iliad* and the *Odyssey* by the ancient Greek poet Homer are two of the most famous epic poems in the Western world. *Gilgamesh*, *Beowulf*, and *Paradise Lost* are other famous epic poems.

9 ▶ Silent Movies

When motion pictures were first invented, they could only show images. They could not transmit sound. Therefore, all early films were silent movies. In order to guarantee that the audience understood what was happening, moviemakers used several methods. First, the actors overacted, or emoted, to ensure that the meanings of their actions were understood. In addition, cue cards, which had written dialogue or explanations, were used. Silent movies were quite popular, and Charlie Chaplin became the most famous actor in them. In 1927, the first "talkies"—movies with sound—began appearing, so silent movies quickly disappeared.

10 ▶ Ancient Greek Comedies

The ancient Greeks often enjoyed dramatic performances. Among them were comedies. These were plays that incorporated humor and were meant to amuse and entertain their audiences. There were several comedic writers who achieved fame. The best known of them was Aristophanes. Several of his plays have survived in their entirety. These include *Lysistrata* and *The Clouds*. Much of Aristophanes' work incorporated social commentary. He enjoyed making fun of the most famous people in Greece as well as the political issues of his time.

11 ▶ Frescoes

One unique type of art is the fresco. This is a painted work, but artists do not make it on canvas. Instead, they paint on plaster that is then attached to walls. There are two major types of frescoes. They are buon and secco frescoes. Buon frescoes are painted on wet plaster. So the artist has a limited amount of time to finish the painting. As soon as the plaster dries, no more painting can be done. Secco frescoes, on the other hand, are done on plaster that is already dry. A medium is used in the paint so that it adheres to the plaster.

12 ▶ Dramatic Productions

Plays are a kind of dramatic production. They are written either in prose or in verse, but they are intended to be performed on stage. Actors and actresses perform various roles in the play, which lets them tell the story. There are many different genres of plays. They can be comedies, tragedies, histories, and satires, among others. In the Western world, the history of dramatic productions goes back to the time of the ancient Greeks. Since then, there have been countless dramatic productions written and performed. In history, Williams Shakespeare is arguably the most famous of all playwrights.

- **abstract** (adj) nonrepresentational; not realistic in appearance
- **airy** (adj) light
- **ancestor** (n) an object, idea, or event that acts as a forerunner or inspiration for something that comes later
- **apply** (v) to put on
- **argue** (v) to have a verbal fight or disagreement
- **audience** (n) the people in attendance at some kind of a performance
- **ballet** (n) a dramatic performance in which the performers often dance
- **beautify** (v) to make more beautiful or better looking
- **bruise** (n) a contusion; a discoloration on the body
- **brushstroke** (n) the stroke an artist makes with a brush while painting
- **clay** (n) a kind of soil that is often very thick
- **constitute** (v) to comprise; to make up
- **contour** (n) the outline of a body or a part of a body
- **convey** (v) to communicate; to impart
- **craftsman** (n) an artisan; a person who is good at making things
- **depth** (n) complexity
- **dialogue** (n) spoken lines in a work
- **distress** (n) anxiety; suffering
- **drab** (adj) dull; lifeless
- **dread** (n) fear
- **dreary** (adj) boring; monotonous
- **elder** (n) an older, often respected, person in a group
- **element** (n) an aspect; a part of something
- **entitle** (v) to give a name to
- **exhibition** (n) a display; an exhibit
- **explosion** (n) a detonation
- **evolve** (n) to change or develop slowly over time; to transform
- **facial** (adj) relating to the face
- **fame** (n) renown; celebrity
- **fashionable** (adj) popular; in style
- **feature** (v) to portray; to depict
- **fortune** (n) a large amount of money
- **forum** (n) a medium
- **frighten** (v) to scare; to make afraid
- **function** (v) to operate; to be in use
- **garner** (v) to gain; to collect; to glean
- **icon** (n) an image; a symbol
- **indisputable** (adj) unable to be argued; undeniable
- **innovative** (adj) new; novel
- **inspire** (v) to motivate
- **limited** (adj) restricted to some degree

- **lyrics** (n) the words to a song
- **master** (n) a person who excels at a certain trade or work
- **masterpiece** (n) a great work of art
- **objective** (n) a goal
- **offer** (v) to propose
- **opera** (n) a dramatic performance in which the performers often sing their parts
- **pacing** (n) the rate or speed of a performance
- **pale** (adj) ashen; excessively white
- **patron** (n) a person who sponsors someone or something, often related to the arts
- **percussion instrument** (n) a musical instrument such as a drum that is hit with a hand or stick
- **perspective** (n) a viewpoint
- **pitch** (n) the degree of a tone or sound
- **portray** (v) to depict; to show
- **popularity** (n) the act of being liked or approved of by others
- **practitioner** (n) a person who does something specific, often a profession
- **preserved** (adj) saved; conserved; remaining in one's original condition
- **reasoning** (n) logic
- **recognition** (n) acknowledgement
- **replace** (v) to take on a role that previously belonged to someone or something else
- **respect** (n) admiration
- **ritual** (n) a rite
- **sacred** (adj) holy
- **scar** (n) a marking on a body; a blemish; a wound
- **scream** (n) a high-pitched yell of fear
- **semblance** (n) a look; an appearance
- **shaman** (n) a person who acts as a connection between the real world and the spiritual world
- **shock** (v) to surprise greatly; to stun
- **shun** (v) to avoid
- **somber** (adj) serious
- **sponsor** (v) to provide another person with money to do a job often related to the arts
- **stand out** (v) to be obvious; to be apparent
- **startling** (adj) surprising; shocking
- **theatrical** (adj) relating to the theater
- **tone** (n) a pitch; a sound
- **upbeat** (adj) lighthearted
- **verify** (v) to prove to be true
- **version** (n) a particular form or type of something
- **visual** (n) something that can be seen
- **vivid** (adj) bright; colorful

✿ Choose the word or phrase closest in meaning to the highlighted part of the sentence.

1   Since the eyes can convey emotions, it is important for the audience to see them clearly.
   Ⓐ interpret
   Ⓑ understand
   Ⓒ express
   Ⓓ include

2   Perhaps these are depictions made by tribal elders to instruct the younger members in how to hunt.
   Ⓐ images
   Ⓑ lessons
   Ⓒ photographs
   Ⓓ directions

3   Impressionists preferred vivid colors and shunned the dark and drab ones used by realists.
   Ⓐ primary
   Ⓑ imaginative
   Ⓒ bright
   Ⓓ excessive

4   When other artists copied their styles, this also increased their fame.
   Ⓐ created
   Ⓑ imitated
   Ⓒ exhibited
   Ⓓ explained

5   These scholars argue that people would not have decorated places in which they did not live.
   Ⓐ scientists
   Ⓑ instructors
   Ⓒ clergymen
   Ⓓ academics

6   The movement itself was incredibly diverse.
   Ⓐ quite
   Ⓑ specifically
   Ⓒ systematically
   Ⓓ seriously

7   They could also be long epic poems, chansons, or other tales that told the deeds of great heroes from the past.
   Ⓐ ideas
   Ⓑ promotions
   Ⓒ feats
   Ⓓ proposals

8   And some might even utilize it to create the semblance of blood on their bodies.
   Ⓐ fact
   Ⓑ appearance
   Ⓒ scent
   Ⓓ awareness

9   Collecting art also became fashionable.
   Ⓐ expensive
   Ⓑ exclusive
   Ⓒ trendy
   Ⓓ clarified

10 Human and animal voices can also be included to shock or frighten an audience.
   Ⓐ inspire
   Ⓑ scare
   Ⓒ connect with
   Ⓓ distract

11 The most influential of all medieval musical instruments was the lute.
   Ⓐ expensive
   Ⓑ complicated
   Ⓒ significant
   Ⓓ uncommon

12 At other times, artists have received some measure of recognition during their lifetimes.

(A) amount
(B) article
(C) action
(D) approach

13 Some of the songs were even meant to frighten the enemy, which would give the singers the advantage in battle.

(A) surprise
(B) strategy
(C) clash
(D) edge

14 Many actors apply makeup around their eyes to make them stand out.

(A) put on
(B) establish
(C) create
(D) look up

15 If the music is more upbeat and lively, the audience will likely feel more lighthearted.

(A) sensational
(B) cheerful
(C) somber
(D) sinister

16 Still, music is above all intended to entertain.

(A) meant
(B) composed
(C) attracted
(D) timed

17 Ultimately, while there was some disagreement, it was generally agreed that the use of bright colors, short brushstrokes, and light in outdoor scenes constituted the main ideals of the movement.

(A) reported
(B) approved
(C) listed
(D) comprised

18 They then performed rituals as they drew the paintings on the walls.

(A) songs
(B) research
(C) hunts
(D) rites

19 The music and the sound effects are added in postproduction after everything has been filmed.

(A) recorded
(B) shown
(C) featured
(D) edited

20 Typically, a lute had four or five pairs of strings that were plucked.

(A) pressed
(B) hit
(C) pulled
(D) blown on

Part B

Chapter 03   Archaeology and Anthropology

Archaeology and anthropology focus on the study of prehistoric and ancient humans. Archaeologists study ancient people by researching the ruins, artifacts, and written texts left by past civilizations. Anthropologists focus on the development of humans over time. They conduct research on humans' beliefs, cultures, and social and physical development. People in both areas of study engage in fieldwork to do hands-on research to learn about the past. They must do a lot of guesswork because of the lack of written records. Therefore, they cannot confirm much of their work. Instead, they make educated guesses about past people and civilizations.

Mastering **the Question Types**

A

☑ Vocabulary   ☐ Fill in a Table   ☐ Factual Information   ☐ Negative Factual Information   ☑ Prose Summary
☐ Insert Text   ☐ Reference   ☑ Rhetorical Purpose   ☐ Sentence Simplification   ☐ Inference

Ancient Burial Customs

Archaeologists believe humans have been burying their dead for at least 50,000 years. The oldest intentional burial site ever found is in Israel. It dates back around 10,000 years. By unearthing tombs and graves from the past, archaeologists have managed to make many discoveries about burial customs from people in ancient cultures.

The Egyptians are widely known for converting their dead into mummies. One reason this was done was the hot, dry climate in the desert. It made mummification a practical way to bury people. In other locations around the Mediterranean Sea and in Europe, people buried their dead in the ground without mummifying them. Burial was, for example, practiced by the Greeks, the Romans, and the Celts. In India, however, Hindu culture often required that the deceased be <u>cremated</u>. Then, their ashes were spread into the Ganges River.

³➡ As a general rule, the dead were buried with various possessions of theirs. In ancient Egypt, wealthy individuals as well as pharaohs were buried in tombs with huge amounts of treasure, food, clothes, weapons, and other personal items. There were more than 5,000 relics found in the tomb of King Tutankhamen, which was discovered by Howard Carter in 1922. Among them were priceless artifacts made of gold. The Celts, among others, also buried their dead with personal items of great value.

Due to beliefs in the afterlife, people in ancient cultures had unique traditions. The Greeks would place a coin under the tongue of the deceased. This was to be given to Charon, a mythological figure who was a ferryman. He transported the dead across the river Styx and took them to the <u>underworld</u>. But he required payment of one coin. The Egyptians would bury food and drinks with the dead so that they would have nourishment in the afterlife.

Glossary
cremate: to burn a dead body down to ash
underworld: the place where the spirits of people went after they died

1 The word "converting" in the passage is closest in meaning to

   (A) appearing

   (B) requiring

   (C) transforming

   (D) exchanging

2 Why does the author mention "Howard Carter" in paragraph 3?

   (A) To name him as the person who found King Tutankhamen's tomb

   (B) To state that he was a world-famous archaeologist in the 1900s

   (C) To describe some of the 5,000 ancient Egyptian artifacts he unearthed

   (D) To discuss his theory on why the Egyptians mummified the dead

3 *Directions:* An introductory sentence for a brief summary of the passage is provided below. Complete the summary by selecting the THREE answer choices that express the most important ideas of the passage. Some sentences do not belong because they express ideas that are not presented in the passage or are minor ideas in the passage. *This question is worth 2 points.*

People in ancient cultures had some unique practices when it came to burying the dead.

Answer Choices

[1] People in many places in Europe and the Mediterranean buried the dead with various valuables.

[2] The tomb of King Tutankhamen was found with more than 5,000 relics, including gold items.

[3] Some civilizations, such as the Hindu culture in India, cremated people after they died.

[4] One burial practice that was common in ancient Egypt was to turn the dead into mummies.

[5] The first intentional burial site has been dated back to around 10,000 years ago.

[6] The ancient Greeks would bury the dead with a coin while the Egyptians buried them with food and drinks.

Summarizing　Complete the summary by using the words or phrases given in the box.

a coin	buried their dead	unique customs	their possessions

Humans have been burying the dead for around 50,000 years and had _____ in ancient times. The Egyptians turned people into mummies. But other cultures, such as the Greeks, the Romans, and the Celts, _____ . People were often buried with some of _____ . King Tutankhamen's tomb had more than 5,000 relics, and the Celts buried people with valuable personal items. The Greeks put _____ under the tongue of the deceased. And the Egyptians buried people with food and drinks.

Mastering **the Question Types**

B

☐ Vocabulary   ☑ Fill in a Table   ☐ Factual Information   ☑ Negative Factual Information   ☐ Prose Summary
☐ Insert Text   ☐ Reference   ☐ Rhetorical Purpose   ☐ Sentence Simplification   ☑ Inference

Ancient Greek Pottery

The ancient Greeks had a massive pottery industry. And they almost always painted designs on their pottery, particularly those used as decorations. Fortunately for archaeologists, huge numbers of Greek ceramics of all types have survived to the present day. This has provided them with a wealth of information about Greek pottery. The Greeks had several design styles, yet experts have determined that three were the major ones. They are, in chronological order, the geometric style, black-figure pottery, and red-figure pottery.

2→ From around 1000 B.C. to 700 B.C., the geometric style of pottery dominated. This was particularly true for Athens. No matter what kind of pottery was made, it was almost always decorated. The designs on the ceramics made by the Greeks were done with geometric figures. During this period, animal and human designs were **stylized** into shapes such as triangles and squares. This period also had a tremendous influence on later styles.

Around 700 B.C. in the Greek city-state of Corinth, the next major style emerged. It was known as black-figure pottery. The decorations in this style were actually made before the pottery was fired in the **kiln** a final time. As the pottery was cooking, the design turned black while the rest of the pot remained the original color of the clay, which was usually red.

4→ Black-figure pottery remained popular for around 150 years until it was surpassed by red-figure pottery. This style was created in Athens and was found to be much easier to work with than black-figure pottery. Essentially, the artists painted the background black. They then painted the outlines of the details of the pictures. The rest was left alone. Then, the pot was fired, so the picture turned red. Since this style permitted the artists to show more detail, it quickly became popular.

Glossary

stylize: to design; to form
kiln: an oven that is used to bake pottery

1   According to paragraph 2, which of the following is NOT true of the geometric style of pottery?

     (A) The figures created were done with regular shapes.

     (B) It was the first of the three major styles of Greek pottery.

     (C) It remained a major style in Greece for a millennium.

     (D) It featured pictures of living creatures on the pottery.

2   In paragraph 4, the author implies that Athens

     (A) collected the best pottery in ancient Greece

     (B) was where pottery was introduced to Greece

     (C) opposed the use of black-figure pottery

     (D) was influential on ancient Greek pottery

3   ***Directions:*** Select the appropriate statements from the answer choices and match them to the style of pottery to which they relate. TWO of the answer choices will NOT be used. ***This question is worth 4 points.***

Answer Choices	STYLE OF POTTERY
[1] Allowed artists to present many details	**Geometric Style**
[2] Was popular for a century and a half	•
[3] Is the style most frequently found by archaeologists	•
[4] Had the undecorated parts of the pottery turn red	**Black-Figure Pottery**
[5] Utilized triangles and squares for figures	•
[6] Was developed in a place other than Athens	•
[7] Was the third major style to be developed	•
[8] Had an important effect on later styles of pottery	**Red-Figure Pottery**
[9] Included decorations such as people and flowers	•
	•

Summarizing   Complete the summary by using the words or phrases given in the box.

squares	the geometric style	firing the pot	the level of detail

There were three major styles of pottery in ancient Greece. The first was _____ . It used shapes such as triangles and _____ to draw animals and people. The second was black-figure pottery. For it, artists made decorations prior to _____ in the kiln. This turned the design black and the pot red. Later, red-figure pottery was used. The pot turned black while the designs stayed red. Red-figure pottery was popular because of _____ it permitted.

Famines in Ancient Cultures

In ancient times, some cultures that seemed to be vibrant suddenly ceased to exist. There is usually a lack of evidence to explain why. They were not destroyed by warfare. Nor did natural disasters such as volcanic eruptions or earthquakes occur. This absence of solid evidence has led many archaeologists to conclude that famine—a lack of food—caused them to disappear.

²→ In the Americas, famines happened with regularity in ancient times. In some cases, the cultures completely died out. This is thought to be what occurred to the Anasazi, a tribe that started to dominate what is now the southwestern United States around 900. The Anasazi created their own unique culture. They farmed, hunted, made pottery, and traded with other tribes. They flourished as a people. Yet around 1130, they went into decline and quickly vanished. It is thought that decades of drought caused this. Due to crop failures, the Anasazi were unable to feed themselves. They may have even turned to **cannibalism**. By the 1200s, all of the Anasazi had died of starvation, moved elsewhere, or been absorbed into other tribes.

Unlike the Anasazi, other pre-Columbian American cultures did not suffer so greatly. Instead, some just slowly declined culturally due to famines. The most famous of them is the Maya Empire. The Mayas founded a large, cultured empire in the Central American rainforests. They had a golden age from around 300 to 900. **1** Then, Mayan culture began to dissolve from within. They were not **bested** in war by other tribes. **2** Many experts instead believe that the Mayas suffered from years of famine. **3** This likely happened since the soil they farmed on was poor due to their slash-and-burn land-clearing techniques. **4** While they did not disappear at once, they went into a slow decline. By 1500, the Maya Empire was no more.

Glossary

cannibalism: the practice of eating one's own species

bested: to be defeated, typically in battle

1 Which of the sentences below best expresses the essential information in the highlighted sentence in the passage? *Incorrect* answer choices change the meaning in important ways or leave out essential information.

(A) According to archaeologists, famines are responsible for a large number of extinct cultures.

(B) When no one is sure why a civilization vanished, then the most likely reason that it occurred is famine.

(C) Archaeologists may cite famine as a reason for vanished cultures when there is no other evidence.

(D) When a culture disappears, many archaeologists are quick to give the reason for this as a lack of food.

2 According to paragraph 2, which of the following is true of the Anasazi?

(A) They ate members of the tribes they captured in battle.

(B) They were the leading culture in their area for some time.

(C) They absorbed members of other tribes into their own.

(D) They were overcome by famine as well as war.

3 The word "them" in the passage refers to

(A) the Anasazi

(B) other pre-Columbian American cultures

(C) famines

(D) the Mayas

4 Look at the four squares [■] that indicate where the following sentence could be added to the passage.

Soil cleared in this manner frequently produced crops for only a couple of years.

Where would the sentence best fit?

Summarizing Complete the summary by using the words or phrases given in the box.

evidence	famines	dominated	drought

Vibrant cultures in the past sometimes suddenly disappeared. When there is no _____ for warfare or natural disasters, archaeologists often blame this on _____. In pre-Columbian America, there were many famines. Around 900, the Anasazi _____ a region in the modern-day southwestern United States. But they went into decline and disappeared by 1200. Many believe that _____, which led to famine, caused this. The Maya Empire was similarly affected. It likely experienced years of famine. It did not quickly disappear but went into a slow decline.

The Spread of Agriculture

Most anthropologists believe agriculture was independently developed in several locations. Among the first places were the Middle East, China, central Africa, New Guinea, and parts of Central and South America. From there, it spread all over the world. As a result, today, people farm land in virtually any area suitable for growing crops. However, agriculture did not simultaneously develop in these places. Instead, people discovered how to do it at various times in the past. In addition, due to reasons such as differences in soil, temperature, and rainfall, the first crops people raised varied from place to place.

²→ Humans are thought to have developed agriculture first in the Middle East. They did this in the region around the Tigris and Euphrates rivers. Scholars are not sure how people learned to farm. One of the most widely accepted theories is that bands of humans discovered that certain wild plants they ate grew in the same places every year. Through <u>rudimentary</u> experiments, people learned that the seeds could be taken and planted elsewhere, and then new plants would grow. From this humble beginning, people discovered farming.

³→ In the Middle East, the first major plant humans cultivated was wheat. Later, they domesticated lentils, chickpeas, flax, and barley. Knowledge of farming then spread from its place of origin. Both seeds and farming methods were taken to North Africa and Europe and also toward India. It is thought that farming first reached India around 9000 B.C. and Egypt by 7000 B.C. Most archaeologists claim that people began farming in southern Europe at the same time they were doing so in Egypt.

Farming was first practiced in China around 8000 B.C. Chinese farmers initially grew rice and millet. From China, knowledge of rice farming spread to India. In both regions, rice farming was <u>reliant</u> on the seasonal heavy monsoon rains. The next major place to develop farming was New Guinea. This happened around 7000 B.C. The plants that were first grown there are unknown, yet they may have been sugarcane or certain root plants.

Around 5000 B.C., people began farming in Central Africa and South and Central America. In Africa, the main crops were rice and sorghum. As for the Americas, the natives raised several crops. **1** The first European explorers discovered natives growing potatoes, tomatoes, corn, squash, and beans. **2** The Aztecs of Central America introduced plants and farming methods to tribes in North America. **3** The Incan people, who lived in the Andes Mountains, spread farming methods throughout South America. **4** In fact, Christopher Columbus and later explorers from the Old World arrived to find intensive agriculture going on in the New World.

Glossary
rudimentary: basic; elementary
reliant: dependent

NOTE

Before humans discovered agriculture, they were hunter-gatherers. So they hunted animals for food and collected wild grains and fruits to eat. They also lived nomadic lives. They followed herds of animals as they migrated from place to place. This let them have a constant food supply.

After humans discovered agriculture, they began to live in small villages. These were the first human settlements. The first villages and towns were in the Middle East.

Farming gave humans a more regular food supply. It also let people devote more time to pursuits other than gathering food. This is what led to the rise of civilization.

Even today, rice farmers in Asia depend on the monsoon rains to grow their crops.

Tomatoes were among the crops in the New World that were unknown in the rest of the world. Yet tomatoes did not become popular anywhere other than in the New World until many years later.

1 Why does the author mention "the Tigris and Euphrates rivers" in paragraph 2?

    (A) To claim that their fertile land was good for farming

    (B) To show where some people in the Middle East lived

    (C) To say that it was the location of the first civilization

    (D) To name the area where farming first developed

2 According to paragraph 3, which of the following is true of agriculture?

    (A) People in southern Europe started it around 7000 B.C.

    (B) Barley was the first plant that people began to cultivate.

    (C) It was practiced in Egypt before people in India did it.

    (D) Early farmers learned to raise both grains and fruits.

3 Look at the four squares [■] that indicate where the following sentence could be added to the passage.

Some of these crops were new to the foreign visitors, who introduced them to their native countries when they returned home.

Where would the sentence best fit?

4 *Directions:* Select the appropriate statements from the answer choices and match them to the farming location to which they relate. TWO of the answer choices will NOT be used. *This question is worth 3 points.*

Answer Choices	FARMING LOCATION
① Learned about rice farming from the Chinese	**Middle East**
② Was one of the last original places to discover agriculture	•
③ First farmed several different types of grains	•
④ Is said to be the place where people first learned to farm	**India**
⑤ Required large amounts of rain to raise some crops	•
⑥ Might have learned to raise root plants before any others	•
⑦ Instructed others in South America how to farm the land	**Central America**
	•

Summarizing Complete the summary by filling in the blanks.

Farming likely _____ in several places around the world at different times. The first place people learned how to farm was _____ . People there discovered agriculture and _____ elsewhere. They raised wheat and other plants. People in India learned about farming in 9000 B.C., in China around 8000 B.C, and in New Guinea around 7000 B.C. About 5000 B.C., farming was learned in Central Africa and South and Central America. People in the Americas grew _____ .

The Hohokam Tribe

From 300 to 1500, the Hohokam people occupied much of the land in what is now Arizona in the Southwestern United States. The Hohokams originated from the south in Mexico. For some reason, though, they migrated north to the area around the Gila and Salt rivers called the Tucson Basin. They were hunter-gatherers but also farmed the land. In fact, they utilized a unique irrigation system to help them grow crops. The Hohokams survived for over a millennium but had disappeared as a people by the time the first Spanish explorers arrived in the region in the 1600s.

2➡ While the Tucson Basin is mostly desert today, this was not true when the Hohokams lived there. Instead, it received some rainfall, <u>retained</u> water well, and had more vegetation than today. The streams and rivers then did not dry up completely during the summer. Finally, the region had a high water table. Thus the area likely had more than 200 days a year when there was sufficient water to grow crops.

The Hohokams changed the farming method used in the Tucson Basin. Previously, native tribes had planted crops on the <u>flood plains</u>. This was risky since flash floods could wash the crops away. The Hohokams established farms above the flood plains. To water their land, they devised a system of irrigation canals. These ingenious canals were so plentiful that they crisscrossed the region and provided ample amounts of water to the fields.

The Hohokams primarily raised corn, squash, beans, and cotton. They planted their crops in March and harvested them in July. Corn, their major crop, comprised an important part of their daily diets. They either ate it on the cob or dried it and ground it into flour. They used the flour to make bread and dumplings. They also utilized cotton as a food source and to make clothing. Cotton seeds were dried, ground, and made into cakes. The fibers were spun, and clothes were made from them. In addition to farming their food, the Hohokams ate meat—mostly rabbit and deer—and fish plus the seeds and fruits of wild plants.

Although the region saw occasional periods of drought, this did not cause the Hohokams to die out. Instead, they disappeared through assimilation into other tribes. This started in 1100 when they lost contact with their traditional homeland in Mexico. By 1500, much of their cultural distinctiveness was gone. Most of the Hohokams had joined other tribes and assumed their characteristics. Today, the only proof of their existence is the ruins archaeologists have found in the Southwestern United States.

NOTE

There have been many different tribes that lived in the area today covered by the American Southwest. One well-known tribe was the Anasazi, who lived there around the same time as the Hohokam.

The modern-day city of Tucson, Arizona, sits in the middle of the Tucson Basin. In addition, Saguaro National Park, a large desert area with many enormous cacti, is in the same area.

Flash floods can be very dangerous in deserts or dry environments. Because the ground is so dry, water does not soak into it easily. So even small amounts of rain can cause sudden, dangerous floods.

In general, the Hohokams obtained about half of their food from farming. Many times, they grew enough food that they could trade the surplus with other tribes.

In many cases, like that of the Anasazi, tribes were not assimilated by others. Instead, changes in the environment or warfare either killed the tribe members or forced them to move to other places.

Glossary

retain: to keep; to maintain
flood plain: an area around a river that often gets flooded during rainy conditions

1 Which of the sentences below best expresses the essential information in the highlighted sentence in the passage? *Incorrect* answer choices change the meaning in important ways or leave out essential information.

Ⓐ In spite of existing as a people for a millennium, the Hohokams were no match for the Spanish, who came in the 1600s.

Ⓑ When the Spanish came in the seventeenth century, the thousand-year existence of the Hohokams had already ended.

Ⓒ After the Spanish arrived, they defeated the Hohokams in battle and ended the natives' millennium-long reign.

Ⓓ The Spanish arrived in the 1600s to see the end of the Hohokams, who had lived as a tribe for a thousand years.

2 Which of the following can be inferred from paragraph 2 about the Tucson Basin?

Ⓐ There are places in it today where rivers and streams run.

Ⓑ The land there is not as fertile today as it once was.

Ⓒ It has expanded in size as desertification has occurred.

Ⓓ It rained so much in the past that many forests grew there.

3 The word "ample" in the passage is closest in meaning to

Ⓐ plentiful　　　　　　　　　　　Ⓑ exact

Ⓒ necessary　　　　　　　　　　Ⓓ conservative

4 *Directions:* An introductory sentence for a brief summary of the passage is provided below. Complete the summary by selecting the THREE answer choices that express the most important ideas of the passage. Some sentences do not belong because they express ideas that are not presented in the passage or are minor ideas in the passage. *This question is worth 2 points.*

The Hohokam people survived in the Tucson Basin thanks to their farming methods, but they slowly disappeared as a people over the course of several centuries.

Answer Choices

① While other tribes lived in the same area, the Hohokams were the dominant group for centuries.

② There were many droughts in the Hohokam's land, but these did not cause the Hohokams to vanish.

③ The Hohokams raised corn and cotton, which gave them both food and fibers to make clothes with.

④ The Hohokams' irrigation methods enabled them to provide enough water for all of their crops.

⑤ When the Hohokams lost touch with their ancestral homeland, their culture started declining until it vanished.

⑥ The Tucson Basin receives much less rainfall today than it used to, so it is less hospitable to people today.

Summarizing　Complete the summary by filling in the blanks.

From 300 to 1500, the Hohokam tribe dominated _____, an area that is now in the southwestern United States. It received enough rainfall then, so the land was good for farming. The Hohokams used canals to _____. They raised crops such as corn, squash, beans, and cotton. They relied heavily on corn but also _____ cotton. They used cotton for both food and clothing. The Hohokams were assimilated _____ over a period of about 400 years.

Mastering **the Subject**

Minoan Culture

The eastern part of the Mediterranean Sea has witnessed the rise and fall of many great cultures. For 1,500 years—from 2600 to 1100 B.C.—the Minoan culture was one of them. The Minoans lived on Crete, an island located southeast of Greece. A literate and artistic people, they built an impressive civilization. They traded with other cultures. And they became wealthy. When their civilization came to its mysterious end, they were among the most advanced people in the <u>Levant</u>.

Modern archaeologists have learned about Minoan civilization from two main sources. The ruins of palaces and other buildings are the first. The Minoans decorated their buildings with frescoes, a type of painting made with plaster. Frescoes are useful for studying the past since they do not decay as easily as paintings or paper documents do. They have therefore provided archaeologists with numerous pictorial views of Minoan life. The second source of information comes from records written on stone tablets. The Minoans developed a writing system called Linear B. Although it was a mystery for years, it was decoded in the twentieth century. As a result, the stone tablets could be read and translated. Most concern administrative matters, so they provide an <u>invaluable</u> look at how Minoan rulers organized their kingdoms.

³➡ Together, these clues present a coherent picture of Minoan life. The Minoans were farmers, fishermen, and traders. An island people, they relied heavily on the sea. They lacked a powerful navy as they used their sailing vessels for fishing and trading. They are known to have sailed to Egypt, Syria, and Greece since Minoan artifacts have been found in all three areas. The Minoans traded many goods, including copper and tin. They may have done the same with gold and silver. Their maritime trade made them wealthy and let them lead luxurious lives. Archaeologists have uncovered many signs pointing to the lives of leisure many Minoans enjoyed thanks to their wealth.

⁴➡ Unfortunately for the Minoans, their civilization suddenly vanished. The reason remains unknown to archaeologists. One possibility is a natural disaster. Crete often gets hit by earthquakes. They even destroyed some Minoan cities. Some speculate that a powerful earthquake may have caused enough death and destruction to have wiped out Minoan culture as a whole. Others believe a volcanic eruption in the Mediterranean may have killed the Minoans. And others think a seafaring culture visited Crete and conquered the Minoans. These are all merely guesses. What is known for sure is that the Minoans disappeared. While their culture would later influence others—particularly the Greeks—the Minoans themselves were no more.

NOTE

In ancient Greek mythology, King Minos lived on Crete. Minos was considered both a lawmaker and cruel tyrant. Beneath his castle was the Labyrinth, where the Minotaur, a monster with the head of a bull and the body of a man, was kept. It was later killed by the Greek hero Theseus.

Other artifacts from Minoan civilization have survived. These include gold and silvery jewelry, ivory ornaments, and ceramics.

Linear B was deciphered in 1952. Michael Ventris, a British archaeologist, was the man who did that.

In recent years, Minoan-style frescoes have been unearthed in Israel. This shows that the Minoans had a strong influence in the eastern part of the Mediterranean Sea as well.

A volcanic eruption on the modern-day island of Santorini—called Thera in the past—may have ended Minoan civilization. It might have caused a tsunami that destroyed many coastal areas.

Glossary

Levant: the lands located along the eastern shores of the Mediterranean Sea

invaluable: precious; of great importance or value

1 The word "They" in the passage refers to

(A) The Minoans

(B) Frescoes

(C) Paintings

(D) Paper documents

2 According to paragraph 3, which of the following is NOT true of the Minoans?

(A) They used military ships to dominate the Mediterranean Sea.

(B) Some of them amassed very much wealth through maritime trade.

(C) Their merchants sailed across the Mediterranean Sea to many places.

(D) Some of the goods that they traded were raw materials.

3 The author discusses the vanishing of Minoan civilization in paragraph 4 in order to

(A) put the most viable theories about their disappearance in order

(B) claim that it is the biggest unsolved mystery about the Minoans

(C) list some possible explanations for why the Minoans disappeared

(D) explain how the Minoans influenced others after they were gone

4 *Directions:* An introductory sentence for a brief summary of the passage is provided below. Complete the summary by selecting the THREE answer choices that express the most important ideas of the passage. Some sentences do not belong because they express ideas that are not presented in the passage or are minor ideas in the passage. *This question is worth 2 points.*

For a millennium and a half, the Minoans built a seafaring merchant culture that made many of its people rich, but they suddenly vanished for an unknown reason.

Answer Choices

1 Linear B, the language of the Minoans, was finally translated by scholars during the twentieth century.

2 Minoan sailors visited areas throughout the Mediterranean Sea, where they engaged in trade with the people there.

3 Natural disaster and warfare are two possible reasons why the Minoans ceased to exist as a culture.

4 Although the Minoans sailed all over the Mediterranean Sea, they did not have a strong navy to protect their merchant ships.

5 Minoan aristocrats constructed large palaces thanks to the wealth they accrued from trading in copper, tin, and other metals.

6 The written and painted sources from Minoan times show that some of the people led lives of wealth and luxury.

Summarizing   **Complete the summary by filling in the blanks.**

The Minoans lived on the island of Crete from around 2600 to 1100 B.C. Archaeologists have learned about them because of the ruins of their palaces and _____, their writing system. The Minoans used ships to trade all over _____. They traded metals and other goods, which _____. Minoan culture suddenly vanished around 1100 B.C. No one is sure what happened. There may have been _____ that destroyed their culture, or they could have been invaded by another people.

How the Pyramids Were Built

Part of the Giza Pyramid Complex

¹→ Most archaeologists agree that the Egyptians built the pyramids as tombs for their pharaohs—Egyptian kings. Yet the process by which they were made is uncertain. Some of the largest pyramids, such as the Great Pyramid at Giza, contain almost a million large square blocks. Some blocks weigh several tons apiece. The primary question facing archaeologists is how the Egyptians managed to shape, move, and place so many large blocks without advanced machines or electrical power. Some archaeologists believe they know the truth: The Egyptians used human and animal power as well as their knowledge of math and engineering to build the pyramids.

²→ The first task was the cutting of the massive stones, which were mostly granite and limestone. These stones were hewed from **quarries** found up and down the Nile River. The soft limestone was easy to cut with copper tools. Granite is much harder, so it required tougher tools. Those were made of dolerite, a hard, volcanic rock. Using copper and dolerite tools, Egyptian workers shaped the stones into the appropriate sizes. To cut the stones out, the workers made holes and drove wooden pegs into them. Then, they poured water into the holes. This made the wooden pegs expand, and the stones subsequently cracked.

³→ Next, the cut stones had to be moved. Stones from quarries far away were brought to the Nile, loaded onto barges, and transported on water. Those closer to the site were moved by muscle power. Teams of people and oxen placed the stone blocks on wooden sleds. Most pyramids were made from 2700 to 1700 B.C. At that time, the Egyptians were ignorant of the wheel, which would have made transporting the stones easier. Instead, they **lubricated** the wooden sleds. This made the pathways as smooth as possible. People and oxen then dragged the loads to their destinations.

⁴→ Placing the stones presented another problem. As a pyramid grew higher, large stones had to be raised to higher elevations. Most evidence suggests that large ramps were used for this purpose. Experts, however, disagree on what kind of ramp was used. Some believe a single ramp that became progressively higher and wider—to strengthen it—was made. Others claim that a series of ramps spiraled their way up around the pyramid. **1** Whatever the case, the ramps were made of earth and stone and had smooth tops. **2** The sleds carrying the stones were dragged up the ramps, and the stones were then put in their proper positions. **3** Once construction was complete, the ramps were dismantled. **4**

5➜ The final question concerns the laborers who built the pyramids. Slaves were surely involved. But many experts believe free Egyptian peasants did most of the work. They were offered incentives to work, and the pharaohs made sure they had shelter and adequate food supplies. Perhaps 20,000 to 30,000 people simultaneously worked on a single pyramid. Building them was a tremendous logistical undertaking. They took years to construct. The Great Pyramid at Giza itself required at least twenty-three years to make. Constructing a pyramid actually took so long that most pharaohs began building their tombs as soon as they attained power so that their resting places would be ready for them when they died.

Glossary
quarry: a place where rocks used for construction are cut
lubricate: to oil or grease something in order to make it smoother or slippery

1 According to paragraph 1, the construction of the pyramids is a mystery to archaeologists because

    Ⓐ the Egyptians did not use modern construction techniques

    Ⓑ they do not know how the Egyptians moved such large stones

    Ⓒ the Egyptians are not thought to have used any pack animals

    Ⓓ ancient descriptions of their construction have not been translated

2 In paragraph 2, the author uses "dolerite" as an example of

    Ⓐ a stone that can cut granite

    Ⓑ something harder than copper

    Ⓒ a construction material for the pyramids

    Ⓓ a kind of ore found in Egypt

3 According to paragraph 2, which of the following is NOT true of the process used to cut rocks from quarries?

    Ⓐ A multistep process was necessary for hard rocks.

    Ⓑ Workers lifted the stones out with wooden pegs.

    Ⓒ It required tools harder than the rocks being extracted.

    Ⓓ It was simple to extract some of the rocks.

4 The word "ignorant" in the passage is closest in meaning to

    Ⓐ unaware

    Ⓑ unknown

    Ⓒ unintelligent

    Ⓓ uninspired

5 In paragraph 3, the author implies that the Egyptians

    Ⓐ used oil they pumped to lubricate the sleds

    Ⓑ invented the wheel after they built the pyramids

    Ⓒ relied more on oxen than people to push their carts

    Ⓓ built ships that could carry heavy loads

6 According to paragraph 4, which of the following is true of the ramps used while building the pyramids?

    Ⓐ They were made out of stones from the quarries.

    Ⓑ They became higher as construction continued.

    Ⓒ They were left in place after the pyramids were finished.

    Ⓓ They were oiled when the sleds were dragged up them.

7 According to paragraph 5, which of the following is true of the construction of the pyramids?

    Ⓐ Most pyramids required around two decades to complete.

    Ⓑ The people who worked on them were all compensated.

    Ⓒ Tens of thousands of people worked on them at the same time.

    Ⓓ The pharaohs abused the majority of people working on them.

8   Which of the sentences below best expresses the essential information in the highlighted sentence in the passage? *Incorrect* answer choices change the meaning in important ways or leave out essential information.

    (A) When a pharaoh took power, he usually started building a pyramid to be buried in because of the length of time it took to make one.

    (B) The pharaohs were concerned with having a tomb to be buried in, so they began to construct theirs at some point in their lives.

    (C) To guarantee that their pyramids would be complete when they died, Egyptian pharaohs spared no expense while constructing them.

    (D) The pyramids served as tombs for the pharaohs, who made them the most important construction project during their lives.

9   Look at the four squares [■] that indicate where the following sentence could be added to the passage.

The materials in the ramps could then be used for other construction projects nearby.

Where would the sentence best fit?

> Click on a square [■] to add the sentence to the passage.

10 ***Directions:*** An introductory sentence for a brief summary of the passage is provided below. Complete the summary by selecting the THREE answer choices that express the most important ideas of the passage. Some sentences do not belong because they express ideas that are not presented in the passage or are minor ideas in the passage. ***This question is worth 2 points.***

> Drag your answer choices to the spaces where they belong.
> To remove an answer choice, click on it. To review the passage, click on **View Text**.

While archaeologists are not positive they know how the pyramids are built, many believe it was a process that required humans, animals, and ingenuity.

-
-
-

Answer Choices

1 In order to get the hardest stones out of the quarries, a method using wooden pegs and water was devised by the Egyptians.

2 The Egyptians constructed enormous ramps to bring the stones up to the highest parts of the pyramids.

3 The pyramids were some of the largest manmade structures in the world for thousands of years until the time of the Renaissance.

4 The pharaohs built the pyramids so that they could be entombed in them once they died and went to the afterlife.

5 The stones used for the pyramids were transported on sleds that were dragged by either humans or animals.

6 Some people have suggested that the Egyptians required alien or advanced technology in order to build the pyramids.

Star Performer Subject Topics | Archaeology and Anthropology

1 Sumerian Culture

One of the world's first cultures was founded in Sumer. Its people became known as the Sumerians. Sumer was a group of ancient city-states located around the Tigris and Euphrates rivers in the Middle East. Sumerian culture first arose sometime between 4500 and 4000 B.C. Two of its earliest cities were Eridu and Uruk. The people were successful farmers thanks to the irrigations methods they used. The Sumerians developed their own language, which they recorded. The epic poem *Gilgamesh* comes from this culture. They also had many temples in which the Sumerian people worshipped a number of gods and goddesses.

2 The Maya

One of the greatest Mesoamerican cultures was the Maya. They lived in Central America in the area covered in part by modern-day Guatemala, Honduras, and Belize. Evidence of the Maya goes back to at least 1000 B.C. They flourished as a culture from 300 to 900 A.D. The Maya founded large numbers of minor kingdoms. They farmed the land, but they also engaged in trade. The Maya developed fairly advanced cities, which were used by the aristocracy and priestly classes. They were also well versed in architecture, math, and astronomy. For unknown reasons, their culture declined, and they disappeared by 1500.

3 Animal Domestication

Humans have domesticated, or tamed, animals since around 9,000 B.C. It is believed that the first animals to be tamed were dogs. Sheep and goats were also tamed by humans early on. Humans tamed animals for several reasons. Some—such as horses and oxen—could do work for them. Others—such as sheep, goats, cattle, and chickens—could provide food for them. And dogs could provide both protection—as guard animals—and companionship. Different cultures domesticated various animals. The animals they tamed depended mostly on which ones lived in a particular area.

4 Migrations to the Americas

Anthropologists generally agree that humans first evolved in Africa. From there, they spread to the rest of the world. The last two continents to be settled were North and South America. There are two theories on how people migrated there. Some believe people sailed ships from Polynesian islands to the Americas. But many disregard this theory. Most believe the first humans migrated over a land bridge in the Bering Sea. This connected modern-day Siberia in Asia and Alaska in North America. This happened around 16,000 to 13,000 years ago during the last ice age. Afterward, humans wandered south to populate both continents.

5 Archaeological Methods

Archaeologists have two major ways in which they learn about the past. The first is to read. They may read primary sources, which were written by people when the events occurred. Or they may read secondary sources, which were written by people after the events occurred. But many events from the past are not recorded. This is particularly true for prehistoric cultures. In these cases, archaeologists must go on site and excavate areas. They search for ruins and other evidence of past civilizations and cultures. Then, they analyze and interpret what they find to help them understand the past.

6 Cultural Diffusion

All cultures develop at different paces. For instance, humans did not all develop civilization at once. Instead, it arose first in certain areas of the world. Then, it spread to other people and places. This is known as cultural diffusion. Sometimes it is called transcultural diffusion. Ideas, religions, technology, languages, and many other features spread from culture to culture through diffusion. Knowing about diffusion can be helpful to archaeologists. For example, it can suggest when a culture developed writing. It can also explain how a culture developed a certain technology.

7 ► Neanderthal Man

There have been many ancestors of modern man. One of these was Neanderthal Man. The Neanderthals lived mostly in Europe, the Mediterranean region, and parts of Asia. They lived around 120,000 to 30,000 years ago. They were about the size of the average modern human. But they were very muscular and much more powerful. They had larger brains than modern humans, yet they were not as intelligent. At some point, they came into contact with modern humans. But the Neanderthals could not adapt as quickly as modern humans did. So they eventually died out.

8 ► The Fertile Crescent

The Fertile Crescent was a region in Africa and the Middle East. It started at the Nile River in Egypt. It stretched across the Syrian Desert to the Tigris and Euphrates rivers. Today, much of that area is desert and uninhabitable land. Thousands of years ago, it was more hospitable and teemed with life. It was where the first human civilizations arose around 10,000 years ago. The Egyptian, Babylonian, and Mesopotamian cultures were all located there. In the Fertile Crescent, men finally stopped living nomadic lives. Then, they learned farming and began to build cities.

9 ► The Stone Age

The earliest human prehistoric age is called the Stone Age. This was the period when humans began making stone tools. Different stones were used for different tools. Hard stones were used to make weapons and cutting tools. Softer stones were used for other kinds of tools. Archaeologists have divided the Stone Age into three major periods. They are the Paleolithic, Mesolithic, and Neolithic periods. During these three periods, which lasted thousands of years, human knowledge improved. Humans went from mastering fire to developing metallurgy during these periods. As the Neolithic Period ended, humans had started making metal tools.

10 ► Hunter-Gatherers

Early hominids and primitive humans were all hunter-gatherers. They did not know how to farm the land. So they had to hunt or gather food in order to survive. These people also lived nomadic lives. Typically, they hunted large herds of animals. Many of these animals migrated throughout the year. So the hunter-gatherers followed the herds as they migrated. Some of them also fished when they were near water. They further supplemented their diets by eating various fruits, vegetables, and grains that they found growing in the wild.

11 ► Australopithecus

Modern man, called *Homo sapiens*, has evolved over millions of years. One of man's earliest ancestors was Australopithecus. There were seven species of them. They all lived in Africa somewhere between 4.4 and 1.2 million years ago. They belonged to the family *Hominidae*, which includes humans and their closest relatives. They were bipeds, so they walked on two feet. Their faces and skulls had some similarities with humans'. But they were tinier and had smaller brains than modern humans. Little is known about Australopithecus because of a lack of evidence. Yet it is believed that modern man evolved from them.

12 ► Riverside Civilizations

Most early human civilizations developed along rivers. The Mesopotamians arose by the Tigris and Euphrates rivers. Egyptian civilization originated beside the Nile River. The Indus Valley people settled next to the Indus River. And cities in China grew up by the Yellow River. Water was crucial to early people. Not only did they drink it, but they also used it to water their crops once they learned farming. They kept their animals near rivers to provide them with water as well. And water was an easy way both to travel and to transport goods from place to place.

- **absorb** (v) to take into; to soak up
- **afterlife** (n) life after death
- **artifact** (n) an object of historical value; a relic
- **artistic** (adj) creative; having to do with art
- **background** (n) a backdrop
- **barge** (n) a flat-bottomed boat used to transport goods
- **bury** (v) to put something such as a body in the ground and to cover it with earth
- **ceramic** (n) pottery
- **chronological** (adj) having to do with time
- **coherent** (adj) clear
- **conquer** (v) to defeat; to win against; to overcome
- **crack** (v) to break apart; to crumble
- **crisscross** (v) to interlace; to cut back and forth across something
- **decade** (n) a period of ten years
- **deceased** (n) a dead person
- **decline** (v) to decrease in value or importance
- **decode** (v) to decipher
- **decoration** (n) an ornament; something that is intended to make another object better looking
- **devise** (v) to create; to come up with; to think of
- **diet** (n) the food that one eats on a daily basis
- **dissolve** (v) to fall apart; to crumble
- **distinctiveness** (n) individuality; uniqueness
- **document** (n) an official paper
- **domesticated** (adj) tamed
- **dominate** (v) to rule over; to control
- **drag** (v) to pull something, often a heavy object
- **drought** (n) an extended period of time without rainfall
- **earthquake** (n) the sudden shaking of the earth; a tremor
- **elevation** (n) altitude; height
- **emerge** (v) to arise
- **eruption** (n) the explosion of something, such as a volcano
- **establish** (v) to build; to create
- **failure** (n) the nonperformance of something, such as crops
- **famine** (n) an extended period of time in which crops do not grow
- **fire** (v) to bake pottery in a kiln
- **flash flood** (n) a sudden flood caused by an intense period of rainfall
- **fresco** (n) a kind of painting that is done on plaster

- **grave** (n) the place where someone is buried
- **harvest** (v) to reap; to collect plants that are ripe
- **hew** (v) to cut
- **homeland** (n) the place where a person or group of people is from
- **humble** (adj) modest
- **impressive** (adj) large; incredible
- **ingenious** (adj) clever; brilliant
- **intensive** (adj) concentrated; rigorous
- **invaluable** (adj) precious; of great worth
- **irrigation** (n) a process in which water for farming is brought from one place to another
- **kingdom** (n) the land that is ruled by a king
- **literate** (adj) able to read and write
- **logistical** (adj) relating to logistics, which is the obtaining of supplies
- **maritime** (adj) naval; relating to the sea
- **millennium** (n) a period of one thousand years
- **monsoon** (n) a heavy seasonal rain
- **mummy** (n) the preserved body of a person as practiced by the ancient Egyptians
- **mysterious** (adj) unexplained; unusual
- **mythological** (adj) imaginary; relating to something from myths or stories from the past
- **native** (n) a person who lives in a specific region
- **peasant** (n) a person of very low status
- **pharaoh** (n) an ancient Egyptian king
- **priceless** (adj) invaluable; being of great worth or value
- **progressively** (adv) increasingly; becoming greater in size or scope
- **proof** (n) evidence that something is true or correct
- **pursue** (v) to engage in, as in an activity or a hobby
- **raise** (v) to grow, as in crops
- **risky** (adj) dangerous
- **seafaring** (adj) oceangoing
- **speculate** (v) to propose; to postulate; to believe
- **spiral** (v) to move around in a circular motion
- **spread** (v) to move from one place to another
- **starvation** (n) hunger
- **sufficient** (adj) enough
- **technique** (n) a way of doing something
- **treasure** (n) something that is of great value
- **unearth** (v) to dig up from under the ground
- **vegetation** (n) plant life
- **witness** (v) to see something as it occurs; to observe

✿ Choose the word or phrase closest in meaning to the highlighted part of the sentence.

1   This absence of solid evidence has led many archaeologists to conclude that famine—a lack of food—caused them to disappear.

    Ⓐ visual
    Ⓑ concrete
    Ⓒ written
    Ⓓ buried

2   They were offered incentives to work, and the pharaohs made sure they had shelter and adequate food supplies.

    Ⓐ sufficient
    Ⓑ extravagant
    Ⓒ nutritious
    Ⓓ tasty

3   Cotton seeds were dried, ground, and made into cakes.

    Ⓐ eaten
    Ⓑ crushed
    Ⓒ rolled
    Ⓓ cooked

4   There were more than 5,000 relics found in the tomb of King Tutankhamen, which was discovered by Howard Carter in 1922.

    Ⓐ valuables
    Ⓑ weapons
    Ⓒ jewels
    Ⓓ artifacts

5   In the Middle East, the first major plant humans cultivated was wheat.

    Ⓐ adapted
    Ⓑ picked
    Ⓒ ate
    Ⓓ grew

6   An island people, they relied heavily on the sea.

    Ⓐ solely
    Ⓑ greatly
    Ⓒ fiercely
    Ⓓ somewhat

7   As the pottery was cooking, the design turned black while the rest of the pot remained the original color of the clay, which was usually red.

    Ⓐ stayed
    Ⓑ turned
    Ⓒ rejected
    Ⓓ assumed

8   They have therefore provided archaeologists with numerous pictorial views of ancient Minoan life.

    Ⓐ illustrated
    Ⓑ substantial
    Ⓒ accurate
    Ⓓ cartoonish

9   The streams and rivers then did not dry up completely during the summer.

    Ⓐ erode
    Ⓑ eradicate
    Ⓒ exterminate
    Ⓓ evaporate

10   The sleds carrying the stones were dragged up the ramps, and the stones were then put in their proper positions.

    Ⓐ correct
    Ⓑ individual
    Ⓒ elevated
    Ⓓ distinctive

11 In some cases, the cultures completely died out.

Ⓐ sporadically
Ⓑ entirely
Ⓒ individually
Ⓓ rapidly

12 Archaeologists have uncovered many signs pointing to the lives of leisure many Minoans enjoyed thanks to their wealth.

Ⓐ recognized
Ⓑ portrayed
Ⓒ discovered
Ⓓ theorized

13 Today, the only proof of their existence is the ruins archaeologists have found in the Southwestern United States.

Ⓐ research
Ⓑ belief
Ⓒ evidence
Ⓓ legend

14 It made mummification a practical way to bury people.

Ⓐ useful
Ⓑ popular
Ⓒ relevant
Ⓓ simple

15 Granite is much harder, so it required tougher tools.

Ⓐ larger
Ⓑ more advanced
Ⓒ more suitable
Ⓓ stronger

16 In both regions, rice farming was reliant on the seasonal heavy monsoon rains.

Ⓐ weathered
Ⓑ cyclical
Ⓒ periodical
Ⓓ occasional

17 This likely happened since the soil they farmed on was poor due to their slash-and-burn land-clearing techniques.

Ⓐ hard
Ⓑ barren
Ⓒ dry
Ⓓ unproductive

18 Building a pyramid actually took so long that most pharaohs began building their tombs as soon as they attained power so that their resting places would be ready for them when they died.

Ⓐ crypts
Ⓑ cemeteries
Ⓒ graveyards
Ⓓ shrouds

19 As a result, today, people farm land in virtually any area suitable for growing crops.

Ⓐ visual
Ⓑ accepted
Ⓒ appropriate
Ⓓ fortunate

20 No matter what kind of pottery was made, it was almost always decorated.

Ⓐ pretty
Ⓑ cooked
Ⓒ glazed
Ⓓ adorned

Part B

Chapter 04   Education, Sociology, and Psychology

Education, sociology, and psychology are three prominent social sciences. Education is concerned with both learning and teaching, so its practitioners focus on teaching and learning methods in their research. Sociology studies human societies, both past and present. Sociologists try to understand how societies develop, organize, progress, and function. They often make comparisons between past and present human societies. Psychologists are interested in learning about how people think and what makes them think in certain ways. They may examine mental issues that people have. These three fields are different, yet they all emphasize humans, their thought processes, and the results of their thoughts.

Mastering **the Question Types**

A

☑ Vocabulary   ☐ Fill in a Table   ☐ Factual Information   ☐ Negative Factual Information   ☑ Prose Summary
☐ Insert Text   ☐ Reference   ☑ Rhetorical Purpose   ☐ Sentence Simplification   ☐ Inference

The Effects of Advertisements on Children

Businesses constantly advertise their products to encourage people to purchase them. Many focus on advertising to children. According to some experts, the average child is exposed to about 40,000 advertisements each year. This includes advertisements on television and the Internet and in newspapers and magazines. These experts have determined that ads have both positive and negative effects on children.

² → Some ads focus on positive values such as honesty. These ads can encourage children to be truthful to others. There are also ads that encourage children not to drink, smoke, or take illegal drugs and to live healthy lives. And some ads, particularly those for products based on advanced technology, inform children about new innovations. In that regard, they help educate young people about society. Those are all ways in which ads can be beneficial to young people.

Nevertheless, experts argue that ads have many more negative effects on children. For example, **junk food** ads, such as those for breakfast cereals, snacks, and fast food, are often aimed at children. They may feature healthy, attractive people consuming the products. The children watching those ads assume the actors actually use the products. So they see no harm in trying the products themselves. They do not realize that eating too much junk food will make them overweight. This is one cause of the high rates of youth obesity in modern times.

Another negative aspect of ads is that some show people engaging in dangerous behavior. As an example, skateboard commercials often show people performing dangerous stunts. The ads may have **disclaimers** stating that people should not try the moves at home because they could get hurt. Still, children ignore those warnings and attempt the same tricks. This has resulted in many children being injured and even hospitalized.

Glossary

junk food: food that is high in calories but has little or no nutritional value
disclaimer: a statement stating that a person or group does not take responsibility for something

1   In paragraph 2, why does the author mention "honesty"?

    Ⓐ To argue that it cannot be found in most advertisements

    Ⓑ To compare this value with some more negative ones

    Ⓒ To complain that few advertisements focus on this trait

    Ⓓ To focus on a beneficial aspect of some advertisements

2   The word "stunts" in the passage is closest in meaning to

    Ⓐ styles

    Ⓑ feats

    Ⓒ rides

    Ⓓ races

3   ***Directions:*** An introductory sentence for a brief summary of the passage is provided below. Complete the summary by selecting the THREE answer choices that express the most important ideas of the passage. Some sentences do not belong because they express ideas that are not presented in the passage or are minor ideas in the passage. ***This question is worth 2 points.***

Advertisements can have both positive and negative effects on children.

Answer Choices

⓵ A large number of children have begun using illegal drugs on account of certain advertisements.

⓶ Some ads that show dangerous acts encourage children to imitate them and then get hurt.

⓷ Misleading ads for certain unhealthy foods have likely caused many children to become overweight.

⓸ A lot of advertisements educate children about the world and teach them how to act properly.

⓹ Children may see more than 40,000 advertisements in different formats on a yearly basis.

⓺ Some ads introduce aspects of advanced technology to children to help them learn about it.

Summarizing   Complete the summary by using the words or phrases given in the box.

new innovations	try the stunts	focus on advertising	become overweight

Businesses _____ to children so much that they may see 40,000 ads a year. Ads can be positive. Some show positive values such as honesty and introduce advanced technology and _____ to children. But junk food ads can show healthy, attractive people. Children think those actors use the products, so they try them and then _____. Other ads show dangerous behavior such as skateboard stunts. Despite warnings in the ads, children _____ and then get hurt and may be hospitalized.

John Dewey and Education

¹➡ John Dewey was an American philosopher and educational **reformer**. He lived from 1859 to 1952. He was involved in many fields. But most people remember his work in education. Dewey felt that the educational system was ineffective. During his time, most students learned by listening to teachers lecturing in classrooms. They took notes. Then, they studied the lessons for their exams. Dewey disliked this system. He thought this style of learning offered no practical experience. So he wrote a book entitled *Experience and Education*. In his work, he outlined his philosophy of education.

Dewey wrote about what he called experiential education. Others refer to it as progressive education. Its main elements are doing projects and taking a hands-on approach to learning. Dewey was eager for students to do activities. He also stressed doing group work and problem solving. He wanted students to learn about various issues. They would discuss these issues together. Then, they would try to devise an effective solution. If students tested possible solutions, Dewey felt they could find the best way to solve any problem.

³➡ Dewey's ideas on education became popular. They influenced several generations of educators. Even today, people still try to **implement** his ideas. As a result, several new types of education have been developed. These include outdoor education, service learning, and environmental learning. In outdoor education, students take part in outside activities. Two examples are camping and hiking. They teach students about nature. They also give students hands-on experience at being outdoors. Service learning gets students to do work in their communities. This may take the form of assisting the elderly or the poor. Environmental learning occurs when students work on environmental issues. Recycling and forest management are two of these.

Glossary
reformer: a person who attempts to make changes to something
implement: to put into practice

1 In paragraph 1, the author's description of the state of education during John Dewey's time mentions all of the following EXCEPT:

(A) How teachers instructed their students

(B) How students benefitted from the system

(C) How students had their knowledge tested

(D) What students did while their teachers lectured

2 In paragraph 3, which of the following can be inferred about John Dewey's teaching philosophy?

(A) Instructors that follow it use several teaching methods.

(B) It takes people many years to learn how to use it.

(C) He came up with his ideas by teaching elementary school.

(D) The most important part of it is environmental learning.

3 *Directions:* Select the appropriate sentences from the answer choices and match them to the aspect of John Dewey's teaching philosophy to which they relate. TWO of the answer choices will NOT be used. *This question is worth 3 points.*

Answer Choices

1 Students may spend time outdoors.

2 Some students are involved in community work.

3 Students should do hands-on activities.

4 Dewey wrote a book called *Experience and Education*.

5 There are many new types of education today.

6 Students work together with others.

7 There were many fields that interested Dewey.

JOHN DEWEY'S TEACHING PHILOSOPHY

Principles

•

•

Influences on Educators

•

•

•

Summarizing Complete the summary by using the words or phrases given in the box.

| a hands-on approach | environmental learning | American education | forms of education |

John Dewey was an American educator. He disliked the state of _____ during his life. At that time, teachers lectured, students took notes, and the students took tests. Dewey preferred _____ to education. He also liked group work and problem solving. Many educators were influenced by Dewey, so they developed new _____ . These included outdoor education, service learning, and _____ . These types of education let students do activities they would not normally get an opportunity to do in the classroom.

Mastering **the Question Types**

☐ Vocabulary ☐ Fill in a Table ☑ Factual Information ☐ Negative Factual Information ☐ Prose Summary
☑ Insert Text ☑ Reference ☐ Rhetorical Purpose ☑ Sentence Simplification ☐ Inference

Villages and Towns in the Middle Ages

¹➡ Most historians agree that the Roman Empire fell in 476. This began the period in Europe known as the Middle Ages. They would last until the Renaissance started around 1400. At the start of the Middle Ages, civilization declined. There was a lack of learning, and urban centers began crumbling. Many historians refer to this bleak period as the Dark Ages. Over time, society began to rebuild itself. But rather than live in cities, people mostly lived in small villages. The local nobles typically controlled these people and ruled them under a system known as <u>feudalism</u>.

Life under the feudal system was hard for most peasants. The villagers worked their own land and provided labor for their noble's land. The noble lived in a castle or large manor house, and his word was law. **1** Religion, in the guise of the Catholic Church, played a major role in people's lives. **2** The villages were isolated yet self-sustaining. **3** So the villagers made their own food, clothes, and whatever else they needed. **4** Coined money was rare, so much trade was done by the <u>barter system</u>.

However, as the Middle Ages progressed, conditions improved. Both trade and population increased. Many villages became towns. As trade became more common, some townsmen became wealthy and powerful. These individuals were free men and owed no labor service to their local nobles. They still had to pay a part of their earnings to the nobles. Eventually, however, these free townsmen formed guilds of craftsmen and merchants, which enabled them better to control business and trade in their local areas. The guildsmen became the most powerful members of their towns and often established local governments. This system of local town government began to spread and eventually helped make feudalism die out in much of Europe.

Glossary
feudalism: a social system that was practiced during medieval Europe
barter system: a system in which people trade goods and services for other goods and services rather than for money

1   According to paragraph 1, which of the following is true of the Dark Ages?

    Ⓐ They happened at the start of the Middle Ages.

    Ⓑ They were a time when society started rebuilding.

    Ⓒ They took place before the Roman Empire fell.

    Ⓓ Many people lived in cities during this period.

2   The word "They" in the passage refers to

    Ⓐ Many villages

    Ⓑ Towns

    Ⓒ Some townsmen

    Ⓓ Their local nobles

3   Which of the sentences below best expresses the essential information in the highlighted sentence in the passage? *Incorrect* answer choices change the meaning in important ways or leave out essential information.

    Ⓐ Since the townsmen had control over local trade, they were able to organize into specialized groups.

    Ⓑ A lot of merchants and other individuals organized themselves into groups that were known as guilds.

    Ⓒ The people in many towns were interested in coming up with ways to control the economy better.

    Ⓓ Some people in the town established guilds, which gave them more power over the local economy.

4   Look at the four squares [■] that indicate where the following sentence could be added to the passage.

In fact, the Church was arguably more important to the people than their local noble was.

Where would the sentence best fit?

Summarizing   **Complete the summary by using the words or phrases given in the box.**

established local governments	feudalism	the Dark Ages	provide services

After the Roman Empire fell, the Middles Ages began. The first part was called _____.
This was a time when cities disappeared and people lived in villages. They lived under a system called
_____. In it, the villagers were under the control of the local noble. They had to
_____ for him. However, as the Middle Ages progressed, this changed. Some men became
wealthy merchants and craftsmen. They started to form guilds and later _____. These men
helped end feudalism throughout Europe.

Mastering **the Subject**

Urban and Rural Neighborly Relationships

Humans have historically lived in rural communities. Yet once the Industrial Revolution began in the 1700s, people began to move away from rural areas and into cities. As a result, in many countries, a majority of the population now lives either in cities or suburbs. Nevertheless, many countries, such as the United States, still have sizable rural populations. Life in urban and rural areas is quite different. This is particularly obvious in how neighbors in both places relate to and interact with one another.

2→ The types of dwellings people in both regions have account for some of the differences. In villages and small towns, most people live in private houses. They have yards and gardens and spend time outdoors, where they often encounter their neighbors. They chat with their neighbors about various topics. They also invite their neighbors to barbecues, parties, and other social gatherings. This lets them become close to one another. In cities, however, many people live in cramped apartments. They rarely see their neighbors except on the elevator or in the lobby. They might only greet or nod even to their next-door neighbors instead of getting to know them better. Ironically, while **urbanites** live closer to one another, they know their neighbors much less than people in rural areas do.

3→ People in rural areas do not always get along with one another. Yet in rural settings, the bonds between neighbors are stronger. One reason is that many people in rural areas are related. It is not surprising to find several common **surnames** for people living in a certain area. Many are brothers, sisters, cousins, uncles, and aunts. This is much rarer in cities. Additionally, in rural areas, even unrelated people frequently attend the same schools, play on the same sports teams, and engage in the same activities. While this happens in cities, the level of interaction with neighbors is not nearly as high as it is in rural environments.

The level of trust in both places differs. Those in rural communities are more likely to know and trust one another. In contrast, there is less trust between neighbors in urban areas. This has led to the strange phenomenon in which one can more easily get aid in a sparsely populated rural area than in a city with millions of people. People in rural areas are highly likely to offer assistance to those in need because they are liable to know the person who needs help. This is not true in cities, where pleas for assistance often go ignored.

NOTE

In most developed countries, the percentage of people living in rural areas is extremely small. In some cases, it can be between ten and twenty percent of a country's population.

One feature of cities is high-rise buildings that may be forty, fifty, sixty—or even more—stories high. Rural areas frequently have few buildings that rise even more than ten stories high.

In the United States, many people in rural areas can trace their ancestry back several generations. These people are also often familiar with their neighbors as well as their neighbors' ancestors who lived in their area.

There have been several documented cases of people in urban areas being attacked, raped, and even killed while others do nothing to stop their attackers. Witnesses to these events often state that they did not call the police or try to help because they assumed that others would do so.

Glossary
urbanite: a person who lives in an urban area
surname: a last name

1   In paragraph 2, the author of the passage implies that urbanites

    (A) have smaller homes than people in rural areas

    (B) would prefer to live in regions with fewer people

    (C) are uninterested in being friends with their neighbors

    (D) cannot afford to purchase large homes

2   According to paragraph 3, which of the following is NOT true of people living in rural areas?

    (A) A large number of them are related to one another.

    (B) They always have friendly relations with one another.

    (C) They participate in many social activities together.

    (D) They have a high level of interaction.

3   The word "sparsely" in the passage is closest in meaning to

    (A) normally

    (B) consistently

    (C) easily

    (D) lightly

4   *Directions:* Select the appropriate statements from the answer choices and match them to the location of the people to which they relate. TWO of the answer choices will NOT be used. ***This question is worth 3 points.***

Answer Choices	LOCATION OF PEOPLE
1 Go to social events with their neighbors	**Rural Area**
2 Might rarely interact with one another	•
3 Often have strong relationships with one another	•
4 Hardly know who their neighbors are	•
5 Spend large sums of money to buy their homes	**Urban Area**
6 Live next door to people they are related to	•
7 Tend to be more helpful to one another	•

Summarizing   Complete the summary by filling in the blanks.

Nowadays, people live in both urban and rural areas. But _____ between the people in each place are different. People in rural areas often have homes, spend time outside, and get to _____. People in urban areas frequently live in apartments and rarely see their neighbors. Those in rural areas have _____ because they are related and do many activities together. They trust one another more. So people in rural areas are more likely to _____ than people in cities.

Childhood Memories

People have many experiences as children. But when they become adults, they have trouble recalling these events. Few people have any memories prior to turning three years of age. After that age, most childhood memories are related to life-changing incidents. So people may remember their first day of school or the death of a relative. But more <u>traumatic</u> incidents, such as car wrecks, may be totally forgotten. There are several theories about why people lose their childhood memories. The best-regarded one is that children develop in stages, so people's early memories never solidly form in the first place.

2➡ Jean Piaget, a Swiss philosopher, proposed the most-accepted theory of children's development. Piaget conducted extensive studies on children of all ages. He realized that children develop their abilities in different stages. Prior to turning twelve, most children are still developing mental skills such as reason and logic. Their development also includes their memories. Most experts agree that babies fewer than two years old have almost no ability to retain memories. Even children three years of age can only retain a mere handful of them. In fact, until a person's teenage years, most early memories concern life-changing events.

Studies of adults who suffered a distressing incident during their childhood have shown varying results concerning their memories. Some adults remember being in an accident while others do not. Some adults claim to remember suffering abuse as children even when they were younger than three years old. Yet there is little evidence to support these supposed memories. **1** Conversely, other adults who really were abused have no memory of these events. **2** In other studies, some experts looked at adults who had been in wars as children. **3** Most remembered the war or events from it. **4** These included the deaths of their parents and soldiers visiting their towns or villages. Sadly, most wanted to forget those memories but could not.

Most child experts conclude that the ability to remember events from one's past is selective. It <u>**hinges on**</u> each person's individual experiences. Memories prior to two years of age are impossible to retain whereas other childhood memories depend on the actual incident itself. In many cases, people seem to have blocked traumatic memories. Perhaps this act shelters them from reliving horrible events in their past. Yet others are unable to erase memories of war or death no matter how much they may desire to. Overall, experts have determined that there is no conclusive answer as to why some people remember the past while others do not.

NOTE

Other types of memories that people may recall are moving to new areas, special birthday parties, sporting events, and various natural disasters such as hurricanes or tornadoes.

Jean Piaget conducted all kinds of research on children. He is well known for his theory of cognitive development, which divides the stages during which children learn various skills into four distinct groups.

Unfortunately, these false claims of abuse have led to some families being destroyed and some individuals being imprisoned on false charges.

Some doctors have used hypnosis therapy to unblock people's minds and to get them to remember certain memories from the past. However, this remains an imperfect science.

Glossary
traumatic: disturbing; shocking
hinge on: to depend on; to be determined by

1 According to paragraph 2, which of the following is true of Jean Piaget?

    Ⓐ Many people believe that his ideas on children are correct.

    Ⓑ He conducted research on the lives of Swiss children.

    Ⓒ He determined that all babies, even young ones, have memories.

    Ⓓ The research he did was mostly concerned with teenagers.

2 Which of the sentences below best expresses the essential information in the highlighted sentence in the passage? *Incorrect* answer choices change the meaning in important ways or leave out essential information.

    Ⓐ Some incidents are so traumatic that people can recall them no matter how young they were at the time.

    Ⓑ No one can remember memories before turning two, but some childhood memories may be kept.

    Ⓒ Depending upon the memory, some people are able to remember events from when they were two years old.

    Ⓓ Research has determined that it is not possible to remember anything before a person turned two.

3 Look at the four squares [■] that indicate where the following sentence could be added to the passage.

In all likelihood, these people have fabricated memories and convinced themselves that they are real.

Where would the sentence best fit?

4 *Directions:* An introductory sentence for a brief summary of the passage is provided below. Complete the summary by selecting the THREE answer choices that express the most important ideas of the passage. Some sentences do not belong because they express ideas that are not presented in the passage or are minor ideas in the passage. *This question is worth 2 points.*

Research has shown that people are unable to retain any of their earliest childhood memories but may remember events from later in their childhood.

Answer Choices

1. Most of the memories a person has before becoming a teen involve crucial events in that person's life.

2. While some people might remember a death in their childhood, they might forget something like a car accident.

3. Jean Piaget's research on children proved that their abilities develop in different stages as they get older.

4. Some people want to forget about memories of tragic events, but they find that they are unable to.

5. Sometimes children suffer unfortunate events such as being in war zones or having their parents die.

6. The majority of experts agree that people cannot retain any memories of their lives before they turned two.

Summarizing   Complete the summary by filling in the blanks.

People have difficulty remembering anything before they turn _____. One reason was discovered by Jean Piaget. He learned that children's abilities develop in stages. One is memory. People have _____ from two years of age or younger, and they have only selective memories after that until their teens. In addition, adults may or may not remember _____ from their childhood. In some cases, they make fake memories or want to forget something but cannot. Sometimes, though, they can block _____.

Mastering **the Subject**

Family and Farms in Colonial America

1→ In early colonial America during the 1600s and 1700s, most people lived on farms. They lived in family units with everyone working together. Farmers and their sons plowed the land, planted crops, and raised animals. Mothers and daughters took care of the household and any new babies. Children were educated as best as their parents could manage. Yet schooling beyond a basic level was not possible for most children in farm families. The farm was the center of life, so most people rarely traveled far from it. But as America's population grew, a desire to find and settle new lands split many colonial families.

2→ Daughters were expected to marry and to start their own families. Those that did not primarily remained with their parents for their entire lives. Sons were expected to have families of their own, too. But land was also crucial for sons. As the colonial population increased, land became <u>scarce</u>. During that period, sons usually inherited their fathers' land. However, if a father lived a long life, his sons could become grown men and still be waiting for their inheritance. And if a family had many sons, the land they were to receive could be small. This made many families follow the practice of primogeniture. So only the oldest son inherited any land. While this ensured that farms remained large, it left nothing for second and third sons.

Many of these sons sought their fortunes elsewhere. Some became merchants or other professionals, but most remained farmers. They looked for new places outside of the original thirteen colonies. This desire for land resulted in the expansion of America. First, settlers <u>breached</u> the Appalachian Mountains in the east and begin filling the land between the mountains and the Mississippi River. Then, after the establishment of the United States, immigrants began arriving in large numbers. The 1800s saw a vast expansion of the country's population. Many immigrants became farmers and moved westward to settle uninhabited lands.

As sons left their family farms, family units began splitting. Due to distance and the slow means of communication available at the time, many of them lost contact with their families back in the east. For many, traveling west was equivalent to their ancestors leaving Europe to go to the New World. Just as their ancestors never returned to their homelands, very few of these sons ever went back to their families in the east. Instead, they stayed in the west, where they started their own farms and families in a new land.

> **NOTE**
>
> Many early American farms were almost completely self-supporting. The farmers, their wives, and their children could do the wide variety of tasks needed to keep their farms operational.
>
> Some fathers insisted upon giving all of their sons some amount of land. However, because the parcels of land were so small, unless the father was rich and owned a great amount of land, the sons often had difficulty supporting themselves.
>
> During the early 1800s, the area from the Atlantic Ocean to the Mississippi River quickly filled up with people, and these areas all joined the United States as individual states.
>
> From the 1850s onward, many people—Americans and immigrants—crossed the Mississippi River and headed west toward the Pacific Ocean. There, they settled the land and made their own fortunes.

Glossary

scarce: rare

breach: to go past; to break through

1   In paragraph 1, all of the following questions are answered EXCEPT:

    (A) Why did many colonial families split up?

    (B) What kinds of work did American farmers do?

    (C) Where did children in farm families attend school?

    (D) Who took care of babies in colonial American times?

2   The author discusses "primogeniture" in paragraph 2 in order to

    (A) explain why most American farms were very large

    (B) give a reason why some sons abandoned their family farms

    (C) criticize the practice of giving all of the land to the oldest son

    (D) stress that women rarely inherited anything from their fathers

3   The word "them" in the passage refers to

    (A) sons

    (B) family farms

    (C) family units

    (D) their families

4   *Directions:* An introductory sentence for a brief summary of the passage is provided below. Complete the summary by selecting the THREE answer choices that express the most important ideas of the passage. Some sentences do not belong because they express ideas that are not presented in the passage or are minor ideas in the passage. *This question is worth 2 points.*

American farm families traditionally stayed together, but many sons began leaving their farms and headed west for a new beginning.

Answer Choices

[1] Many families did not keep in touch with one another once the young children began to move far away from their homes.

[2] Primogeniture was the practice of allowing only the oldest son to inherit the land from the father.

[3] As many young men traveled elsewhere, large parts of the American frontier began to be populated.

[4] In the seventeenth and eighteenth centuries, American farm families stayed on their farms and all worked together.

[5] Second and third sons inherited no land, so they left their family farms in order to find some land of their own.

[6] A large number of immigrants arrived in America in the 1800s and helped settle the western frontier.

Summarizing   Complete the summary by filling in the blanks.

In colonial America, families lived on farms and worked hard to support one another. _____ were expected to get married and to start their own families. Sons also expected to inherit land. But many Americans _____, so only the oldest son got any land. The younger sons left the farms and headed west. They wanted _____. These sons helped populate the western part of the United States. They lost contact _____, but they started new lives of their own.

TOEFL **Practice Test**

Suburban Migration

Houses in an American suburb

1→ Suburbs are small cities or towns near large metropolitan areas. Despite being close to cities, suburbs are dissimilar to them. They are primarily residential areas, so most of their buildings are homes and apartments. There are also schools and shopping districts. But there are seldom factories or other signs of industrialization. In addition, suburbs have few office buildings. Those that are located in the suburbs are restricted to certain areas.

2→ Suburbs are attractive to people residing in metropolitan areas for two main reasons. First, they offer people the opportunity to become homeowners. While real estate prices are often outrageously high in metropolitan areas, housing costs in suburbs are much lower. Houses in suburbs are also usually much bigger than those in cities. And many suburban houses have yards, which add to their appeal. This is especially true when a couple has young children. The second main reason why suburbs are attractive is that they are regarded as oases of peace and safety from the city. Suburbs have few tall buildings, unlike cities. They have no factories **spewing** pollution. And they have more open green spaces, less noise, and much less crime than urban centers. Couples with young children or who are looking to start families frequently find these advantages reason enough to move to the suburbs and to become homeowners there.

3→ Another appealing feature of suburbs is their proximity to the metropolitan area's center. This short commute permits many **suburbanites** to keep their jobs, which are often high paying, at offices in the city. They also have access to all of the advantages of the city—shopping centers, theaters, museums, and galleries—without having to live there. At the end of the day, people can retreat to their safe, comfortable, and quiet suburban homes. Making this easier is the fact that many suburbs are linked to metropolitan areas by extensive transportations systems. These include highways, bus and subway lines and commuter trains.

4→ On the negative side, suburbs are often considered relatively boring by those who live there. Children and teens often find that there is little to do among the endless blocks of similar houses. **1** Since most suburbs are filled with residences, there is little room for places of entertainment. **2** Many suburbs have a single shopping mall with a movie theater to serve as the entertainment district. **3** Still, for many adults, these negative aspects are outweighed by the advantages of the suburbs. **4**

5➜ In the United States, one disturbing aspect of suburbs in their early years was the racial segregation that took place in them. Many suburbs were populated almost exclusively by white upper- and middle-class people. Few minorities lived in them. This was especially true in the 1950s and 1960s. White families moved to the suburbs while black and Hispanic families remained in the inner cities. So too did the hundreds of thousands of immigrants who came to the U.S. during those decades. In recent years, though, more integration has occurred. Now, many suburbs are no longer the exclusive domains of white families. Instead, they include minority families as well.

Glossary

spew: to expel
suburbanite: a person who lives in a suburb

1 According to paragraph 1, which of the following is true of suburbs?

 (A) They are more rural than urban in nature.

 (B) There are office buildings located throughout them.

 (C) The schools in them are known for their quality.

 (D) They are mainly places for people to live in.

2 Which of the sentences below best expresses the essential information in the highlighted sentence in the passage? *Incorrect* answer choices change the meaning in important ways or leave out essential information.

 (A) Life in the suburbs is ideal for young couples who are interested in starting their own families.

 (B) A large number of families in the suburbs are those with young children who moved there to take advantage of suburban life.

 (C) It is possible for young couples to purchase homes in the suburbs so that they can raise their children there.

 (D) The advantages of the suburbs make them appealing places for young families to buy homes.

3 According to paragraph 2, people prefer to live in the suburbs because

 (A) they like to get to know their neighbors

 (B) they can save money when buying homes

 (C) the schools are located close to their houses

 (D) homes in the cities often lack backyards

4 Which of the following can be inferred from paragraph 2 about the suburbs?

 (A) There is a lack of manufacturing jobs in them.

 (B) They have almost no crime in them.

 (C) Anyone can afford to purchase a house in them.

 (D) People there buy their homes instead of renting them.

5 The word "proximity" in the passage is closest in meaning to

 (A) nearness

 (B) approach

 (C) continuation

 (D) estimate

6 According to paragraph 3, which of the following is NOT true of suburbanites' commutes?

 (A) They require the use of cars.

 (B) They are mostly convenient.

 (C) They may be done by train.

 (D) They do not take a long time.

7 In paragraph 4, the author uses "a single shopping mall" as an example of

Ⓐ an exclusive place for buying products

Ⓑ a negative aspect of suburbs

Ⓒ a place of entertainment

Ⓓ an area near many residences

8 According to paragraph 5, in the 1950s and 1960s, most suburbs were filled with white families because

Ⓐ minorities were discouraged from moving to them

Ⓑ most minorities lived in urban areas

Ⓒ immigrants preferred to live in rural areas

Ⓓ racial segregation was the law at that time

9 Look at the four squares [■] that indicate where the following sentence could be added to the passage.

There may be restaurants and bars near the mall, but they are often few in number.

Where would the sentence best fit?

Click on a square [■] to add the sentence to the passage.

10 **Directions:** An introductory sentence for a brief summary of the passage is provided below. Complete the summary by selecting the THREE answer choices that express the most important ideas of the passage. Some sentences do not belong because they express ideas that are not presented in the passage or are minor ideas in the passage. **This question is worth 2 points.**

Drag your answer choices to the spaces where they belong.
To remove an answer choice, click on it. To review the passage, click on **View Text**.

Many people find suburbs more appealing places to live in than metropolitan areas for a number of different reasons.

-
-
-

Answer Choices

① Most cities have an extensive transportation network that connects them with the suburbs and makes commuting easy.

② Minorities rarely moved to the suburbs for several decades, but they have begun doing so in recent years.

③ Raising children in the suburbs is pleasant because they are safe, clean, and have little crime.

④ Some people find the suburbs to be uneventful because there is a lack of entertainment to be found in them.

⑤ The cost of purchasing a house in the suburbs is much less than the price of a house in a big city.

⑥ Big cities provide people with access to theaters, museums, galleries, and other places of cultural interest.

1 **The Montessori Method**

Educators sometimes devise new teaching methods. This was what Maria Montessori, an Italian educator, did. Her method was designed for children of very young ages. Essentially, the teacher is an observer. The students are left to learn at their own pace. In the classroom, there are many things of interest for the students. As the students try to use various items, the teacher can explain them or answer questions about them. In this method, the natural curiosity and desire to learn of each student typically determines how much a student will learn.

2 **The Effects of the Printing Press on Society**

In the 1450s, Johannes Gutenberg changed society forever. His invention of the printing press caused this change. Thanks to him, books became much easier to produce. The printing press could rapidly make large numbers of books at fairly low prices. As a result, more people had access to books. This helped increase the literacy rate in society. As more people became educated, a new age in human civilization began. Since that time, humans have made more discoveries and become more educated in general than ever before.

3 **Human Interaction**

Since humans first evolved, they have lived in groups. Humans are social animals. Most of them require dealings with one another. In fact, most societies are designed around humans interacting with one another. For instance, humans typically live together in family units consisting of both adults and children. They also tend to live in areas near other people. These places can be small villages or enormous metropolitan areas. Interacting with other humans provides them with company, comfort, and safety. Some people get by with minimal interaction with others. But these loners are in the minority.

4 **The Rise of Universities**

During the late Middle Ages, small groups of scholars began coming together and forming schools. In the past, many teachers had wandered from place to place to find pupils. But, suddenly, teachers began to establish universities. In 1119, there was a university founded in Bologna, Italy. Within 200 years, there were universities in many cities throughout Europe. They mostly prepared young men for life in the clergy. However, some taught other skills, such as medicine or law. These universities provided a structured education for many people. And they served as the basis for today's modern universities.

5 **Misconceptions**

People may form misconceptions because of an incomplete understanding of a situation. This causes them to come to a mistaken conclusion about something. For instance, perhaps a woman is giving a presentation. A man who did not sleep much the night before yawns during the presentation. The woman giving the presentation may believe her talk is boring. In fact, the man is not bored; he is simply tired. Still, the woman may form a misconception about her performance. She may tell a joke or do something to make her speech more interesting when there is, in fact, no reason to do so.

6 **Sign Language**

Some people are deaf and thus unable to hear. Others are mute, so they cannot speak. These people cannot communicate through oral language. Throughout much of history, they have had problems, especially in times when most people could not read or write. Today, however, they can communicate through sign language. Sign language involves the manipulation of a person's hands and face, as well as other body movements, to communicate with others. By using various hand movements, people can speak to others without using oral language.

7 ▸ Linguistics

The study of language is known as linguistics. Yet linguists are not merely interested in speaking other languages. They are also interested in how languages function. They focus on aspects of language such as grammar, syntax, and pronunciation. Many of them explore connections between various languages, particularly with regard to words that one language borrows from another. And some linguists go back to study the history of languages. They try to determine how they evolved and when certain words and phrases were invented and first came to be used by people.

8 ▸ Short-Term and Long-Term Memory

A person's memory is that individual's ability to retain information or past experiences. There are two basic kinds: short-term memory and long-term memory. Anything a person learns or does goes into that individual's short-term memory. Often, this information is unimportant, so the person quickly forgets it. Short-term memories can be lost within seconds of being acquired in many cases. Other memories, however, are important. Perhaps the person is making a conscious effort to remember something. In that case, it will enter a person's long-term memory. These memories can last for minutes or years. It depends upon how important the memory is to the person.

9 ▸ Nuclear and Extended Families

Most people live together in families. In most societies, the nuclear family is the most typical method of organization. A nuclear family consists of a mother, a father, and their children. These families often stay together for a couple of decades until the children are old enough to leave and to form their own families. In some societies, people are organized as extended families. An extended family is one that includes distant relatives such as grandparents, grandchildren, aunts, uncles, cousins, nieces, and nephews. These families tend to be more common in Asian societies.

10 ▸ Emotions and Behavior

Humans can experience many emotions. Among them are happiness, sadness, nervousness, and anger. In many instances, emotions and behavior are intimately connected. For instance, a happy person may treat others with kindness. Meanwhile, a sad or angry person may either ignore people or treat them badly. A nervous person, on the other hand, might act in ways that are atypical for that individual. The person may have trouble speaking, act foolishly, or engage in behavior that is odd. Since people experience various emotions, their behavior is not constant. Instead, it tends to change along with their moods.

11 ▸ Teaching Methods

At school, students are instructed by their teachers. Teachers use various means to enable their students to learn. Their ways of instructing students are called teaching methods. Observation is one such method. Students simply observe something being done—a science experiment perhaps—and imitate it. Rote is another method. Teachers explain something, and students memorize it. Others use the question-and-answer method. Students ask questions, to which teachers provide answers. The explanation method is also popular. Teachers explain various facts to their students. As a general rule, teachers use several teaching methods to instruct their students.

12 ▸ Advertisements

Providers of goods and services are interested in selling them. So they must promote their products to customers. One way of doing this is by using advertisements. Through the use of ads, sellers seek to encourage people to pay money for their products. Thus they need to find the best ways to make their products appealing. Advertisements may use famous pitchmen—celebrities who attest to the value of a product. They may try to associate their product with something positive, such as money or health. Or they may simply extol the benefits of their products in their advertisements.

- **abuse** (n) mistreatment; cruelty
- **access** (n) the right to enter someplace or to use something
- **advertise** (v) to promote a service or product in an attempt to get people to purchase it
- **aid** (n) assistance; help
- **approach** (n) a method of doing something
- **attractive** (adj) appealing
- **block** (v) to stop; to prevent
- **bond** (n) a tie; a connection
- **colonial** (adj) relating to a colony
- **community** (n) a neighborhood; an area in which many people live
- **commute** (n) the daily trip from one's home to one's workplace and then back home again
- **conclude** (v) to come to a determination about something
- **control** (v) to rule over; to command
- **conversely** (adv) in opposition; on the other hand
- **cramped** (adj) lacking room
- **distressing** (adj) alarming; worrisome
- **domain** (n) a province; an area; a realm
- **earning** (n) the money a person makes
- **elderly** (n) old people
- **endless** (adj) having no ending; perpetual
- **engage** (v) to participate in; to do
- **erase** (v) to remove; to delete
- **equivalent** (n) comparable; equal
- **evidence** (n) proof
- **expansion** (n) an enlarging
- **experiential** (adj) observed; practical
- **extensive** (adj) widespread; detailed
- **gallery** (n) a museum that displays works of art
- **gathering** (n) a meeting; a get-together
- **generation** (n) an age group
- **guildsman** (n) a member of a guild
- **hands-on** (adj) practical
- **homeland** (n) one's home country or area; the place where a person is from
- **ignore** (v) not to pay attention to
- **immigrant** (n) a person who moves to another country
- **industrialization** (n) the act of developing industry in a place
- **inherit** (v) to receive upon the death of another
- **inheritance** (n) the possessions one receives upon the death of another
- **influence** (v) to have an effect on
- **innovation** (n) an invention; something that is newly created

- **integration** (n) the act of mixing two or more separate groups of people
- **isolated** (adj) alone; solitary
- **labor** (n) work, often of the manual variety
- **lack** (n) an absence of something
- **last** (v) to continue
- **logic** (n) reason
- **manor house** (n) a large estate
- **merchant** (n) a vendor; a person who sells things for a living
- **metropolitan** (adj) relating to a large urban area
- **noble** (n) a member of the royalty; a titled person
- **oasis** (n) a haven; a sanctuary; a place of safety
- **obesity** (n) the condition of being very fat or weighing too much
- **outrageously** (adv) excessively; too much
- **outweigh** (v) to be of greater importance than something else
- **overweight** (adj) fat; weighing too much; being larger than one should be
- **particularly** (adv) quite; very
- **plea** (n) a request; an appeal
- **population** (n) the number of people in a certain area
- **progressive** (adj) in favor of progress or advancement
- **real estate** (n) land or buildings
- **relate** (v) to connect with another; to understand
- **relive** (v) to go through something a second time
- **remain** (v) to stay with
- **retain** (v) to remember; to keep
- **residential** (adj) relating to a home
- **rural** (adj) relating to the countryside
- **schooling** (n) the education one is taught at a school
- **segregation** (n) the dividing of people based on certain qualifications, such as race
- **selective** (adj) choosy; discriminating
- **self-sustaining** (adj) self-sufficient; able to survive on one's own
- **split** (v) to divide
- **suburb** (n) a small city next to a larger one
- **suffer** (v) to endure; to go through
- **test** (v) to try out; to experiment with
- **townsman** (n) a person who lives in a town
- **truthful** (adj) honest
- **uninhabited** (adj) not lived in by any others
- **urban** (adj) relating to the city
- **value** (n) a characteristic that is regarded as positive by society

⛢ Choose the word or phrase closest in meaning to the highlighted part of the sentence.

1   In cities, however, many people live in cramped apartments.

   (A) expensive
   (B) run-down
   (C) crowded
   (D) overpriced

2   The guildsmen became the most powerful members of their towns and often established local governments.

   (A) influenced
   (B) elected
   (C) founded
   (D) bribed

3   Still, children ignore those warnings and attempt the same tricks.

   (A) overlook
   (B) laugh at
   (C) consider
   (D) refuse

4   Those that are located in the suburbs are restricted to certain areas.

   (A) approved
   (B) constructed
   (C) planned
   (D) limited

5   Perhaps this act shelters them from reliving horrible events in their past.

   (A) enables
   (B) protects
   (C) reminds
   (D) strengthens

6   Many immigrants became farmers and moved westward to settle uninhabited lands.

   (A) unknown
   (B) unpopulated
   (C) undiscovered
   (D) uninvited

7   Dewey felt that the educational system was ineffective.

   (A) impressive
   (B) outdated
   (C) useless
   (D) overwhelming

8   Since most suburbs are filled with residences, there is little room for places of entertainment.

   (A) buildings
   (B) factories
   (C) offices
   (D) homes

9   Studies of adults who suffered a distressing incident during their childhood have shown varying results concerning their memories.

   (A) upsetting
   (B) life-changing
   (C) minor
   (D) permanent

10 The villagers worked their own land and provided labor for the noble's land.

   (A) work
   (B) taxes
   (C) materials
   (D) improvement

11 This desire for land resulted in the expansion of America.

   (A) creation
   (B) freeing
   (C) enlarging
   (D) rebelling

12 They may feature healthy, attractive people consuming the products.

   (A) intelligent
   (B) stylish
   (C) resourceful
   (D) good-looking

13 Children and teens often find that there is little to do among the endless blocks of similar houses.

   (A) expanding
   (B) continual
   (C) enlarging
   (D) dull

14 Nevertheless, many countries, such as the United States, still have sizable rural populations.

   (A) actual
   (B) considerate
   (C) large
   (D) perpetual

15 But rather than live in cities, people mostly lived in small villages.

   (A) always
   (B) preferably
   (C) distinctly
   (D) primarily

16 This may take the form of assisting the elderly or the poor.

   (A) feeding
   (B) restricting
   (C) aiding
   (D) approaching

17 People in rural areas are highly likely to offer assistance to those in need because they are liable to know the person who needs help.

   (A) likely
   (B) sure
   (C) apparently
   (D) visibly

18 But as America's population grew, a desire to find and settle new lands split many colonial families.

   (A) created
   (B) involved
   (C) overcame
   (D) divided

19 These ads can encourage children to be truthful to others.

   (A) request
   (B) approve
   (C) demand
   (D) inspire

20 But more traumatic incidents, such as car wrecks, may be totally forgotten.

   (A) incidents
   (B) crashes
   (C) warnings
   (D) purchases

Part B

Chapter 05 Economics

Economics is a social science concerned with the production, distribution, and consumption of goods and services. Microeconomics and macroeconomics are two main fields in economics. Microeconomics examines minor and individual aspects of the economy. Macroeconomics is broader and focuses on economics on the national or global level. Economists often try to understand how economic systems act and react with one another. There are many fields in economics. Some economists examine production and distribution methods. Others look at the history of economics or how politics and economics are related. And others research aspects of finance and their effects on the economy.

Mastering **the Question Types**

☑ Vocabulary   ☐ Fill in a Table   ☐ Factual Information   ☐ Negative Factual Information   ☑ Prose Summary
☐ Insert Text   ☐ Reference   ☑ Rhetorical Purpose   ☐ Sentence Simplification   ☐ Inference

Medieval Guilds

In Europe during the Middle Ages, certain groups of craftsmen started to form associations. These were called guilds. They were an attempt to regulate the craftsmen's specific professions. They attained a good measure of power in Europe and existed for centuries. Only when the Industrial Revolution began did they finally decline in power and influence.

² → All sorts of guilds were formed. There were ones for carpenters, masons, bakers, and blacksmiths, among others. When one was established, its members had a number of goals. They wanted to protect their rights, to set standards of skill and payment, to prevent nonmembers from doing business in an area, and to train apprentices. The guilds collected **dues** from their members. They also had officers who tended to their affairs. When a man joined a guild, he had to vow to follow its rules. In return, he received all of the benefits of a full member.

Guilds established monopolies in their region. They prevented outsiders—by force if necessary—from conducting business without their permission. This was an early form of protectionism. It eliminated competitors and helped standardize prices. The guilds and their members jealously guarded their monopolies. This guaranteed them employment and a constant income. Unfortunately, this lack of competition discouraged innovation. So many professions with guilds never developed new methods. Or the ones that did make advances did so very slowly.

Guilds were dominant during the Middle Ages and the Renaissance. But as technology began to improve, they lost power. After the Industrial Revolution got underway in the 1700s, many machines were made that could do better, faster, and cheaper work than master craftsmen. This led to the guilds' **undoing**. Soon afterward, they had all but disappeared from Europe.

Glossary

due: a fee a person must pay to become a member of an organization
undoing: downfall; failure; destruction; demise

1 In paragraph 2, the author discusses what guilds sought to do in order to

    Ⓐ compare guild members with nonmembers

    Ⓑ explain what caused them to arise in the Middle Ages

    Ⓒ show how they benefitted their members

    Ⓓ prove that guilds' officers were useful

2 The word "eliminated" in the passage is closest in meaning to

    Ⓐ removed

    Ⓑ killed

    Ⓒ expelled

    Ⓓ defeated

3 ***Directions:*** An introductory sentence for a brief summary of the passage is provided below. Complete the summary by selecting the THREE answer choices that express the most important ideas of the passage. Some sentences do not belong because they express ideas that are not presented in the passage or are minor ideas in the passage. ***This question is worth 2 points.***

During the Middle Ages, guilds were powerful organizations of craftsmen that regulated workers in many different fields.

Answer Choices

1. Guilds focused on protecting the rights of various individuals, including masons, bakers, and blacksmiths.

2. Craftsmen had to pay dues to their guilds in order for them to be permitted to become members.

3. During the Industrial Revolution, guilds began to lose influence and eventually completely disappeared.

4. The monopolies that guilds established prevented outsiders from taking business away from their members.

5. All guild members had to agree to follow the rules and regulations that were proclaimed by the guilds.

6. There was little progress during the Middle Ages because guild members were not interested in doing research.

Summarizing   Complete the summary by using the words or phrases given in the box.

train new apprentices	protected	craftsman	monopolies

Guilds were associations of _____ that formed during the Middle Ages. There were guilds for carpenters, masons, bakers, blacksmiths, and many others. Guilds tried to regulate the way that craftsmen worked. They _____ their members and helped them _____. Guilds formed _____, which helped their members. However, these monopolies discouraged innovation. After the Renaissance ended, guilds slowly began losing power. During the Industrial Revolution, they mostly disappeared.

☐ Vocabulary   ☑ Fill in a Table   ☐ Factual Information   ☑ Negative Factual Information   ☐ Prose Summary
☐ Insert Text   ☐ Reference   ☐ Rhetorical Purpose   ☐ Sentence Simplification   ☑ Inference

Some Early Effects of the Industrial Revolution

The Industrial Revolution began in Great Britain in the 1700s. From there, it eventually spread around the world. In Great Britain, it caused the immediate advance of society. There were countless benefits for the British people. The Industrial Revolution's effects were not always positive though. In fact, there were a <u>multitude</u> of problems that sprung up because of it. Every country dealt with its problems in its own way. In Great Britain, many of the solutions were effective.

²➜ As Great Britain industrialized, there was a dramatic population shift. People abandoned the countryside for the cities. But poor urban planning resulted in overcrowded housing conditions. This, in turn, caused an increase in both disease and crime. The factories that employed people burned coal to produce steam to run their machinery. This created air pollution, which caused an increasing number of health problems among people. The factories also had poor safety standards, so accidents were frequent. Factory workers not only got injured but also died. On top of all this, many British factories utilized child labor.

³➜ The British government recognized that these problems existed. Its politicians then took steps to improve the lives of the country's citizens. For instance, efforts at better urban planning were made. The newer parts of cities that were built were designed much better and provided more space for people. Improvements in medical science made people healthier while more police <u>patrolled</u> the streets to keep crime under control. Laws were passed to reduce pollution levels. Safety procedures for factories were implemented, and child labor laws were passed. These mandated both that children work less and that they attend school. While the problems caused by the Industrial Revolution were not all solved, these steps managed to make its effect on Britain more of a positive than a negative one.

Glossary

multitude: a large number; a great amount
patrol: to guard; to walk around while protecting something

1 According to paragraph 2, which of the following was NOT a disadvantage of the Industrial Revolution?

(A) Only adults were hired to work in factories.

(B) Many employees died while they were working.

(C) A great deal of pollution was created by factories.

(D) People had to live very closely with their neighbors.

2 Which of the following can be inferred from paragraph 3 about the British government?

(A) It raised taxes to pay for programs to help its citizens.

(B) It was more concerned with the economy than with education.

(C) It was eager to decrease the amount of crime in the country.

(D) It continued to permit young children to work in factories.

3 *Directions:* Select the appropriate sentences from the answer choices and match them to the causes and the effects of the problems that started during the Industrial Revolution. TWO of the answer choices will NOT be used. *This question is worth 3 points.*

Answer Choices

1 Factories created a large amount of air pollution.

2 Urban planning caused new parts of cities to be better designed.

3 The Industrial Revolution first started in Great Britain.

4 Laws were passed that required children to be educated.

5 Children were obligated to work in factories to earn money.

6 Many sectors of society advanced during the Industrial Revolution.

7 Social issues such as more crime and diseases occurred.

PROBLEMS IN THE INDUSTRIAL REVOLUTION

Cause

•

•

•

Effect

•

•

Summarizing Complete the summary by using the words or phrases given in the box.

attend school	overcrowded	factories	air pollution

The Industrial Revolution started in Great Britain in the 1700s. It had many negative effects. British cities became _____, which increased crime and disease rates. Factories created _____, which made people sick. Workers were hurt or killed in _____, and even children worked in them. The British government acted to solve these problems. It designed cities better and hired more police. Pollution levels were reduced, and factories became safer. And children had to work fewer hours and _____.

Mastering **the Question Types**

C

☐ Vocabulary   ☐ Fill in a Table   ☑ Factual Information   ☐ Negative Factual Information   ☐ Prose Summary
☑ Insert Text   ☑ Reference   ☐ Rhetorical Purpose   ☑ Sentence Simplification   ☐ Inference

The Economic Effects of the Suez Canal

In the 1400s, Europeans began sailing around Africa to reach India and the Far East. The desire to reach India further inspired Christopher Columbus to sail west across the Atlantic Ocean. These sailors were interested in trading for spices, silk, and other exotic goods in Asia. The journeys were long and dangerous. Many ships never reached their final destinations. Overland routes were slow and dangerous, too. And merchants could only carry limited amounts of goods.

The water route from Europe to Asia became dramatically shorter in 1869. This happened when the Suez Canal opened. **1** It ran through Egypt and connected the Mediterranean Sea with the Red Sea, which empties into the Indian Ocean. **2** With an initial transit time of forty hours, the Suez Canal greatly shortened the trip from Europe to Asia. **3** This had many positive economic effects. **4**

³➡ In its first year of operation, the Suez Canal averaged two transits a day. 100 years later, more than fifty ships passed through it daily. As the years went by, the sizes of the ships also increased. So the **tonnage** transported increased from 440,000 tons a year to more than a billion tons annually nowadays. Petroleum, coal, ore, metal, grain, and wood are some of the main items transported. At its peak, nearly one million people a year **transited** through the canal. That number has decreased today due to the ease of air travel though.

Shorter travel times and safer trips have resulted in cheaper prices. While a single ship could once carry a fortune in spices, prices have declined thanks to the canal. There is also a wider range of products available in both Europe and Asia since freighters can carry huge amounts of goods. Today, fifteen percent of global shipping passes through the canal, making it vital to the global economy.

Glossary

tonnage: the amount of weight carried by a ship
transit: to pass through

1   Select the TWO answer choices from paragraph 3 that identify the effects of the Suez Canal each year in modern times. *To receive credit, you must select TWO answers.*

    Ⓐ A variety of items are transported through the canal.

    Ⓑ Approximately half a million tons of goods pass through it.

    Ⓒ More than one million people travel through the canal.

    Ⓓ Large ships carrying around a billion tons of goods go through it.

2   Which of the sentences below best expresses the essential information in the highlighted sentence in the passage? *Incorrect* answer choices change the meaning in important ways or leave out essential information.

    Ⓐ Freighters going from Asia to Europe transport all kinds of different products for stores to sell.

    Ⓑ The carrying abilities of freighters have made many kinds of goods available in Europe and Asia.

    Ⓒ There are many large ships that carry goods through the canal between Europe and Asia.

    Ⓓ European goods transported to Asia have increased the number of products available in many countries.

3   The word "it" in the passage refers to

    Ⓐ fifteen percent

    Ⓑ global shipping

    Ⓒ the canal

    Ⓓ the global economy

4   Look at the four squares [■] that indicate where the following sentence could be added to the passage.

Today, ships can pass through the Suez Canal in less than half that amount of time.

Where would the sentence best fit?

Summarizing   **Complete the summary by using the words or phrases given in the box.**

various exotic goods	prices of goods	forty hours	one billion tons

For centuries, sailors wanted to go from Europe to Asia to trade for _____. But the journey was long and dangerous. In 1869, the Suez Canal in Egypt opened and made the voyage shorter. Initially, it only took _____ to transit the canal. Large numbers of ships began passing through the canal daily, and today, more than _____ of goods go through it. The canal has made the _____ lower, and there are more products available for people to purchase.

Mechanization and the American Economy

During its colonial history, America was a land of farmers. But, today, the United States is one of the world's most industrialized countries. The change from an agrarian culture to an industrialized one began mostly after 1850. It continues to do this. During the mid- to late-1800s, there were several developments that caused the mechanization of the U.S. to begin in earnest.

Some years after the Industrial Revolution started in Great Britain, it crossed the Atlantic Ocean to the U.S. Machines became a part of American life. This was more so in northern states than in southern ones. Still, mechanization proceeded rather slowly. Then, in the mid-1800s, a period called the Second Industrial Revolution began. This greatly accelerated the speed of American industrialization.

[3]➡ The Second Industrial Revolution saw innovations in many fields. There were advances in the electric, steel, chemical, and petroleum industries. Developments in these fields dramatically altered society. For instance, experiments on electricity let it be used as a power source. Electric lights, for one, were introduced during this period. Improvements in steel allowed taller and stronger buildings to be made. This led to the erecting of skyscrapers. They now feature on the **skylines** of almost every mid-sized American city. New inventions and discoveries concerning chemicals led to advances in fields as diverse as medicine and refrigeration. Then, oil was discovered—first in Pennsylvania and later in other states. People began using it as an energy source. It was notably used for the internal combustion engine, which was installed in the newly invented automobile.

These advances helped the U.S. develop with astonishing speed. Yet they were not enough to industrialize the country. There were other factors involved. One of the most crucial was the availability of raw materials. The U.S. was rich in raw materials, such as iron, coal, oil, and timber. These raw materials were often located near the factories that needed them. And those that were found far away were transported over the United States' expanding railway lines or across its many waterways. Fueled by an abundance of raw materials, American factories churned out huge amounts of finished products.

One other major factor helped the U.S. industrialize: immigration. The 1800s saw a flood of immigrants come to America's shores. Most hailed from Europe. These immigrants numbered in the millions. They provided the **manpower** that factories required. Coupled with advances such as the assembly line, immigrants helped lead the U.S. to an unprecedented period of industrialization during the latter half of the 1800s.

NOTE

Most early Americans were farmers. Even after America began to industrialize, the majority of the country's citizens lived in rural areas.

The Industrial Revolution began in Great Britain in the early 1700s. It then went to America and other places in Western Europe.

There were many prominent American inventors during this period. They included Samuel Morse, who worked on the telegraph, Alexander Graham Bell, who invented the telephone, and Thomas Edison, who invented the electric light and many other inventions.

The huge amount of raw materials in the United States has always benefitted it. Even today, the country has enormous fossil fuel reserves, vast forests full of timber, and large supplies of various metals.

In the 1800s, the population of the United States rose dramatically. The main reason for this was immigration.

Glossary
skyline: the outline of buildings against the sky in a city's downtown area when seen from afar
manpower: work that is done by people

1   The word "erecting" in the passage is closest in meaning to

     (A) leasing

     (B) designing

     (C) removing

     (D) building

2   According to paragraph 3, which of the following is true of the Second Industrial Revolution?

     (A) There were more innovations in it than in the first Industrial Revolution.

     (B) The changes that occurred during it greatly altered society.

     (C) It made the cost of using various energy sources cheaper than before.

     (D) The most important changes were in the field of transportation.

3   The word "those" in the passage refers to

     (A) inventions

     (B) other factors

     (C) raw materials

     (D) factories

4   ***Directions:*** An introductory sentence for a brief summary of the passage is provided below. Complete the summary by selecting the THREE answer choices that express the most important ideas of the passage. Some sentences do not belong because they express ideas that are not presented in the passage or are minor ideas in the passage. ***This question is worth 2 points.***

In the middle of the 1800s, the Second Industrial Revolution occurred in the United States, and it, along with other factors, helped the country industrialize at a rapid pace.

Answer Choices

1 The abundance of raw materials in the United States provided factories with the materials they needed to make finished products.

2 An increase in the number of immigrants in the nineteenth century enabled factories to hire enough people to make their products.

3 The Industrial Revolution started in Great Britain, and then it spread from there to other countries around the world.

4 People began to use refrigerators to preserve their food, and this helped them enjoy much better diets.

5 There were great advances made in the steel and petroleum industries during the middle of the nineteenth century.

6 A vast majority of Americans were farmers or lived in rural areas for most of the country's history.

Summarizing   Complete the summary by filling in the blanks.

The United States _____ around 1850 when the Second Industrial Revolution began.
There were advances in _____ industries. The discovery of oil in the U.S. let people use it
in _____ . The U.S. had large amounts of raw materials, including iron, coal, oil, and timber.
Factories used them to make finished products. Finally, in the 1800s, millions of immigrants moved to the U.S.
Many worked in factories and _____ that helped the country industrialize.

Mastering **the Subject**

Patents

Once an inventor creates something, that person almost always applies for a patent. This is a claim to ownership of an invention. It gives the owner—typically the inventor—the exclusive right to use the patented item. Patents are generally good for anywhere between a few years to several decades. When something is patented, anyone wishing to use it must pay the owner for the privilege. The payment is a royalty. Having people pay royalties helps protect the rights of the patent holder. Ever since they were first used, patents have served as a major factor in economic progress.

2→ Patents are not modern creations but existed in ancient times. There are records showing patents were <u>granted</u> as far back as ancient Greece. In more recent times, the first recorded use of a patent came in 1474 in Venice, Italy. This was during the Renaissance, when more modern notions began to be used. As time progressed, patents were used more often. In the 1600s and 1700s, patent laws were written and passed in both Great Britain and the United States. Since the Industrial Revolution, a time when many inventions were made, came to those two countries faster than to most others, it is unsurprising that both nations took efforts to protect the works of their inventors. People in Britain and the U.S. were concerned about the theft of ideas. Realizing the importance of inventors to their economies, they sought to protect inventors' rights and to enable them to profit as well. In many cases, these laws helped. In others, such as the invention of the cotton gin by Eli Whitney, they did not. While Whitney's invention <u>revolutionized</u> the cotton industry, he received virtually no royalties. People simply copied his design without paying him at all.

3→ Still, governments tried to enforce patents. They did this for three reasons. First, awarding patents provided people with an incentive to innovate and to conduct research. Inventing and making new discoveries are time consuming and costly. Knowing their work will be protected by a patent can inspire people to continue their efforts. Second, patents encourage inventors to show their work to the public. This gives others the opportunity to see new ideas and technology. Once the patent expires, other people can either improve upon these inventions or make even better creations. Finally, patents give incentives to corporations to fund expensive research. Patents are often awarded to corporations for long periods of time. So companies can profit from their inventions for years. Knowing this, they become more willing to invest money, manpower, and time into developing new products.

NOTE

In general, a patent holder can determine how much the royalties must be. However, if the royalties are too expensive, people will not use the invention. This encourages the patent holder to make royalty requests.

Despite the existence of patents, many people simply ignored them and never paid royalties. Even today, this is a problem in many countries throughout the world.

Eli Whitney's cotton gin was so simple that most people felt there was no need to pay him royalties. Other people took his invention and improved upon it or altered it in various ways.

One requirement for patents today is that the person must document exactly how the patented item works so that another person would be able to duplicate it. This requires a person to show all of the work that was put into making the object. Later, when the patent expires, anyone is able to use the inventor's work for free.

Glossary
grant: to give; to bestow upon
revolutionize: to change dramatically

1 Which of the sentences below best expresses the essential information in the highlighted sentence in the passage? *Incorrect* answer choices change the meaning in important ways or leave out essential information.

    Ⓐ Unsurprisingly, a couple of nations led the effort not only to advance the Industrial Revolution but also to protect the people who made new inventions.

    Ⓑ The Industrial Revolution happened first in several countries, and these same countries were, unsurprisingly, the ones that looked after inventors' rights.

    Ⓒ Because many inventions were made in the Industrial Revolution, governments became more interested in protecting inventors and their creations.

    Ⓓ It is natural that both countries tried to protect inventors' works since the Industrial Revolution started in them more quickly than in other places.

2 In paragraph 2, why does the author mention "Eli Whitney"?

    Ⓐ To state that he made little money from his invention

    Ⓑ To show how he changed the world with the cotton gin

    Ⓒ To explain why the government paid him no royalties

    Ⓓ To describe his feelings about making no money from the cotton gin

3 According to paragraph 3, which of the following is NOT true of why governments tried to enforce patents?

    Ⓐ They wanted inventors to explain how their inventions worked.

    Ⓑ They helped convince inventors to spend time working on new projects.

    Ⓒ They enabled some people to become wealthy from their inventions.

    Ⓓ They encouraged corporations to pay money for costly research.

4 *Directions:* An introductory sentence for a brief summary of the passage is provided below. Complete the summary by selecting the THREE answer choices that express the most important ideas of the passage. Some sentences do not belong because they express ideas that are not presented in the passage or are minor ideas in the passage. *This question is worth 2 points.*

Since ancient times, patents have protected the rights of inventors by giving them ownership of their inventions and by enabling them to collect royalties from their creations.

Answer Choices

1 The enforcing of patents by governments encouraged inventors to work harder and to share their work with others.

2 Eli Whitney was one of many whose inventions transformed society yet never profited.

3 Patents existed in ancient Greece and Renaissance Italy and were used to protect the inventors of various things.

4 The royalty rate that inventors are paid by people using their creations varies depending upon what the item is.

5 Many people stole the ideas or designs for certain inventions, so they never paid royalties to their creators.

6 The British and U.S. governments began looking after inventors' rights.

Summarizing   Complete the summary by filling in the blanks.

A patent gives its creator _____. Then, the patent holder receives royalties when others use the invention. Patents date back to _____. However, they were not well protected until Great Britain and the United States began enforcing them during _____. Still, inventors often received few royalties for their inventions. Governments have many reasons to enforce patents. Patent enforcement encourages inventors to work hard and to _____ with others. It also persuades corporations to spend money on research.

Mastering **the Subject**

China's Economic Development

In modern times, China is a world power. It has a thriving economy that increases at high rates virtually every year. Today, China's trillion-dollar-a-year economy is the envy of many nations. In the past, China was also one of the world's most powerful countries. Yet for a long time in between, China's economy wallowed in misery. It endured an extended period of decline and stagnation. While the Industrial Revolution modernized many countries' economies, it bypassed China. This was on account of several <u>obstacles</u> there.

²➜ China is a huge country. This long hampered its economic progress. There were several reasons for this. Due to a lack of infrastructure in terms of roads, waterways, and railways, traveling there was a laborious process. This caused many problems. Communications were inefficient and slow. Transporting goods was even slower. And ruling such a large land was a difficult task. For instance, many Chinese dialects were incomprehensible to one another. This kept the people from being united. It also slowed down the country's development.

China's population also frequently retarded its growth. Over a billion people today, it stood at hundreds of millions in the 1800s and 1900s. Most of its people were subsistence farmers. In the West, the Industrial Revolution brought about many advances in farming technology. These increased crop yields. **1** Thus fewer people were needed to produce more food. **2** But progress came late to China. **3** Even today, farming methods in some places mirror those used in past centuries. **4** With such a huge amount of its labor force dedicated to farming, China had problems developing economically.

Finally, China's history often worked against it. In the 1800s, European colonial powers wielded enormous influence there. They exerted control over many parts of China. After the Europeans left, the Japanese entered. Thus China was frequently in a state of conflict with foreign powers on its own territory. For instance, from 1920 to 1949, there was almost constant <u>turmoil</u>—in the forms of war and revolution—in China. Due to the chaos, the national economy could not develop.

Peace came in 1949 after Communist forces under Mao Zedong triumphed against Chinese Nationalist forces. Mao then attempted a rapid modernization of the economy. This was called the Great Leap Forward. In reality, it was a huge step backward. The Chinese tried doing too much too quickly. Their economy was severely disrupted. Communist policies against free enterprise dramatically hindered economic progress. It was only after Mao's death in 1976 that the Chinese government changed its methods. This was when the economic boom period that China is still experiencing got underway.

Glossary
obstacle: a hindrance; something that is blocking another thing; a barrier
turmoil: disorder; chaos

NOTE

The Chinese often referred to their country as the "Middle Kingdom." To them, this indicated that they were the center of the world. This name was a result of the importance that China had in the world centuries ago.

The eastern part of China has always been better developed than the rest of the country. This includes the cities of Beijing and Shanghai. Today, this coastal region is experiencing an economic boom, yet many interior regions in China are still quite poor.

One of the main economic benefits of the Industrial Revolution was that it freed people from having to farm to survive. Thus the surplus laborers were able to find work in factories. This greatly helped many countries industrialize.

In the mid-nineteenth century, there were two wars in China involving European powers. They were the First Opium War and the Second Opium War. They mostly involved Britain and France.

In recent years, China's economy has been expanding at rates of over 10% annually.

1 In paragraph 2, the author implies that China's size

    Ⓐ made it a formidable opponent in war

    Ⓑ was a major factor in dividing the country

    Ⓒ resulted in it having a diverse geographical area

    Ⓓ made constructing roads in the cities difficult

2 The word "hindered" in the passage is closest in meaning to

    Ⓐ deterred

    Ⓑ influenced

    Ⓒ augmented

    Ⓓ considered

3 Look at the four squares [■] that indicate where the following sentence could be added to the passage.

Even with a smaller number of farmers, more food than ever was produced thanks to these advances.

Where would the sentence best fit?

4 *Directions:* Select the appropriate sentences from the answer choices and match them to the factors that slowed down Chinese economic development. TWO of the answer choices will NOT be used. *This question is worth 3 points.*

Answer Choices	FACTORS IN CHINA'S ECONOMIC DEVELOPMENT
1 The Japanese moved into China after the departure of the Europeans.	**Population**
2 Many European nations were involved in China in the 1800s.	•
3 The people living in China spoke a number of different dialects.	•
4 There were many conflicts and revolutions within China itself.	**History**
5 Most of China's people engaged in subsistence farming.	•
6 Communications and transportation were historically very slow.	•
7 A lack of farming technology prevented people from doing work other than farming.	•

Summarizing   Complete the summary by filling in the blanks.

Today, China is a leading world power and was a great country in the past. For many centuries though, it was poor with numerous problems. Its size made _____ throughout the country difficult. Its enormous population was mostly involved in _____ since the country industrialized very late. China's history was troubled. _____ were both involved in its internal affairs. There was a revolution in China as well. Finally, in 1976, after _____, China's economy began to improve.

The Salt Trade in Venice

The entrance to the port of Venice

1 ➔ During the Middle Ages, the city-state of Venice was a great European power. In northern Italy by the Adriatic Sea, Venice derived its power—and wealth—from trade. Of great importance was the salt trade. Its leaders and merchants obtained a salt monopoly covering much of northern Italy. The Venetians were ruthless as they built their monopoly. They raided cities and destroyed rival salt production centers. Eventually, using their peerless navy, they seized control of the local salt trade.

2 ➔ Salt was a valued commodity in the Middle Ages. It could preserve meat, fish, and products such as butter. Salted food let people keep a reserve in case of bad harvests. There were two sources available: salt from dried seawater and from salt mines. Sea salt can be obtained when seawater evaporates. Salt mines exist where outcrops of rocks contain salt. This salt comes from ancient lakes or seas that dried up and were covered by layers of earth. Salt from mines is generally of a higher quality than sea salt.

3 ➔ Recognizing the value of salt, the Venetians sought to control the local trade. They tried making their own salt works to evaporate seawater. However, the low-lying areas around the islands Venice is built on are vulnerable to storms. So the rainy weather caused problems for them. For centuries, the Venetians made salt, yet it was never very profitable. They were also outcompeted by others with more reliable sources of salt.

4 ➔ The Venetians tried establishing a monopoly by disrupting other local sources of salt. In 932, they attacked the city of Comacchio, located near Ravenna on the Adriatic Sea. Comacchio was under the control of Ravenna and had long been a center of salt production. The Venetians killed most of the inhabitants there and destroyed the salt works. This initiated a long period of conflict between Venice and Ravenna. Eventually, the Venetian navy defeated Ravenna. Then, the Venetians enacted a ban on salt from Ravenna in northern Italy.

Venice's other great rival in the salt trade was Genoa, which was located on the western side of Italy. The Venetians, with their strong government and more cold-blooded methods, were the ultimate victors in this rivalry. **1** By the 1200s, they controlled the northern Italian salt trade. **2** Around this time, they mostly abandoned trying to produce salt. **3** Instead, they decided to make money by trading salt from other sources. **4** The Venetians began forcing all ships trading salt in the Adriatic to pass through their port. Once there, the salt was subjected to high taxes. For example, at one time, a Venetian merchant paid one ducat—the Venetian currency—for a ton of salt. Shipping costs to Venice were about three ducats a ton. Before the salt was taken out of Venice, a tax was imposed on it. After the tax had been levied, the price had risen to thirty-three ducats a ton. The farther along the trade route it went, the higher its price grew. Customers had no choice but to pay the cost since having salt was literally a matter of life or death. It was in this way that Venice controlled the salt trade for the next several centuries.

Glossary
peerless: without equal
ban: a prohibition on some activity

Part B | 141

1 The word "derived" in the passage is closest in meaning to

(A) utilized

(B) requested

(C) attained

(D) observed

2 According to paragraph 1, which of the following is true of Venice?

(A) Its own ships often transported salt throughout the Adriatic Sea.

(B) It used violence in order to improve its economic situation.

(C) It was the sole supplier of salt all throughout Italy.

(D) The salt trade provided Venice with the majority of its income.

3 In paragraph 2, all of the following questions are answered EXCEPT:

(A) Where did people get salt from in the past?

(B) How is sea salt in comparison to salt from mines?

(C) What was the main reason people needed salt in the past?

(D) How were people able to extract salt from the ocean?

4 In paragraph 2, the author implies that people in Venice

(A) preferred salt that was mined to sea salt

(B) lived near several productive salt mines

(C) paid reduced prices when they purchased salt

(D) ate a variety of foods seasoned with salt

5 In paragraph 3, why does the author mention the Venetian "salt works"?

(A) To stress how successful they were at evaporating seawater

(B) To explain where in the city they were located

(C) To discuss the methods that they used to make salt

(D) To note that the Venetians tried to obtain their own salt

6 According to paragraph 3, the Venetians encountered problems in getting salt from the sea because

(A) the weather there was often bad

(B) they lacked the necessary technology

(C) the Adriatic Sea's waters were not very salty

(D) rivals attacked their salt production centers

7 According to paragraph 4, the city of Ravenna

(A) attacked sailors from Comacchio at times

(B) defeated the Venetians and dominated the salt trade

(C) often engaged in hostilities against Venice

(D) was destroyed by raiders from Venice in 932

8   The word "imposed" in the passage refers to

   (A) levied

   (B) considered

   (C) reimbursed

   (D) proposed

9   Look at the four squares [■] that indicate where the following sentence could be added to the passage.

   This monopoly directly led to Venice becoming one of the greatest powers in all of Europe.

   Where would the sentence best fit?

   Click on a square [■] to add the sentence to the passage.

10 *Directions:* An introductory sentence for a brief summary of the passage is provided below. Complete the summary by selecting the THREE answer choices that express the most important ideas of the passage. Some sentences do not belong because they express ideas that are not presented in the passage or are minor ideas in the passage. *This question is worth 2 points.*

   Drag your answer choices to the spaces where they belong.
   To remove an answer choice, click on it. To review the passage, click on **View Text**.

   During the Middle Ages, the city-state of Venice recognized the importance of salt, so it created a monopoly on the salt trade in northern Italy.

   -
   -
   -

Answer Choices

1. Venice had to deal with rivals in other places in Italy in order to establish a monopoly in the salt trade.

2. Venice eventually lost control of the salt trade when new trade routes to India were opened, so ships began avoiding the Adriatic Sea.

3. While the Venetians were not very successful at evaporating salt from the sea, they found other ways to dominate the salt trade.

4. People in the Middle Ages needed salt to help preserve their food since there were no advanced methods of refrigeration then.

5. The Venetians used violence, such as when they attacked Comacchio, to prevent other city-states from dealing in the salt trade.

6. The price of salt increased dramatically the farther along the trade route that it went from Venice to the rest of Europe.

1 ▸ Railroads and the Economy

Products are often manufactured in factories. However, these products must then be transported to markets where they can be sold. In many cases, railroads carry the goods. The reason is that railroads can easily transport many goods quickly and cheaply. Since the invention of the railroad in the 1800s, railroads have helped improve the economies of cities. One example is Chicago, a city located at a crossroads between the east and west. Chicago's railroads let people transport raw materials and finished products all over the United States. This helped make Chicago one of the American Midwest's most important cities.

2 ▸ The Steam Engine

One of the most important inventions in the Industrial Revolution was the steam engine. Two men were crucial to its development. The first was Thomas Newcomen. In 1712, he built a steam engine. Years later, by 1790, James Watt had made several improvements on it. The result was that the steam engine was used in many different industries. People utilized it for mining, the textile and other industries, and especially in transportation. Steam engines were eventually used to run trains and steamships. The result was that transportation—for people and products—became much faster and cheaper.

3 ▸ Governments and Economics

Most governments get involved in their nations' economies. In some cases, the government directly controls the economy. These may be socialist or communist economies. However, in capitalist societies, the amount of government interference is much less. Adam Smith, the noted economist from the eighteenth century, believed that government involvement in the economy should be as little as possible. He was in favor of *laissez-faire* economics. In other words, he thought that the economy would take care of itself and that government involvement would only cause problems and not actually solve them.

4 ▸ Trade Routes

Much trade is done over long distances. People must transport their products either over land or on water to reach a market where they can sell them. In most cases, the people transporting the products take the same routes again and again. These are called trade routes. Efforts are often made to keep trade routes safe and open. This enables products to move swiftly from one place to another. The Silk Road was one of history's most famous trade routes. It was a series of roads and paths that went over land from Europe all the way to China.

5 ▸ The Cotton Gin

In the eighteenth century, cotton was an important crop. People used it to make clothes. However, the cotton fibers were difficult to separate from the cotton seeds. But in 1793, Eli Whitney invented the cotton gin. This machine could easily separate large amounts of cotton fibers. Overnight, the economy of the American South changed. Many farmers began planting cotton. They made huge profits from growing it. However, cotton is a labor-intensive plant. Therefore, large numbers of African slaves were imported to work on the Southern plantations. Eventually, slavery would help lead to the American Civil War from 1861 to 1865.

6 ▸ The Assembly Line

For much of history, people made products very inefficiently. One person usually did every step required to make a product. This changed in the late 1800s when some people began using the assembly line. It became a popular manufacturing method in the early 1900s thanks to Henry Ford. Ford used the assembly line to make automobiles. The cars were placed on a long conveyor belt. They moved slowly down the line. Individual workers did one task to help build each car. This let workers specialize and work more efficiently. Thanks to the assembly line, making products became faster, cheaper, and easier.

7 The Effect of Inventions on the Economy

Throughout history, there have been inventions that have greatly changed society and the economy. This was especially true in the twentieth century. Many times, new inventions have a dramatic effect on the economy. For instance, airplanes were invented in the early 1900s. As advances in airplane technology were made, entirely new industries arose. Today, the aerospace industry employs hundreds of thousands of people all over the world. Computers, the Internet, and other related industries have also improved the economies of numerous countries. In the future, new inventions will likely have a positive effect as well.

8 Raw Materials vs. Finished Goods

Many economies depend greatly on the buying and selling of raw materials and finished goods. Raw materials are natural resources. They include metals such as gold, silver, and iron. They include energy sources such as coal, oil, and natural gas. They can also include timber and water. Some countries are rich in natural resources while others have few of them. Finished goods, on the other hand, are products that people make from raw materials. Various industries in many countries manufacture finished products from raw materials. These help contribute to the well-being of the nations' economies.

9 Capitalism

Capitalism is an economic system. In capitalism, the means of production are owned by private individuals or by corporations. The government either does not own any or owns very few means of production. In addition, the ownership of private property is stressed in capitalism. Finally, the objective of people and corporations is to make a profit. In most cases, people and corporations take portions of their profits and reinvest them. They do this in order to earn even more money. The United States has a capitalist economy. So do many other countries around the world.

10 Industrialization

For most of history, people relied upon either humans or animals to do work. However, when the Industrial Revolution began in the 1700s, there was a change. Many machines started doing work instead. This began the process of industrialization. Essentially, people developed manufacturing techniques that were done by machines but operated by humans. These machines were faster and more efficient than humans. This eventually led to the development of mass-production methods, which are regularly used today. Many countries around the world have been fully industrialized and no longer depend upon human or animal power to do work.

11 Trade during Ancient Times

In ancient times, people in different cultures frequently traded with one another. However, trade was often limited because of slow transportation methods. Most trade products during ancient times were transported over water. But ancient ships often only sailed near the coast and not on open water. Many ships also sank due to storms and poor construction. There were two major results of this. Trade with faraway regions took great deal of time to complete. And the objects traded with people in these places were typically expensive. Nevertheless, many ancient cultures in Europe and Asia engaged in trade with lands in distant places.

12 Tariffs

Tariffs are a kind of tax. They are frequently referred to as duties or customs. Governments usually levy tariffs on both imported and exported items. In many cases, tariffs are levied because of protectionism. For instance, people in some countries can make products cheaper than those in other countries. However, when they export their cheaper products, the governments of many countries levy tariffs on these products. This increases the prices of the products. In doing so, the governments are protecting their own domestic industries. This can make domestic manufacturers more competitive with foreign manufacturers.

- **accelerate** (v) to speed up; to go faster
- **agrarian** (adj) relating to land
- **ban** (n) a prohibition against something
- **blacksmith** (n) a person who makes objects made of iron
- **blessing** (n) approval
- **boom period** (n) a time of great economic expansion
- **bypass** (v) to go around; to avoid
- **canal** (n) a manmade waterway connecting two bodies of water
- **carpenter** (n) a person who makes objects from wood
- **chaos** (n) disorder; confusion
- **claim** (n) a declaration
- **competitor** (n) a person against whom one vies or competes for something
- **conduct** (v) to carry out; to implement
- **countless** (adj) numerous; many
- **currency** (n) money
- **derive** (v) to gain; to get; to attain
- **disrupt** (v) to bother; to interrupt; to pester
- **diverse** (adj) wide-ranging; varied
- **enact** (v) to begin; to start; to implement
- **enforce** (v) to put into force; to make sure that a rule or rules are followed
- **exert** (v) to make an effort; to apply
- **expire** (v) to end; to run out of time
- **factory** (n) a place where various products are manufactured
- **flood** (n) a large number
- **fortune** (n) a very large amount of money
- **hail** (v) to come from
- **hamper** (v) to harm; to affect in a negative manner
- **harvest** (n) the time when farmers gather their crops from the fields
- **illegal** (adj) against the law
- **immigration** (n) the act of a person moving from one country to another
- **implement** (v) to use; to enact
- **impose** (v) to levy; to charge
- **incentive** (n) an enticement; something that encourages one to do better
- **income** (n) money earned
- **incomprehensible** (adj) unintelligible; not understandable
- **inefficient** (adj) wasteful; incompetent
- **industrialize** (v) to develop industries

- **inspire** (v) to motivate a person to do better
- **inventor** (n) a person who creates new products
- **invest** (v) to spend money in an attempt to earn more money at a later time
- **laborious** (adj) difficult; hard
- **leading** (adj) principal; main; very important
- **levy** (v) to charge, usually a tax
- **machinery** (n) equipment
- **mason** (n) a person who works with stones and bricks
- **measure** (n) an amount
- **mechanization** (n) industrialization; the replacement of human labor with machine labor
- **merchant** (n) a person who buys and sells goods
- **outcompete** (v) to do better than another person; to best; to win against
- **overcrowded** (adj) having too many people; overpopulated
- **ownership** (n) possession
- **payment** (n) money given to another for a good or service
- **privilege** (n) a right
- **profit** (v) to earn or make money
- **protectionism** (n) the act of taking care of one's interests
- **raw material** (n) a natural resource that has not yet been turned into a finished product
- **refrigeration** (n) the act of cooling off an area
- **retard** (v) to slow down; to hold back
- **rival** (n) an opponent
- **royalty** (n) money paid for the use of something a person has created
- **skyscraper** (n) a very tall building that is often many stories high
- **spread** (v) to expand; to become larger; to move from one place to another
- **stagnant** (n) unmoving
- **steel** (n) a form of iron that has been made stronger and which is often used in construction
- **subsistence** (adj) survival
- **tend** (v) to take care of; to look after
- **thriving** (adj) prosperous; flourishing
- **transform** (v) to change; to alter
- **transport** (v) to move; to carry; to take from one place to another
- **trillion** (n) a thousand billion; 1,000,000,000,000
- **unprecedented** (adj) unique; extraordinary
- **vulnerable** (adj) weak; helpless

👆 Choose the word or phrase closest in meaning to the highlighted part of the sentence.

1 Many ships never reached their final destinations.

Ⓐ ports
Ⓑ owners
Ⓒ missions
Ⓓ objectives

2 It gives the owner—typically the inventor—the exclusive right to use the patented item.

Ⓐ permanent
Ⓑ limited
Ⓒ extended
Ⓓ monetary

3 In Great Britain, it caused the immediate advance of society.

Ⓐ delayed
Ⓑ instant
Ⓒ primitive
Ⓓ constant

4 Around this time, they mostly abandoned trying to produce salt.

Ⓐ endured
Ⓑ thought about
Ⓒ gave up
Ⓓ concentrated on

5 During the mid- to late-1800s, there were several developments in the U.S. that caused the mechanization of the country to begin in earnest.

Ⓐ wholeheartedly
Ⓑ somewhat
Ⓒ in effect
Ⓓ afterward

6 When a man joined a guild, he had to vow to follow its rules.

Ⓐ remember
Ⓑ try
Ⓒ promise
Ⓓ forget

7 Knowing their work will be rewarded with a patent can inspire people to continue their efforts.

Ⓐ force
Ⓑ encourage
Ⓒ mislead
Ⓓ introduce

8 It was notably used for the internal combustion engine, which was installed in the newly invented automobile.

Ⓐ occasionally
Ⓑ severely
Ⓒ fortunately
Ⓓ particularly

9 The Venetians killed most of the inhabitants there and destroyed the salt works.

Ⓐ denizens
Ⓑ guildsmen
Ⓒ workers
Ⓓ artisans

10 Once the patent expires, other people can either improve upon these inventions or make even better creations.

Ⓐ runs out
Ⓑ runs on
Ⓒ runs away
Ⓓ runs after

11 After the Industrial Revolution got underway in the 1700s, many machines were made that could do better, faster, and cheaper work than master craftsmen.

  (A) accepted
  (B) started
  (C) promoted
  (D) returned

12 It has a thriving economy that increases at high rates virtually every year.

  (A) advanced
  (B) mechanized
  (C) prosperous
  (D) mercantilist

13 Every country dealt with its problems in its own way.

  (A) negotiated
  (B) required
  (C) ignored
  (D) handled

14 They were also outcompeted by others who had more reliable sources of salt.

  (A) dependable
  (B) inexpensive
  (C) abundant
  (D) nutritious

15 Petroleum, coal, ore, metal, grain, and wood are some of the main items transported.

  (A) loaded
  (B) carried
  (C) traded
  (D) purchased

16 Eventually, using their peerless navy, they seized control of the local salt trade.

  (A) extensive
  (B) superior
  (C) waterborne
  (D) experienced

17 Even today, farming methods in some places mirror those used in past centuries.

  (A) look at
  (B) imagine
  (C) duplicate
  (D) improve upon

18 They wanted to protect their rights, to set standards of skill and payment, to prevent nonmembers from doing business in an area, and to train apprentices.

  (A) notions
  (B) unions
  (C) levels
  (D) pay scales

19 Realizing the importance of inventors to their economies, they sought to protect inventors' rights and to enable them to profit as well.

  (A) thought
  (B) voted
  (C) had
  (D) looked

20 The Second Industrial Revolution saw innovations in many fields.

  (A) advances
  (B) expansions
  (C) theories
  (D) research

Part B

Chapter 06　Life Sciences

Life sciences focus on the study of living organisms. There are many fields of study. They include biology, marine biology, botany, physiology, zoology, and paleontology. Scientists research organisms such as animals, plants, and other kinds of creatures. They study the organisms' characteristics and their interactions with nature and other organisms. Some scientists examine entire ecosystems and the organisms that live in them. Because there are so many organisms on the Earth, life scientists can study many different fields. Some of them even conduct research on extinct species such as dinosaurs. But most of them focus on plants and animals that are alive today.

Mastering **the Question Types**

☑ Vocabulary ☐ Fill in a Table ☐ Factual Information ☐ Negative Factual Information ☑ Prose Summary
☐ Insert Text ☐ Reference ☑ Rhetorical Purpose ☐ Sentence Simplification ☐ Inference

Snakes' Tongues

1 ➜ Snakes' tongues are unusually shaped, especially when compared to those of other animals. Their tongues are <u>forked</u> as they split in two near the tip so that they look like a two-pronged fork. Some snakes' tongues are only slightly forked, making them barely noticeable. However, other snakes have very obviously forked tongues. Most experts believe that the reason for these forked shapes lies in the snakes' sense of smell.

A snake does not smell with its nose but uses its tongue instead. Each time a snake sticks its tongue out, it smells. Chemical particles in the air from the odors of other animals get stuck on the moisture found on the snake's tongue. The snake then returns its tongue to its mouth. After doing so, the tips of the snake's tongue fit into two holes found in the roof of its mouth. These holes are part of an organ in the mouth called the Jacobson's organ. Snakes utilize it to perceive differences in chemical compositions.

These differences are vital to the snake. By sensing the odors of other animals, the snake can both avoid danger from larger animals and also find food. It can also determine if an enemy is nearby according to its unique smell. The snake can further use this sense of smell to follow the trail of an animal it wants to catch and eat. In addition, male snakes are able to use their tongues to detect the presence of female snakes, which makes their sense of smell crucial to the mating process. Once a male snake finds a female, it rapidly flicks its tongue in and out to try to attract the female. Should she notice, mating—and the <u>**propagation**</u> of the species—will ensue.

Glossary
forked: divided
propagation: multiplication; breeding

1 The author discusses "Snakes' tongues" in paragraph 1 in order to

    Ⓐ prove that all of them have forked tongues

    Ⓑ note that their tongues are forked in various ways

    Ⓒ compare their tongues' shapes with those of other animals

    Ⓓ explain how snakes' tongues have evolved

2 The word "perceive" in the passage is closest in meaning to

    Ⓐ detect

    Ⓑ establish

    Ⓒ taste

    Ⓓ explain

3 *Directions:* An introductory sentence for a brief summary of the passage is provided below. Complete the summary by selecting the THREE answer choices that express the most important ideas of the passage. Some sentences do not belong because they express ideas that are not presented in the passage or are minor ideas in the passage. *This question is worth 2 points.*

Snakes use their tongues to smell with, so this enables them to engage in a wide number of activities.

Answer Choices

1️⃣ Snakes can identify the chemical compositions of various prey animals by using their tongues.

2️⃣ Male snakes utilize their tongues when they are looking for a female of the species to mate with.

3️⃣ All snakes have forks in their tongues, but the amount they are forked differs according to each species.

4️⃣ Snakes' tongues collect chemical particles that an organ in their bodies analyzes and interprets.

5️⃣ The Jacobson's organ, which has two holes in it, is found in the roofs of snakes' mouths.

6️⃣ Snakes that have long tongues are able to smell better than those that have shorter tongues.

Summarizing   Complete the summary by using the words or phrases given in the box.

find females	enemies	split in two	chemical particles

All snakes have forked tongues, so they are _____ near the tip. Their tongues are useful because snakes smell with them. Their tongues collect _____ from the moisture in the air. Then, the Jacobson's organ analyzes the particles to determine what they are. Snakes use this knowledge to avoid _____ and to find food. Males also use their tongues to _____. They flick their tongues in and out when trying to attract female snakes' attention.

Mastering **the Question Types**

B

☐ Vocabulary ☑ Fill in a Table ☐ Factual Information ☑ Negative Factual Information ☐ Prose Summary
☐ Insert Text ☐ Reference ☐ Rhetorical Purpose ☐ Sentence Simplification ☑ Inference

Tundra Vegetation

Tundra is a <u>biome</u> whose primary features are extremely cold temperatures and treeless areas. In many places, there is permafrost. This is subsoil—soil directly beneath the topsoil—that remains frozen all year long. Despite the permafrost and the frigid temperatures, there is still a surprisingly large amount of vegetation in tundra.

²→ Arctic tundra is located in the Northern Hemisphere near the North Pole. It covers an extensive area between the North Pole and the <u>taiga forests</u> that lie farther south. There is tundra in parts of Russia, Canada, the United States, Greenland, and Scandinavia. The permafrost ranges from a couple of centimeters thick to more than 1,000 meters deep in places. In addition, winters are periods of almost constant dark. This combination of factors makes it impossible for trees to grow. Instead, mosses and lichens are the most common form of vegetation. The mosses especially provide sustenance for fauna living in the tundra. In places where the permafrost is not thick, some small plants grow. These include various grasses as well as ferns. Labrador tea, a small evergreen shrub, and bearberry, whose berries are devoured by birds, also grow in arctic tundra.

³→ Alpine tundra can be found in places with high elevations all around the world. For instance, the Himalaya, Alps, and Andes mountains all have alpine tundra in certain areas. While they have permafrost, it is not as thick as it is in the Arctic. These places also lack the nearly perpetual night during winter, so the plant life growing in alpine tundra does not require the hardiness that plants do in other tundra. Some trees actually grow there, but they are dwarf trees, so they grow close to the ground. Numerous flowering plants grow in alpine tundra, too. Among them are purple fringe and pygmy bitterroot.

Glossary
biome: a habitat that has distinct plant and animal life as well as a standard climate
taiga forest: forests with mostly evergreen trees that are found in subarctic lands

1   In paragraph 2, the author's description of arctic tundra mentions all of the following EXCEPT:

    Ⓐ The average depth of the permafrost there

    Ⓑ Some types of plants that grow in it

    Ⓒ Places in the world where it is located

    Ⓓ The most common type of vegetation in it

2   Which of the following can be inferred from paragraphs 2 and 3 about alpine tundra?

    Ⓐ There is more alpine tundra in the world than arctic tundra.

    Ⓑ The temperatures in it often climb above freezing.

    Ⓒ Some parts of it are at very low elevations.

    Ⓓ Plants grow taller in it than in arctic tundra.

3   ***Directions:*** Select the appropriate statements from the answer choices and match them to the type of tundra to which they relate. TWO of the answer choices will NOT be used. ***This question is worth 3 points.***

Answer Choices	TYPE OF TUNDRA
① Has a large number of plants that produce flowers	**Arctic Tundra**
② Has both ferns and grasses that grow in it	•
③ Can support small plants in places with little permafrost	•
④ Has some tall trees because winters are not constantly dark	•
⑤ Can support large numbers of animals with its plant life	**Alpine Tundra**
⑥ Has mosses and lichens as its most common vegetation	•
⑦ Can have some trees growing in it in places	•

Summarizing   Complete the summary by using the words or phrases given in the box.

dwarf trees	high elevations	thick permafrost	frigid temperatures

Tundra is a biome that features _____ and permafrost. Arctic tundra is in northern areas near the North Pole. It can have very _____ as well as winters that are very dark. Because of that, trees do not grow there. Mosses, lichens, grasses, and ferns can grow in it though. Alpine tundra is located in mountainous areas with _____. Its permafrost is not so thick, and winters are not completely dark. Some _____ grow there as well as flowering plants.

Mastering **the Question Types**

- ☐ Vocabulary
- ☑ Insert Text
- ☐ Fill in a Table
- ☑ Reference
- ☑ Factual Information
- ☐ Rhetorical Purpose
- ☐ Negative Factual Information
- ☑ Sentence Simplification
- ☐ Prose Summary
- ☐ Inference

The Cambrian Explosion

1 ➜ For most of the Earth's first four billion years, very few life forms evolved. Then, between 570 and 530 million years ago, many new and complex multi-celled life forms appeared. Scientists call this period the Cambrian Explosion. The term Cambrian comes from the geological name of the period. The word "explosion" refers to the fact that so many organisms appeared in a short time. In fact, the majority of modern life forms have their roots in the Cambrian Explosion. The reason for this has <u>puzzled</u> scientists. Yet they have come up with three theories to explain it.

First, some scientists think that the Earth's oxygen levels increased around the time of the Cambrian Explosion. Since oxygen is a byproduct of photosynthesis in plants, the levels of oxygen on the Earth were initially quite low. This prevented complex organisms from developing. **❶** Gradually, as oxygen levels increased, more complex organisms that were bigger and required greater amounts of oxygen evolved. **❷** Second, some believe there was a mass extinction of life forms prior to the Cambrian Explosion. **❸** This left room for new species gradually to evolve over millions of years. **❹** Third, some believe there was no explosion but that the new life forms were merely the end result of billions of years of evolution.

The main problem with determining the answer is a lack of evidence. The evidence for the Cambrian Explosion depends on fossils. There are many fossils from the Cambrian period but few from the pre-Cambrian period. Some scientists argue that complex life forms already existed but did not <u>fossilize</u>. Fossils usually form from hard body parts, such as bones or shells. If there were no bones or shells on complex pre-Cambrian life forms, they would not have fossilized, which, scientists claim, would explain their absence from the fossil record.

Glossary
puzzle: to confuse
fossilize: to become a fossil

1   According to paragraph 1, which of the following is true of the Cambrian Explosion?

    Ⓐ Some scientists claim it is still going on today.

    Ⓑ Many creatures suddenly appeared during this time.

    Ⓒ Very much geological activity took place during it.

    Ⓓ It took place approximately four billion years ago.

2   The word "some" in the passage refers to

    Ⓐ scientists

    Ⓑ Earth's oxygen levels

    Ⓒ plants

    Ⓓ complex organisms

3   Which of the sentences below best expresses the essential information in the highlighted sentence in the passage? *Incorrect* answer choices change the meaning in important ways or leave out essential information.

    Ⓐ Scientists say that there are no pre-Cambrian fossils because the animals living then lacked bones and shells, which do not become fossils.

    Ⓑ Because the bones and shells failed to fossilize, scientists have very little evidence of any of the animals that lived in pre-Cambrian times.

    Ⓒ Scientists say that the only evidence of pre-Cambrian life forms in the fossil record comes in the form of bones and shells.

    Ⓓ Pre-Cambrian organisms all had bones or shells, which can be proven by looking at the fossil record for that period of time.

4   Look at the four squares [■] that indicate where the following sentence could be added to the passage.

A comet or asteroid striking the planet and creating a global catastrophe could have been responsible for that occurring.

Where would the sentence best fit?

Summarizing   Complete the summary by using the words or phrases given in the box.

a mass extinction   no explosion   oxygen level   fossil evidence

For four billion years, the Earth had few life forms. Then, during the Cambrian Explosion, large numbers of species suddenly appeared. Scientists have three main theories about this. Some say the Earth's _____ increased, so complex life forms appeared. Others say new species evolved because of _____ before this period. And others say there was _____ of species at all. The problem is the lack of _____ from this period, so scientists know little about it.

Mastering **the Subject**

Birds and Egg Numbers

All birds lay eggs that carry their unborn offspring. The mother bird—or sometimes the father—cares for the eggs until they hatch. Some species of birds lay only one egg, but others may lay more than a dozen. Several factors ultimately determine how many eggs a bird lays at once.

²➜ The number of eggs a bird lays is its clutch size. A species' longevity and survival rate help determine its clutch size. Some birds, such as penguins, albatrosses, and ostriches, live for decades. These birds lay a single large egg. Thanks to their long lifespans, they have time to raise and care for this single egg and the chick that hatches from it. It takes all of the parents' time and energy to care for a single egg. If these birds' clutch sizes were larger, their eggs' chances of survival would be reduced. However, birds with shorter life spans typically have larger clutch sizes. This increases the odds that some of the offspring will survive after the parents die.

A second factor is the environment. Scientists have observed that most birds living in harsher climates with seasonal changes have larger clutch sizes. For example, birds in North America and Europe tend to have larger clutch sizes than tropical birds. **1** Scientists believe that, because of the changing seasonal weather conditions in northern climes, the birds' offspring have lower survival rates. **2** Therefore, having more eggs makes it more likely that some offspring will survive. **3** Since tropical climates have less severe weather conditions, birds there lay fewer eggs. **4**

⁴➜ The location of a bird's nest is another factor. Some birds, such as woodpeckers, construct nests inside trees. These birds are cavity nesters. They usually have larger clutch sizes than birds that build nests in the open. In general, open-nesting birds are **vulnerable** to predators such as snakes, which eat eggs and young chicks. It might appear logical for open nesters to have bigger clutch sizes in case some eggs or chicks die, yet they do not. In fact, open nesters frequently have smaller clutch sizes than cavity nesters. Scientists believe the reason concerns the huge amount of time and energy it takes to make and protect eggs and then to raise the chicks. Since open nesters will likely lose some offspring, they lay fewer eggs to help them save energy.

These factors cause each bird species to lay different numbers of eggs. Over time, birds have evolved to lay the ideal number of eggs to **ensure** one thing: that their species will not go extinct but will continue to live and to reproduce.

NOTE

Male emperor penguins are responsible for taking care of their eggs. The males hold the eggs between their feet to keep them warm for up to eight weeks.

In general, small birds live for short periods of time, and large birds live for longer periods of time. About half of all songbirds live for two years or less. Albatrosses, which are large seabirds, may live for forty years. And ostriches, which are very large birds, can live for seventy-five years.

Many places in North America and Europe have cold winters. So most of the birds that live in these areas have clutch sizes of six or more eggs.

Snakes are not the only animals that steal eggs from birds' nests. Foxes and weasels commonly steal eggs. Many species of birds steal eggs from other birds' nests, too.

Glossary
vulnerable: defenseless; exposed to
ensure: to guarantee; to promise

1 In paragraph 2, why does the author mention "penguins, albatrosses, and ostriches"?

  Ⓐ To note that they all care for their offspring

  Ⓑ To claim that they lay eggs only once a year

  Ⓒ To name some birds that have long lifespans

  Ⓓ To prove they are better parents than other birds

2 According to paragraph 4, woodpeckers are cavity nesters because

  Ⓐ they make their homes inside holes in trees

  Ⓑ they build nests that are safe from snakes

  Ⓒ they require large nests for the many eggs they lay

  Ⓓ they peck holes in a large number of trees

3 Look at the four squares [■] that indicate where the following sentence could be added to the passage.

For instance, a wren might lay between six and eight eggs while a toucan may lay only two to four eggs at a time.

Where would the sentence best fit?

4 *Directions:* Select the appropriate sentences from the answer choices and match them to the factor for determining clutch size to which they relate. TWO of the answer choices will NOT be used. ***This question is worth 3 points.***

Answer Choices

① The closeness to predators makes birds lay few eggs.

② Harsh weather makes it likely that birds will have several eggs.

③ Birds living in tropical places tend to lay only a few eggs.

④ This can affect how well the parents take care of the offspring.

⑤ Cavity nesters such as the woodpecker might lay many eggs.

⑥ Birds lay many eggs when they are in a place safe from attack.

⑦ This makes birds lay many eggs to increase their species' chances of survival.

FACTOR FOR DETERMINING CLUTCH SIZE

Longevity and Survival Rate

●

●

Location of the Bird's Nest

●

●

●

Summarizing Complete the summary by filling in the blanks.

All birds lay eggs. However, each species lays varying numbers of eggs. For instance, birds that live a long time, such as penguins, _____ , and ostriches, lay one egg; however, short-lived birds lay _____ at once. Birds in colder places lay many eggs while those in _____ lay fewer eggs. The location of a bird's nest is important, too. _____ , which have nests in safe places, lay many eggs. Open nesters, whose nests are vulnerable to predators, lay only a few.

Mastering **the Subject**

The Stages of Sleep

People experience two distinct types of sleep: rapid eye movement sleep (REM) and non-rapid eye movement sleep (NREM). It is during REM sleep that a person dreams while those experiencing NREM sleep do not dream at all. Both types have <u>specific</u> characteristics, especially concerning their length, the reaction of the body, and the type of brain activity that occurs.

²→ Sleep specialists estimate that approximately eighty percent of sleep is NREM. During a typical seven to eight hour period of sleep, a person may only experience about sixty to ninety minutes of REM sleep. When a person is in NREM sleep, that individual's breathing is slow, and the body's heart rate and blood pressure are low. Additionally, the person's body remains quite still. Brainwave activity also slows since the amount of blood flowing to the brain is reduced.

³→ The three major stages of NREM sleep are Stage 1, Stage 2, and Stage 3. During Stage 1, a person drifts off to sleep. It usually lasts about ten minutes. During this time, the person can be easily awakened. The person may also not realize that he or she is sleeping and may confuse sleepy-induced thoughts with reality. Stage 2 usually lasts about twenty minutes. The body functions, including the metabolism rate, slow down more. The individual falls into a deeper sleep, so it is more difficult to wake a person up in this stage. Yet a loud noise or being shaken roughly is frequently enough to awaken someone. Finally, around thirty to forty minutes after falling asleep, Stage 3 begins. This is the deepest stage of sleep as bodily functions are at their lowest level of activity. If someone manages to awaken a sleeper during this stage, the sleeper will be <u>disoriented</u> and unable to do anything for some time.

In contrast to NREM sleep, where there is no dreaming, dreams occur during REM sleep. Most people experience three to five REM dreaming states per night. This stage is characterized by the rapid fluttering of the eyes under closed eyelids. As for dreams, some last only a few minutes while others can last for an hour. During REM sleep, a person's major voluntary muscle groups are paralyzed. Experts believe this happens to keep the person from harming him or herself while dreaming. There is also a sudden increase in the person's rate of breathing, heart rate, and brain activity. The first REM period is often short, but successive REM sleep periods last longer. Most REM sleep also happens later in the night and right before the person awakens in the morning.

> **NOTE**
>
> According to scientists, most people remember only a very small number of their dreams. This normally happens when a person awakens in the middle of a dream.
>
> A person may be in NREM sleep for a cycle that lasts between ninety and 120 minutes. After this, a person may then go into a period of REM sleep.
>
> Scientists used to say that there were four stages of NREM sleep. However, Stage 3 and Stage 4 were combined into a single stage called Stage 3. So now, according to most scientists, there are only three stages of NREM sleep.
>
> As people age, the percentage of REM sleep that they get decreases. Babies and young children get the greatest percentage of REM sleep. However, teens and adults begin to get less REM sleep. Finally, the elderly get the least amount of REM sleep of people in all age groups.

Glossary
specific: exact; precise
disoriented: confused

1 According to paragraph 2, which of the following is true of NREM sleep?

    Ⓐ It comes after a person first experiences REM sleep.

    Ⓑ It may cause a person's heart rate to slow to almost zero.

    Ⓒ A person experiencing it may sometimes cease breathing.

    Ⓓ It results in the overall slowing of the body's activities.

2 In paragraph 3, the author implies that during Stage 3 sleep, a person

    Ⓐ may experience some level of dreaming

    Ⓑ can only be awakened with great difficulty

    Ⓒ gets more rest than in the other stages

    Ⓓ undergoes it for less than an hour at a time

3 The word "others" in the passage refers to

    Ⓐ eyes

    Ⓑ closed eyelids

    Ⓒ dreams

    Ⓓ a few minutes

4 *Directions:* Select the appropriate statements from the answer choices and match them to the type of sleep to which they relate. TWO of the answer choices will NOT be used. ***This question is worth 3 points.***

Answer Choices	TYPE OF SLEEP
① Results in an increase in breathing and a lowering of blood pressure	**NREM Sleep** ● ● ●
② Is the period when a person may experience dreaming	
③ May be difficult to rouse a person from it	
④ Has three distinct stages that people may go through	**REM Sleep** ● ●
⑤ Only takes up about a fifth of a person's sleeping time	
⑥ Involves a progression from light to very deep sleep	
⑦ May cause a person to forget his or her most recent memories	

Summarizing   **Complete the summary by filling in the blanks.**

People experience four different stages of sleep. Three involve NREM sleep, and the other is REM sleep. _____ occurs when a person goes to sleep. Stage 1 is a light sleep, and Stage 2 is deeper. Stage 3 is a _____. During NREM sleep, the person's bodily functions slow down. The fourth stage is REM sleep. This is when people _____. The person's breathing rate, heart rate, and brain activity _____. A person often goes through all four stages repeatedly while sleeping.

Pinyon Pines and Pinyon Jays

Animals and plants sometimes establish unique relationships. One example is that of the pinyon pine tree and the pinyon jay bird in the southwestern United States. Both the pinyon pine tree and the pinyon jay bird have evolved so that they can use each other in order to survive and to increase their numbers. The pines provide a source of food for the jays while the birds help spread the trees' seeds to new locations.

[2]➜ Pinyon jays consume the seeds from the cones growing on pinyon pine trees. These seeds are a major food source for the birds. Several features of the pinyon pine enable the jays easily to consume the seeds. Firstly, the seeds are larger than other seeds and stay on the tree longer than most other seeds. This makes them more attractive and available for a longer time. Next, the pine's seeds have two **distinct** colors. Seeds that fail to mature are tan colored. Those that have matured and are more edible are dark brown. The jays can distinguish between the two colors and, accordingly, know which seeds to eat and which to avoid.

The jays have some unique physical characteristics that make eating the seeds easier. They lack feathers around the **nostrils** on their beak. Therefore, their beaks can more easily enter the cones where the seeds are located. And none of the sticky substance in the pine cones gets stuck to the birds' beaks either. Lastly, each jay can carry up to forty seeds in its throat. This enables them to take large numbers of seeds from the trees at one time.

Once a jay has a full supply of seeds, it flies away and buries them underground. The jays are extremely active in storing food during fall for the coming winter and spring. In fact, they store thousands of seeds in many locations. Fortunately for them, the birds have good memories and can recall where their food storage places are. After mating in late winter, their chicks hatch in spring. The jays then return to their hidden caches of seeds to provide their chicks with food.

While underground, the seeds are safe from other animals and the harsh weather conditions. The jays also occasionally fail to recover all of the seeds, thereby giving them a chance to germinate. So pinyon pine trees often spring up and start growing in new areas. This mutual relationship between pinyon pine trees and pinyon jay birds has evolved over thousands of years. It gives each species a better chance to increase its numbers and its chances of survival.

> **NOTE**
>
> There are many species of jay birds that live all around the world. In general, they are medium-sized birds that are blue in color. They are also members of the crow family and are sometimes called magpies.
>
> Most pinyon pine trees in the United States grow at elevations over 1,200 meters above sea level. They usually grow to be fewer than ten meters high, but they may live for up to 1,000 years in some cases.
>
> In the past, Native Americans frequently survived by eating the nuts from pinyon pine trees during the winter. The trees' nuts are both nutritious and abundant, so the Native Americans did not lack healthy food during cold weather.
>
> Pinyon pine tree seeds that are left on the ground will not germinate. Only buried seeds do. This is why the actions of the pinyon jays are so important to the reproduction of the pinyon pines.

Glossary

distinct: obvious; apparent; distinguishing
nostril: one of the two external openings in an animal's nose

1 Which of the sentences below best expresses the essential information in the highlighted sentence in the passage? *Incorrect* answer choices change the meaning in important ways or leave out essential information.

- Ⓐ Because of evolution, the changes in the pinyon pine tree helped the pinyon jay bird survive and become more numerous.
- Ⓑ There are more pinyon pine trees than there are pinyon jay birds because of the effects of evolution on both of them.
- Ⓒ Thanks to changes in both the pinyon pine tree and the pinyon jay bird, they can make use of each other to reproduce and to live.
- Ⓓ Pinyon jay birds would never have been able to survive without evolution having affected pinyon pine trees.

2 In paragraph 2, the author's description of pinyon pine tree seeds mentions all of the following EXCEPT:

- Ⓐ The time of the year when they mature
- Ⓑ The two different colors that they have
- Ⓒ Their size in comparison to other tree seeds
- Ⓓ An animal that frequently consumes them

3 The word "caches" in the passage is closest in meaning to

- Ⓐ nests
- Ⓑ holes
- Ⓒ meals
- Ⓓ stores

4 *Directions:* An introductory sentence for a brief summary of the passage is provided below. Complete the summary by selecting the THREE answer choices that express the most important ideas of the passage. Some sentences do not belong because they express ideas that are not presented in the passage or are minor ideas in the passage. *This question is worth 2 points.*

Pinyon pine trees and pinyon jay birds have formed a relationship that lets both of them flourish as species.

Answer Choices

1. The branches of pinyon pine trees often serve as places for pinyon jay birds to build their nests.
2. Pinyon jay birds have made the pinyon pine trees' seeds a major part of their daily diets.
3. Pinyon jay birds can store large numbers of pinyon pine tree seeds in their mouths at a single time.
4. The states in the southwestern United States are where pinyon pine trees and pinyon jay birds mostly live.
5. Pinyon pine tree seeds hidden and forgotten by pinyon jay birds often become adult trees.
6. The color of the pinyon pine trees' seeds lets pinyon jay birds determine whether they are edible or not.

Summarizing Complete the summary by filling in the blanks.

Pinyon pine trees and pinyon jay birds have a _____ relationship. The jays eat many of the _____. The seeds have two separate colors. These indicate which ones are ripe and which are not. The jays have beaks that can easily grab the seeds from the cones. The jays then _____ in the ground. In spring, they dig up the seeds to _____. But the jays occasionally forget about some seeds. These then germinate and become adult trees.

TOEFL **Practice Test**

The Leatherback Turtle

A leatherback turtle at the bottom of the ocean

¹→ The leatherback turtle is the largest of all turtles. Some are as long as two meters and weigh up to 900 kilograms. They are unique in several ways. Some can dive far beneath the ocean's surface. They may migrate thousands of kilometers from their breeding places to their feeding grounds. This supposedly cold-blooded animal can also keep its body warm both in cold, deep ocean water and in cold-water climates.

²→ Leatherback turtles hatch from eggs laid on sandy beaches. The females visit the beach—usually at night—dig a hole, and then lay about thirty eggs. The sand must be warm enough to incubate the eggs to let them survive. So the turtles lay their eggs in the tropics. Beaches on Caribbean and South Pacific islands are among their nesting grounds. The eggs and, later, newly hatched turtles, face numerous dangers. Predators comb the beaches looking for eggs. As baby turtles head toward the water, birds and other predators may eat them, too. Upon successfully reaching the water, the males never return to land. The females do so only to lay eggs, but they do not always visit the same beach. This makes leatherback turtles unusual among migratory animals.

³→ From their birthplaces, the turtles swim thousands of miles to their feeding grounds. Some of these are the east coast of Australia, the North Pacific Ocean between Hawaii and the mainland United States, the west coast of South America, and the North Atlantic Ocean. Adult turtles mostly eat jellyfish. Their favorite species is the lion's mane jellyfish, which, weighing around ten pounds, is one of the largest of its kind.

⁴→ The water in some of their feeding grounds is frigid. However, the turtles have adapted to survive in these conditions. They can maintain body temperatures higher than the surrounding water temperature. Their high metabolic rate enables this. The turtles burn food quickly, which keeps them warm. They then use this warmth to heat their blood. As the blood circulates, the warm blood from the inner body heats the colder blood returning from the outer body. The turtles' large flippers often get extremely cold, but they can stop blood from going to the surface of the flippers if it gets too cold. **1** This prevents extremely cold blood from entering the inner body, where it might harm the turtles. **2** Since they are reptiles, scientists classify them as cold blooded. **3** However, it seems reasonable to accept that their high metabolic rate and ability to stay warm in cold surroundings qualify them as warm-blooded animals. **4**

5→ The turtle has been on the Earth for around 100 million years. However, from the 1960s to the 1980s, it was in danger of extinction. Neither predators nor men hunting the turtles were the biggest threats. Instead, the <u>encroachment</u> of humans on their traditional nesting beaches and their getting caught in fishing nets depleted their numbers. Fortunately, recent efforts to protect the turtles have helped revitalize the species. Now, approximately five to eight thousand leatherbacks are alive around the world. Most live in the Atlantic Ocean and Caribbean Sea. Sadly, the Pacific Ocean leatherbacks are in serious decline and may not recover.

Glossary
comb: to search closely for something
encroachment: an intrusion

1 According to paragraph 1, which of the following is true of the leatherback turtle?

    Ⓐ It can stay submerged underwater for hours at a time.

    Ⓑ Its shell can be up to two meters long in some cases.

    Ⓒ Its breeding and feeding grounds are far from each other.

    Ⓓ Its breeding grounds are found in cold-water areas.

2 The word "incubate" in the passage is closest in meaning to

    Ⓐ heat

    Ⓑ hatch

    Ⓒ protect

    Ⓓ soften

3 According to paragraph 2, which of the following is NOT true of leatherback turtle eggs?

    Ⓐ Many eggs are laid by the turtles at the same time.

    Ⓑ The turtles' eggs are buried in the sand until they hatch.

    Ⓒ They are laid on sandy beaches in warm areas.

    Ⓓ They are frequently eaten by birds before they hatch.

4 In paragraph 3, why does the author mention "the lion's mane jellyfish"?

    Ⓐ To name the world's largest jellyfish

    Ⓑ To emphasize how much it weighs

    Ⓒ To state where it is commonly found

    Ⓓ To say which jellyfish the turtle prefers

5 According to paragraph 4, leatherback turtles can keep warm in cold water because

    Ⓐ they avoid diving too deeply

    Ⓑ they are warm-blooded mammals

    Ⓒ they have a high metabolism

    Ⓓ they eat a large amount of food

6 The word "revitalize" in the passage is closest in meaning to

    Ⓐ recede

    Ⓑ reinvigorate

    Ⓒ reconsider

    Ⓓ recreate

7 According to paragraph 5, leatherback turtles almost became extinct because

    Ⓐ they were affected by pollution in the oceans

    Ⓑ their breeding grounds were invaded by people

    Ⓒ they were hunted by people too much

    Ⓓ their numbers were reduced by various ocean predators

8 In paragraph 5, the author implies that leatherback turtles

(A) no longer get trapped in the nets of commercial fisherman

(B) have completely recovered their previous numbers

(C) are still an endangered species

(D) will soon be extinct in one ocean

9 Look at the four squares [■] that indicate where the following sentence could be added to the passage.

This makes them an exception among the members of the reptile family.

Where would the sentence best fit?

Click on a square [■] to add the sentence to the passage.

10 *Directions:* An introductory sentence for a brief summary of the passage is provided below. Complete the summary by selecting the THREE answer choices that express the most important ideas of the passage. Some sentences do not belong because they express ideas that are not presented in the passage or are minor ideas in the passage. *This question is worth 2 points.*

Drag your answer choices to the spaces where they belong.
To remove an answer choice, click on it. To review the passage, click on **View Text**.

Leatherback turtles are migratory animals that are able to survive in cold environments thanks to some of their unique bodily functions.

-
-
-

Answer Choices

1 By increasing their metabolic rate, the turtles can keep their bodies warm even in frigid conditions.

2 The cold blood in their bodies gets heated by the warm blood from the inner part, which helps the turtles stay warm.

3 Leatherback turtles can weigh almost one ton and may extend up to two meters from tip to tip.

4 Thanks to their unique body structure, the turtles can consume large amounts of jellyfish while they are hunting.

5 While they are no longer in danger of extinction, the turtles' numbers have not recovered from their low levels.

6 The turtles might swim thousands of kilometers from their place of birth to where they feed.

Star Performer Subject Topics | Life Sciences

1 Amphibians

Amphibians are a class of animals that are capable of living both in the water and on land. They are vertebrates, and they are also cold-blooded animals. There are three main groups of amphibians. They are frogs and toads, salamanders, and caecilians, which resemble earthworms. Some scientists believe that amphibians are a link between sea creatures such as fish and land creatures such as reptiles, birds, and mammals. Amphibians have been on the Earth for about 350 million years. During this time, the various species have undergone many evolutionary changes.

2 Microclimates

A large area may have its own climate. But within this region, the climactic conditions may vary from place to place. This creates something called a microclimate. Microclimates may often be just a few meters in diameter. A lack or abundance of sunlight or water may cause them to appear. Differences in the temperature or the soil may create them, too. One example of a microclimate is a deep valley between two mountains. It might get less sunlight and be cooler than the area around it. So a microclimate—one with very different weather than the area around it—forms.

3 Fungus

There are many kinds of fungi, all of which belong to the fungus kingdom. The most common fungi are yeasts, molds, mildews, and mushrooms. Fungi used to be considered members of the plant kingdom; however, scientists gave them their own kingdom later. Fungi differ from plants in many regards. They lack chlorophyll, so they are unable to perform photosynthesis. They also do not have any roots, stems, or leaves. Fungi typically require moist places to live and grow. Some even thrive in aquatic conditions. They also secrete various enzymes, which enable them to obtain nutrition.

4 Animals and Body Temperature

Members of the animal kingdom can be divided into animals that are warm and cold blooded. Warm-blooded animals can maintain their body temperatures. But cold-blooded ones cannot. Warm-blooded animals—such as mammals and birds—can regulate their internal temperatures no matter what the weather conditions. They require a large amount of food to do so. So they must constantly eat. As for cold-blooded animals, these are animals such as reptiles, amphibians, and fish. They cannot regulate their bodies' temperatures. Instead, they rely upon the sun to provide them with warmth. This is why many of them frequently bask in the sun.

5 Crop Modification

For thousands of years, since man discovered agriculture, crop yields were often low. Most increases in crop yields resulted from increasing the amount of land farmed. But in the 1950s, scientists started making vast improvements in the quality of the seeds farmers planted. Norman Borlaug was one of these scientists. He is often called the father of the Green Revolution. He introduced better strains of grain to places. The result was that grain production increased dramatically in many countries, including Mexico and India. Thanks in part to men like him, the world's population has greatly increased in the past century.

6 Bird Migration

Every year in mid and late fall, people in temperate zones observe numerous flocks of birds flying south. When spring comes, the same birds return north to their summer homes. Birds migrate primarily to escape from cold weather and to have access to food sources. In snowy climates, the weather can be too frigid for birds. Likewise, there is less food in cold snow-covered areas. In warm and tropical regions, however, birds can find abundant food. Scientists have long studied bird migration, but they are not yet sure how birds know when they should migrate south or north.

7 ▶ Animal Survival

All animals have one instinct that overrides all of their others: the survival instinct. All animals are either prey or predators. Prey animals get hunted. Predators do the hunting. In order to survive, animals utilize a variety of defenses. Some have sharp teeth or claws to defend themselves. Others have venom in their bites that either kills or injures predators. Some animals use camouflage to hide from predators. And others simply are able to escape predators by using great speed, flight, or swimming or digging ability. There are numerous ways that animals can ensure their survival in the wild.

8 ▶ Plants and Minerals

The quality of the soil that plants are found in determines how well they will grow. Good soil has many nutrients while poor soil does not. All plants require certain amounts of water and sunlight to live. But their roots also need to extract minerals from the ground. These minerals then help the plants grow. Nitrogen is one mineral whose presence in soil helps plants thrive. In addition, plants frequently extract minerals such as potassium and phosphorous. These minerals enable plants to grow taller, to have stronger stems, and to bear more and better fruit.

9 ▶ Moths

Moths are insects that belong to the same scientific order as butterflies. In some ways, they are quite similar to each other. For instance, both moths and butterflies undergo the same four-stage life cycle of egg, larva, pupa, and adult. They also spend their pupa stages in a cocoon while transforming into adults. And they are superficially similar in appearance. However, moths are nocturnal animals, so they are active primarily at night. And they have, on average, wings that are smaller than those of butterflies. Moths also have antennae that look different from butterflies as well as bodies that are thicker.

10 ▶ Plant Defenses

Plants are often consumed—in whole or in part—by various animals, including insects, birds, and mammals. In order to protect themselves, some have developed defenses. Some plants develop physical defenses. Their leaves or stems might grow spines or thorns to protect them from large animals such as deer and cattle. The cactus is one such plant with large spines. Other plants begin to secrete various substances when animals start eating their leaves. This makes the leaves inedible, and thus the animal stops eating. Other plants release chemicals that can be toxic to some creatures, particularly insects.

11 ▶ Coral Reefs

Coral reefs are areas where many corals grow together. They are typically found in the shallow waters of seas and oceans in tropical areas since they cannot live in water cooler than twenty-two degrees Celsius. Coral reefs create vibrant ecosystems that attract a variety of sea creatures. Enormous numbers of species of animals may live in the reefs. Coral reefs have waters with huge amounts of nutrients. They serve as excellent spaces for animals to reproduce and to lay their eggs. And they provide protection from larger predators such as sharks and dolphins, which cannot swim through the razor-sharp coral.

12 ▶ Insect Camouflage

As fairly small creatures, insects are often in danger of being preyed upon by birds, reptiles, mammals, and other insects. Many have therefore developed ways to camouflage themselves. They blend in with their environment to disguise themselves. For instance, many insects use color as camouflage. Moths are often the same color as the trees or rocks upon which they rest. This is also true of grasshoppers, katydids, and butterflies. There are other insects called walking sticks. These actually resemble twigs on trees, so they have no need to hide at all. Animals constantly mistake them for inanimate objects.

- **adapt** (v) to change; to become used to something new
- **beak** (n) the hard, elongated tip of a bird's mouth
- **billion** (n) one thousand million; 1,000,000,000
- **bone** (n) a hard piece of tissue in the body that helps form a skeleton
- **breathe** (v) to take air into the body
- **breed** (v) to reproduce; to mate
- **byproduct** (n) a secondary product created by a reaction such as photosynthesis
- **cavity** (n) a hole; a hollow space
- **characterize** (v) to classify; to consider something as being like something else
- **circulate** (v) to move in a circular way; to flow, as in blood flowing in the body
- **chick** (n) a baby bird
- **complex** (adj) complicated
- **confuse** (v) to puzzle; to make so that one cannot understand
- **consume** (v) to eat
- **distinguish** (v) to tell one apart from another
- **dozen** (n) a group of twelve
- **dream** (v) to have images in one's head while sleeping
- **dwarf** (adj) tiny; smaller than normal
- **edible** (adj) able to be eaten
- **ensue** (v) to happen next; to result
- **evolve** (v) to change slowly in order to adapt to something
- **expert** (n) a person with a great amount of knowledge about a certain topic
- **extinction** (n) the death of a species as a whole
- **far-reaching** (adj) comprehensive; extensive
- **fauna** (n) the animals that live in a certain region
- **feather** (n) the soft outer covering found on most birds
- **feed** (v) to give food to
- **flipper** (n) a fin; an outer limb on an animal which helps it swim
- **flow** (v) to move; to circulate
- **flutter** (v) to flicker; to tremble
- **fossil** (n) the calcified remains of a dead plant or animal
- **freeze** (v) to ice up; to become incredibly cold
- **germinate** (v) to grow; to sprout
- **hatch** (v) to emerge, often from an egg; to be born from an egg
- **lay** (v) to bring forth, as in an egg
- **life form** (n) any kind of living organism

- **lifespan** (n) the period of time that an organism lives
- **longevity** (n) a long life
- **mature** (v) to become ripe; to become edible
- **metabolism** (n) the process by which the body creates energy
- **moisture** (n) wetness; dampness
- **moss** (n) a tiny, flowerless plant that grows on moist soil or on trees or rocks
- **nest** (n) a structure in which a bird lays its eggs and rears its young
- **offspring** (n) children; progeny
- **organ** (n) an important group of tissues, like the heart or brain, in the body
- **organism** (n) any kind of living creature
- **particle** (n) a small piece; a tiny piece
- **predator** (n) an animal that hunts and kills other animals for food
- **prey** (n) an animal that gets hunted by other animals
- **pronged** (adj) split; divided
- **range** (v) to vary in size or amount
- **reduce** (v) to lessen; to decrease
- **reptile** (n) a cold-blooded animal such as a snake, turtle, or lizard
- **result** (v) to occur because of something
- **root** (n) the underground part of the plant that absorbs water and nutrients
- **seed** (n) the fertilized ovule of a plant that enables it to reproduce
- **sense** (v) to detect
- **shell** (n) the hard outer covering of an animal that protects it
- **sleeper** (n) a person or animal that is sleeping
- **soil** (n) ground; earth
- **species** (n) a kind or type of organism
- **spread** (v) to extend; to increase in size, area, or scope
- **stage** (n) a period; a phase
- **sticky** (adj) adhesive; having the properties of glue
- **store** (v) to put away something for use in the future
- **sustenance** (n) something such as food and drink that can keep people or animals alive
- **threat** (n) a danger to someone or something
- **topsoil** (n) fertile earth found at the surface
- **treeless** (adj) having no trees growing in a place
- **tropical** (adj) hot and humid; relating to the tropics
- **unborn** (adj) not yet having been born; still within one's mother's womb

Vocabulary Review

☝ Choose the word or phrase closest in meaning to the highlighted part of the sentence.

1. Third, some believe there was no explosion but that the new life forms were merely the end result of billions of years of evolution.
   (A) absolutely
   (B) possibly
   (C) approximately
   (D) simply

2. Should she notice, mating—and the propagation of the species—will ensue.
   (A) consider
   (B) continue
   (C) result
   (D) remove

3. If the clutch size were larger, the eggs' chances of survival would likely be reduced.
   (A) living
   (B) adapting
   (C) fertilizing
   (D) dying

4. The jays also occasionally fail to recover all of the seeds, thereby giving them a chance to germinate.
   (A) develop
   (B) deteriorate
   (C) decompose
   (D) destruct

5. Sleep specialists estimate that approximately 80% of sleep is NREM.
   (A) students
   (B) physicians
   (C) psychologists
   (D) experts

6. Despite the permafrost and the frigid temperatures, there is still a surprisingly large amount of vegetation in tundra.
   (A) changing
   (B) freezing
   (C) declining
   (D) tropical

7. Experts believe this happens to keep the person from harming him or herself while dreaming.
   (A) moving
   (B) killing
   (C) injuring
   (D) waking

8. Since open nesters will likely lose some offspring, they lay fewer eggs to help them save energy.
   (A) eggs
   (B) stores
   (C) nests
   (D) babies

9. As baby turtles head toward the water, birds and other predators may eat them, too.
   (A) sea creatures
   (B) prey animals
   (C) reptiles
   (D) hunters

10. Fortunately for them, the birds have good memories and can recall where their food storage places are.
    (A) remember
    (B) locate
    (C) recognize
    (D) identify

11 Yet a loud noise or being shaken roughly is frequently enough to awaken someone.

(A) bother
(B) relax
(C) rouse
(D) approach

12 By sensing the odors of other animals, the snake can both avoid danger from larger animals and also find food.

(A) smells
(B) particles
(C) chemicals
(D) tastes

13 This supposedly cold-blooded animal can also keep its body warm in both cold, deep ocean water and in cold-water climates.

(A) clearly
(B) definitely
(C) possibly
(D) allegedly

14 The term Cambrian comes from the geological name of the period.

(A) word
(B) concept
(C) theory
(D) idea

15 Pinyon jays consume the seeds from the cones growing on pinyon pine trees.

(A) remove
(B) transport
(C) swallow
(D) take

16 Labrador tea, a small evergreen shrub, and bearberry, whose berries are devoured by birds, also grow in arctic tundra.

(A) searched for
(B) eaten
(C) avoided
(D) pollinated

17 This prevents extremely cold blood from entering the inner body, where it might harm the turtles.

(A) makes
(B) encourages
(C) stops
(D) pauses

18 Some birds, such as woodpeckers, construct nests inside trees.

(A) build
(B) find
(C) distract
(D) manufacture

19 The main problem with determining the answer is a lack of evidence.

(A) researching
(B) considering
(C) requesting
(D) finding

20 These places also lack the nearly perpetual night during winter, so the plant life growing in alpine tundra does not require the hardiness that plants do in other tundra.

(A) eternal
(B) shortened
(C) dark
(D) frozen

Part B

Chapter 07 Physical Sciences

Physical sciences focus on studying the characteristics, properties, and natures of nonliving things. The primary fields of study in it are chemistry, geology, astronomy, physics, and meteorology. Chemistry is the study of elements and compounds and their properties. Geology focuses on the study of the Earth. This includes examining rocks and minerals. Astronomy is the study of outer space and everything in it, including stars, planets, moons, and other objects. Physics is the study of energy, matter, force, and motion. And meteorology is the study of the weather, what causes it, and how it affects the Earth.

☑ Vocabulary   ☐ Fill in a Table   ☐ Factual Information   ☐ Negative Factual Information   ☑ Prose Summary
☐ Insert Text   ☐ Reference   ☑ Rhetorical Purpose   ☐ Sentence Simplification   ☐ Inference

Earth's Geological Time Scale

Scientists estimate that the Earth is approximately 4.5 billion years old. Yet **humanoid** life forms have been alive for only around four million years. And written records go back only about 5,000 years. To learn about the Earth's history before this time, scientists rely upon various means. These include archaeological evidence, fossils, and several dating methods. From what they have learned, experts have divided the Earth's history into periods based on a geological time scale. They use several units. From longest to shortest, they are supereon, eon, era, epoch, period, and age.

There has been only one supereon. It is the Pre-Cambrian time period. It lasted from the Earth's creation to around 550 million years ago. Within it were three eons: the Hadean, Archean, and Proterozoic. The Hadean Eon ended around 3.8 billion years ago, which was when the first life forms appeared on the planet. The Archean Eon then lasted for a billion years. During this eon, many small organisms, including oxygen-producing bacteria, developed. The oldest known fossils also come from this era. The next eon, the Proterozoic, lasted almost two billion years. It had three distinct eras. They were the Paleo-proterozoic, Meso-proterozoic, and Neo-proterozoic eras. During this extensive eon, the Earth's atmosphere formed. In addition, more complex—yet still very simple—life forms **emerged**.

[3]➡ The Phanerozoic Eon, the current one, was the next eon to follow. It has been divided into three eras: the Paleozoic, Mesozoic, and Cenozoic. The Paleozoic Era began with what scientists call the Cambrian Explosion. For reasons yet unknown, many complex life forms, including small and large plants, insects, and land animals, suddenly developed then. During the Mesozoic Era, the dinosaurs ruled the Earth. They then disappeared around sixty-five million years ago. This gave rise to the Cenozoic Era, which has been dominated by mammals, especially humans.

Glossary

humanoid: having human characteristics
emerge: to arise; to come into being

1   The word "extensive" in the passage is closest in meaning to

   Ⓐ crucial

   Ⓑ lengthy

   Ⓒ unique

   Ⓓ detailed

2   In paragraph 3, why does the author mention "the Cambrian Explosion"?

   Ⓐ To note that many organisms emerged during it

   Ⓑ To claim that it came prior to the Mesozoic Era

   Ⓒ To mention that the dinosaurs developed then

   Ⓓ To emphasize that it was in the Phanerozoic Era

3   *Directions:* An introductory sentence for a brief summary of the passage is provided below. Complete the summary by selecting the THREE answer choices that express the most important ideas of the passage. Some sentences do not belong because they express ideas that are not presented in the passage or are minor ideas in the passage. *This question is worth 2 points.*

Through their studies, geologists have been able to divide the history of the Earth into a number of distinct time periods.

Answer Choices

☐1 The eon currently taking place has been subdivided into three different eras, including the Cenozoic Era.

☐2 Geologists have used fossils, dating methods, and other evidence to come up with the geological time scale.

☐3 The dinosaurs that once ruled the planet vanished from the Earth around sixty-five million years ago.

☐4 While there was just one supereon, geologists have determined that there have been four distinct eons.

☐5 No one knows exactly why so many new life forms suddenly came into existence during the Cambrian Explosion.

☐6 The planet is several billion years old, yet humanoids have been alive for just a fraction of that time.

Summarizing   Complete the summary by using the words or phrases given in the box.

about four million years   atmosphere   dinosaurs   several eons and eras

The Earth is around 4.5 billion years old. While humanoids have only been alive for _____ , geologists have learned much about the Earth's past. They have divided the Earth's history into many time periods. The Pre-Cambrian Supereon was the longest one. It has been divided into _____ . During it, small organisms and the Earth's _____ developed. More advanced life developed during the Phanerozoic Era. The Cambrian Explosion, _____ , and the rise of humans all occurred during it.

Telescopes

¹➜ Telescopes are instruments that allow observers to view distant objects more clearly. Three Dutchmen invented the first telescope in the early 1600s. It was rapidly improved upon by Galileo and, later, others. Since then, several types have been **devised**. The majority of astronomers rely upon two types though. They are refracting and reflecting telescopes.

²➜ Most refracting and reflecting telescopes must gather light to view objects. Refracting telescopes use a series of lenses to do this. Reflecting telescopes, on the other hand, utilize mirrors. The size of the lens or mirror determines how far away distant objects can be seen. The bigger the lens or mirror, the farther the telescope can see. Reflecting telescopes are much better for observing distant objects than refracting telescopes. This is true because once a lens reaches a certain size, the images it presents begin to get distorted. Thus refracting telescopes have definite limits on their sizes. The largest possible lens—one that can return a clear image—is slightly over one meter in diameter. Reflecting telescopes suffer no distortion. They accordingly have no size limit. Currently, the largest is more than ten meters wide.

³➜ While the mirrors in reflecting telescopes do not distort images, they still cannot provide perfect images. Both types must also deal with a difficult-to-avoid problem: the distortion caused by the Earth's atmosphere. And **artificial** lights, which are brightest near cities, make viewing the skies difficult. As a result, many large telescopes are situated on the tops of remote mountains. There, the air is thinner, and there are no nearby city lights. The best telescope for viewing the skies is actually not on the Earth. It is the Hubble Space Telescope. Orbiting the planet, this telescope with a 2.4-meter lens has produced the best images of distant space. It has helped astronomers discover much about the universe.

Glossary
devise: to create; to invent; to come up with
artificial: not natural; made by man

1   According to paragraphs 1 and 2, which of the following is NOT true of telescopes?

    (A) Some of them can have lenses several meters in diameter.

    (B) They cannot view any objects unless they collect light.

    (C) There are only two different types of telescopes.

    (D) They have been improved upon since their inventing.

2   In paragraphs 2 and 3, the author implies that the Hubble Space Telescope

    (A) will fall to the Earth in the future

    (B) is a reflecting telescope

    (C) is difficult to maintain

    (D) was sent into orbit on the Space Shuttle

3   ***Directions:*** Select the appropriate sentences from the answer choices and match them to the type of telescope to which they relate. TWO of the answer choices will NOT be used. ***This question is worth 3 points.***

Answer Choices	**TYPE OF TELESCOPE**
1 Is ideal for looking at objects that are quite distant	**Reflecting Telescope**
	•
2 Was invented during the seventeenth century	•
3 Does not get distorted as it increases in size	•
4 Has a limit on the size of its lens	
5 Has several lenses that let it collect light	**Refracting Telescope**
6 Was used by Galileo to observe the stars and planets	•
	•
7 Gathers light by using mirrors	

Summarizing   Complete the summary by using the words or phrases given in the box.

distant objects   mirrors   distorted images   lenses

The first telescopes were invented in the 1600s. Since then, many improvements have been made. There are two main types of telescopes: reflecting and refracting telescopes. Reflecting telescopes collect light with _____ while refracting telescopes use _____. Reflecting telescopes are good for viewing _____ and have no size limit on their mirrors. Refracting telescopes return _____ when their lenses get too large. The best telescope is the Hubble Space Telescope, which orbits the Earth.

Mastering **the Question Types**

☐ Vocabulary   ☐ Fill in a Table   ☑ Factual Information   ☐ Negative Factual Information   ☐ Prose Summary
☑ Insert Text   ☑ Reference   ☐ Rhetorical Purpose   ☑ Sentence Simplification   ☐ Inference

The Planetary Boundary Layer

The atmosphere consists of five primary layers: the troposphere, the stratosphere, the mesosphere, the thermosphere, and the exosphere. These layers can additionally be divided into smaller parts. For instance, one of the most important sections of the troposphere is the planetary boundary layer (PBL), which is the layer closest to the Earth's surface.

²→ The PBL starts at the surface and rises roughly 1.5 kilometers above the ground. In that relatively small amount of space, the PBL can be divided into three individual layers. First is the surface layer, a thin strip touching the surface. The mixed layer is the middle one of the three. The third layer is the capping inversion layer—also called the <u>entrainment</u> zone—which provides air that is transferred to lower levels.

Because the PBL exists so close to the ground, it is tremendously influenced by various aspects of the surface. **1** These include temperature, wind, <u>convection</u>, and even friction with the land, natural features such as forests, and buildings. **2** Because the wind blows nearly constantly in the PBL, the atmosphere is well mixed with gases. **3** Additionally, of all the atmospheric layers, the PBL is the most susceptible to change. **4** Its weather conditions can change as rapidly as half an hour in some instances.

Another interesting feature of the PBL is that it undergoes dramatic changes during a typical day. When the sun rises on a clear day, air near the surface becomes heated. This warm air goes up yet cools as it ascends into the atmosphere. When it cools off enough, the air descends, creating air circulation. At the same time, the PBL expands when this occurs. When the sun sets, there is cooling, so almost no circulation occurs in the PBL. This causes the PBL to become much smaller and virtually to disappear in some places.

Glossary
entrainment: the transfer of air from the atmosphere into an air current
convection: the movement, often vertical, of atmospheric properties

1   According to paragraph 2, which of the following is true of the PBL?

       Ⓐ The mixed layer is the largest of its three layers.

       Ⓑ It consists of three layers covering a kilometer and a half.

       Ⓒ The entrainment zone is the area nearest the surface.

       Ⓓ Air can be transferred to other levels from the surface layer.

2   Which of the sentences below best expresses the essential information in the highlighted sentence in the passage? *Incorrect* answer choices change the meaning in important ways or leave out essential information.

       Ⓐ The nearness of the PBL to the ground means that parts of the surface affect it.

       Ⓑ The PBL has a great influence on the Earth's surface since the two are so close together.

       Ⓒ The weather near the ground is greatly influenced by the effects of the PBL.

       Ⓓ The weather near the surface is different from the weather in other parts of the PBL.

3   The word "it" in the passage refers to

       Ⓐ the sun

       Ⓑ the surface

       Ⓒ the atmosphere

       Ⓓ the air

4   Look at the four squares [■] that indicate where the following sentence could be added to the passage.

    Pollution is also a major factor, particularly in large cities, where it can have an enormous effect on the weather.

    Where would the sentence best fit?

Summarizing Complete the summary by using the words or phrases given in the box.

where the sun is	the mixed layer	even disappears	closest to the ground

The planetary boundary layer is part of the troposphere and is also the part of the atmosphere _____. The PBL has three parts, the surface layer, _____, and the capping inversion layer or entrainment zone. Many aspects of the surface, including temperature, wind, convection, and friction, affect the PBL. The PBL also changes more than any other part of the atmosphere. The PBL changes greatly during the day depending on _____. At times, it _____ in places.

Pesticides

A pesticide is any substance that kills or controls pests. These include insects, mice, weeds, fungi, bacteria, and viruses. Most pesticides protect crops from the damage that pests cause. Others <u>eliminate</u> disease-carrying insects such as mosquitoes. Despite being highly effective, the usage of some pesticides is controversial since many are made from chemicals some experts believe may harm humans and other animals. In fact, many countries have banned highly effective pesticides. As a result, people are turning to newer types of pesticides.

2→ Pesticides may be a single substance or a mixture of two or more ingredients. There are two primary types: chemical and biological pesticides. Most chemical pesticides kill organisms by <u>disrupting</u> their nervous systems. There are four main types. They are organophosphates, carbamates, organochlorines, and pyrethroids. All four types include numerous pesticides. For instance, DDT, a very lethal pesticide, is an organochlorine. Many chemical pesticides—DDT among them—have been blamed for killing animals and causing damage to humans. As a result, some countries, including the United States, have banned the use of organochlorines.

3→ Chemical pesticides are currently out of favor. So there is a drive to create biologically based ones. These are considered the safer of the two. There are three main types of biological pesticides. They are microbials, plant-incorporated protectants (PIPs), and biochemicals. The first type utilizes a microorganism pest, such as bacteria or fungi, to control another pest. The other pest is usually an insect. For instance, there is a bacterium called bacillus thuringiensis. It can prevent flea and mosquito larvae from becoming mature insects. PIPs, on the other hand, are made by plants. These plants have been genetically modified. This enables them to create the pesticide. When a pest attacks the plant, the pesticide in it kills the pest. Finally, biochemicals are natural substances that can control pests. Pheromones are the most common type. These are chemical signals that insects and other animals use to communicate.

4→ Pesticides work in several ways. Some kill pests. Others disrupt their life cycles. And others merely repel pests. For instance, DDT kills mosquitoes. Some biochemicals prevent pests from reproducing. This decreases the number of pests in a region. Other biochemicals force certain pests to leave an area. Biochemical pesticides that do not kill pests are becoming more common these days. But many chemical pesticides are still used all around the world. DDT, while banned in the U.S. and other nations, is widely sprayed in tropical regions. Despite worries about it harming humans or animals, DDT saves millions of lives every year by killing mosquitoes that carry viruses such as malaria.

Glossary
eliminate: to kill; to wipe out
disrupt: to interfere with; to have an effect on

NOTE

Pesticides are popular with most farmers. They help reduce the amount of farmers' crops that are lost to pests. And they reduce labor costs since farmers do not need to kill pests by hand.

Farmers that grow organic crops use no pesticides at all. This increases the amount of labor they must do. This accounts for the higher prices of organic products.

DDT is one of the most efficient pesticides known to man. However, in the United States, many people blamed it for killing animals, especially birds. This was one of the reasons it was banned in the U.S.

Thanks to new developments in science, it is now possible for people to create a wide range of biological pesticides.

One pesticide that uses a pheromone causes pests to raise an alarm as soon as they sense the pheromone. Believing that they are in danger, the pests flee the area.

Some people are urging the renewed use of DDT, especially in Africa. They claim that the use of DDT keeps the number of cases of malaria down. In the years DDT was not used in Africa, they say that millions of people died unnecessarily.

1   According to paragraph 2, which of the following is true of pesticides?

    (A) They typically have up to three separate ingredients.

    (B) Some of them are not permitted to be used in places.

    (C) Organochlorines are the most lethal of all pesticides.

    (D) There are four different types of biological pesticides.

2   In paragraph 3, the author's description of biological pesticides mentions all of the following EXCEPT:

    (A) The manner in which they work

    (B) Their effects on pests

    (C) How safe they are

    (D) The three primary types of them

3   The author discusses "DDT" in paragraph 4 in order to

    (A) describe its effectiveness

    (B) complain about it being banned

    (C) name some countries that use it

    (D) describe its chemical content

4   ***Directions:*** Select the appropriate statements from the answer choices and match them to the type of pesticide to which they relate. TWO of the answer choices will NOT be used. ***This question is worth 3 points.***

Answer Choices	TYPE OF PESTICIDE
1 Sometimes keeps pests from reproducing	**Chemical Pesticide**
2 Is not permitted to be used in some of its forms in some places	•
3 May sometimes cause harm to people and animals	•
4 Is made up of four primary types	•
5 Is the type preferred by most farmers	**Biological Pesticide**
6 May make use of pheromones	•
7 Can be composed of viruses and other organisms	•

Summarizing   Complete the summary by filling in the blanks.

Pesticides kill all kinds of pests. There are two main types: _____ pesticides. There are four types of chemical pesticides. They typically kill pests. Many, such as DDT, are lethal, but some have been banned because they may be harmful to _____. Nowadays, many people prefer biological pesticides. There are _____ of these. Biological pesticides do not always _____. Sometimes they merely drive them away. All around the world, pesticides such as DDT are commonly used.

Mastering **the Subject**

William Smith's Map of England

¹➡ William Smith was a British geologist who lived from 1769 to 1839. He is famous for creating a map of England that displayed its geological features. Smith wanted to be a surveyor, not a geologist. He began his career working in coal mines and on canals. However, while working, he noticed some layers of rocks in the mines and canal cuttings. Each layer was distinct and appeared to be composed of different types of rock. Over time, Smith realized that this layered pattern repeated itself throughout the country. He also saw fossils in these layers. As he conducted more research, Smith found the same types of fossils in identical layers of rock in many locations.

Smith proceeded to travel across both England and Wales. During the course of his travels, Smith looked for more clues in the cuttings of mines, canals, and railways and in other places with exposed rocks he could observe. From the fossil evidence he found, Smith **surmised** that each rock layer was from a different age in the Earth's past. He concluded that the fossils in each layer were plants and animals from that age. He **formulated** a theory known as the principle of faunal succession. It stated that the fossils in any geological location have a definite sequence in the rock layers.

As Smith gathered his data, he began drawing maps showing his findings. In 1799, he completed his first geological map—a small one. By 1815, he had produced his most famous work. This map showed the geology of all of Wales and England and parts of Scotland. Sadly, Smith failed to protect his work, so his ideas were co-opted by others. This contributed to his financial problems. He went into debt and spent some time in prison. After his release in 1819, Smith could only find work as a surveyor. Fortunately for him, he was recognized as the real creator of the geological map. Thus fame came to Smith—albeit late in his life—so today he is considered the father of British geology.

The usefulness of Smith's work lies in the fields of geology and geological time. His detailed maps laid the foundation for many future studies of geology. In addition, geological maps—such as the ones he made—have numerous applications. They are useful to large-scale engineering projects. These include roads, railways, and canals. They also assist in the search for precious metals and oil. During his lifetime, Smith was not the only person to make geological maps. Yet his ideas on faunal succession were quite unique and helped geologists who came after him.

NOTE

William Smith was mostly a self-educated man. It was his powers of observance that led him to make his discovery of the various rock layers.

Many of the fossils that Smith found were small ones that had lived in the sea. These included mollusks, brachiopods, and ammonites. Their presence in the rock layer also showed that, at one time, much of England had been underwater.

The map that Smith became famous for was later called "The Map that Changed the World." He started drawing it in 1801 but did not publish it until 1815.

Many later geologists relied upon Smith's work. In fact, one, Smith's nephew John Phillips, continued Smith's work and developed some of the first timelines for the Earth's geological history.

Glossary

surmise: to conclude; to state a belief
formulate: to devise; to come up with; to create

1 According to paragraph 1, Smith began studying geology because

- Ⓐ he recognized the potential to become famous in that field
- Ⓑ it was a subject that he had always intended to research
- Ⓒ he was unsuccessful at his work as a surveyor
- Ⓓ he became interested in it while doing other work

2 Which of the sentences below best expresses the essential information in the highlighted sentence in the passage? *Incorrect* answer choices change the meaning in important ways or leave out essential information.

- Ⓐ As Smith worked and traveled, he tried to expose the rocks in many different places.
- Ⓑ By observing rock cuttings in many locations, Smith came up with a new theory.
- Ⓒ Smith looked at exposed rocks in many places as he traveled around the country.
- Ⓓ People working in mines and on canals and railways cut rocks for Smith to observe.

3 The word "co-opted" in the passage is closest in meaning to

- Ⓐ considered
- Ⓑ adapted
- Ⓒ taken
- Ⓓ recalled

4 *Directions:* An introductory sentence for a brief summary of the passage is provided below. Complete the summary by selecting the THREE answer choices that express the most important ideas of the passage. Some sentences do not belong because they express ideas that are not presented in the passage or are minor ideas in the passage. *This question is worth 2 points.*

William Smith observed different rock layers in places all around England, which led him to create several important geological maps of the country.

Answer Choices

1. Smith frequently traveled to various places in Britain, mostly on account of the different jobs he had.

2. Because his work was stolen by others, Smith was unable to pay his bills and was imprisoned for a short time.

3. Smith determined that each layer of rock came from a different geological era in the Earth's history.

4. In 1815, Smith made a map that showed much of Great Britain and was an improvement on his map from 1799.

5. Smith never intended to become a geologist, but he instead first found work as a surveyor.

6. The maps that Smith created were important both to those interested in geology and to people working on other projects.

Summarizing Complete the summary by filling in the blanks.

William Smith was a geologist from England who lived in the 1700s and 1800s. Smith noticed different _____ in places around the country. He realized that each layer came from _____ in the Earth's past. He started making maps of these rock layers. In 1799, he made a small map. But _____, he produced a large map that made him famous. His maps were useful to _____ and helped in the future study of geology.

Lunar Impact Craters

The moon is the Earth's only satellite. One of its dominant characteristics is something that can be seen from the Earth: the large number of craters on its surface. It was once believed that these craters were formed by volcanic eruptions. Today, most astronomers are certain they are impact craters. Thus they were made when asteroids, meteorites, and possibly even comets struck the moon's surface. **1** Since the moon has no atmosphere, the asteroids and other objects failed to burn up—as they often do on the Earth—before hitting the moon's surface. **2** In addition, the moon has no weather. **3** So these impact craters have not eroded but have instead remained well preserved. **4** There are millions of impact craters on the moon's surface. And the number is continually increasing as the moon gets struck by more objects.

Lunar impact craters vary in size. Some are less than a kilometer in diameter. Others are massive. The largest is more than 2,000 kilometers wide and thirteen kilometers deep. An enormous object must have struck the moon to have created that crater. The size and shape of an impact crater depend upon several factors. They are the size, speed, and direction of the object impacting the moon. As one would expect, small, slow objects produce small, shallow impact craters. <u>Conversely</u>, larger, faster objects create more complex, deeper impact craters.

Sometimes, a massive object strikes the moon and causes lunar rocks to be <u>ejected</u> upward. These rocks fall back to the moon's surface, thereby making secondary impact craters. Some areas of the moon have fewer impact craters than others. In particular, the low-lying, flat-looking, dark areas called maria, or seas, have fewer impact craters than do other regions. The reason is that their surface areas are not as old as those in other places.

⁴➡ There are three main types of lunar impact craters: simple, complex, and impact basin craters. A simple impact crater typically is a sunken, bowl-shaped area. Its floor and walls are smooth. A majority of simple craters are less than fifteen kilometers in width and have a depth of less than three kilometers. Complex impact craters are larger. They are between fifteen and 300 kilometers in diameter. They may have uplifts, such as small mountains, rings, or hills, in the centers of their craters. Finally, impact basin craters are the largest of the three. They are more than 300 kilometers in diameter. They are created when huge objects collide with the moon. These impacts can result in widespread geological disruption on the moon and may seriously alter the satellite's appearance.

NOTE

People have long used telescopes to observe the moon's craters. But it was satellites and the *Apollo* moon missions that let astronomers get a closer look at moon craters. They helped prove that the craters had been formed by impacts from space objects.

Some lunar craters are incredibly tiny. When the *Apollo* astronauts brought moon rocks back to the Earth, craters were found in some of them. A microscope was required to see them. These were likely created by particles of dust impacting the moon.

The moon's low gravity—it is one-sixth of the Earth's gravity—often results in secondary impact craters causing only a small amount of damage to the moon.

Many moon craters are so large that they have their own names. The South Pole-Aitken Basin is one of them. It is the largest crater in the entire solar system. The next closest in size is on Mars. However, that crater is 400 kilometers smaller in diameter.

Glossary
conversely: on the other hand; in opposition to
eject: to cast out; to expel

1 The word "their" in the passage refers to

(A) maria

(B) fewer impact craters

(C) other regions

(D) other places

2 In paragraph 4, which of the following can be inferred about lunar impact craters?

(A) Complex impact craters are the ones most frequently found on the moon.

(B) Simple impact craters are caused by relatively small objects from space.

(C) Impact basin craters are found in abundance on the dark side of the moon.

(D) It is possible to see complex impact craters from the Earth without using a telescope.

3 Look at the four squares [■] that indicate where the following sentence could be added to the passage.

On the Earth, generally only the largest meteors fail completely to incinerate in the atmosphere.

Where would the sentence best fit?

4 *Directions:* An introductory sentence for a brief summary of the passage is provided below. Complete the summary by selecting the THREE answer choices that express the most important ideas of the passage. Some sentences do not belong because they express ideas that are not presented in the passage or are minor ideas in the passage. *This question is worth 2 points.*

Objects from outer space frequently strike the moon, and the result of these impacts is the creation of a variety of types of craters.

Answer Choices

1 Astronomers have categorized the majority of lunar impact craters into three distinct classifications.

2 Lunar impact craters can be as small as a kilometer in diameter to more than 2,000 kilometers in diameter.

3 Among the objects that tend to strike the moon are asteroids and meteorites as well as an occasional comet.

4 Some lunar craters are so large that other objects from space crash into them, which creates secondary craters.

5 There are relatively few impact craters in the maria, which are the low-lying, flat parts of the moon.

6 The moon protects the Earth by shielding it from objects that, instead of striking the Earth, collide with the moon.

Summarizing Complete the summary by filling in the blanks.

The moon has been struck by numerous objects from space. These include _____. These impacts have left craters on its surface. The craters range from _____ to more than 2,000 kilometers in diameter. They also vary in shape. This is caused by _____ of the objects impacting the moon. There are three main types of _____: simple, complex, and impact basin craters. The diameters, depths, and shapes of these craters are all different from one another.

Magma

An erupting volcano spewing out lava

1→ Under the Earth's crust, intense heat and pressure create magma by melting rocks and minerals. When magma finds a weak point in the crust, it bubbles to the surface. Sometimes it rises slowly. At other times, it surfaces violently. The end result in both cases is a volcanic eruption. Geologists have three categories for magma. They classify it as basalt magma, andesitic magma, and rhyolite magma. All three types differ in a number of manners.

2→ Basalt magma has the highest temperature. It rises to around 1,200 degrees Celsius. It has a lower silica and gas content than the other two magma types. Due to its low silica content, basalt magma has a low viscosity. As a result, it flows more easily. Chemically, basalt magma is high in iron, magnesium, and calcium yet low in potassium and sodium. The volcanic eruptions it causes are not violent in nature. Rather, the magma oozes to the surface and then flows across the ground. This creates a large area of lava—the name for magma that is aboveground—that spreads out around the volcano. When it cools, the lava forms what is called a volcanic field. Basalt magma flows sometimes produce scoria cones, which are also known as cinder cones. These are volcanic cones generally fewer than 300 meters in height. They are often found near larger volcanic cones.

3→ Andesitic magma is cooler than basalt magma. Its temperature ranges between 800 and 1,000 degrees Celsius. It has a higher silica and gas content than basalt magma. This gives it a higher viscosity. Chemically, it consists of intermediate levels of iron, magnesium, calcium, potassium, and sodium. Volcanic eruptions caused by it can either be flowing—like basalt magma—or more violent, explosive eruptions. When it is a flowing eruption, very thick, rubbery-looking lava flows may result. This leaves enormous fields of volcanic stones when the lava cools. When the eruption is more explosive, a high stratovolcano—a cone-shaped volcano—may be the end result. Scoria cones may also be produced. These eruptions often produce large amounts of falling pumice rocks and ash.

4→ The third type is rhyolite magma, the coolest of the three. Its temperature is anywhere from 750 to 860 degrees Celsius. It has a high silica and gas content. This gives it the highest viscosity of all three types. Its chemical composition has small amounts of iron, magnesium, and calcium and large amounts of potassium and sodium. On account of its high level of gases, rhyolite magma is highly explosive and may cause massive eruptions. Entire volcano tops or sides may be blown away when a volcano erupts. **1** In addition, huge amounts of ash and rock fall from the sky during these eruptions. **2** This magma causes the world's most disastrous volcanic eruptions. **3** This is especially true since a rhyolite magma eruption can cause a pyroclastic flow. **4** This is a massive wall of fast-moving heated ash and gases. It flows down the slope of a volcano and destroys everything in its path. After an eruption, all that may remain of the volcano may be a caldera. This is a large basin-like formation created where a volcano has collapsed on itself.

Glossary
silica: silicon in its dioxide form
ooze: to seep; to move very slowly

1. The word "surfaces" in the passage is closest in meaning to

   (A) expels

   (B) recedes

   (C) emerges

   (D) explodes

2. According to paragraph 1, which of the following is NOT true of magma?

   (A) It has been categorized into three unique types.

   (B) It changes its name when it comes above the ground.

   (C) It is composed in part of rocks and minerals in their liquid forms.

   (D) It remains in the mantle far beneath the Earth's crust.

3. The word "viscosity" in the passage is closest in meaning to

   (A) thickness

   (B) dampness

   (C) oiliness

   (D) greasiness

4. The word "it" in the passage refers to

   (A) a large area of lava

   (B) the volcano

   (C) the lava

   (D) a volcanic field

5. According to paragraph 2, which of the following is true of basalt magma?

   (A) It tends to cause spectacularly violent volcanic eruptions.

   (B) It contains smaller amounts of gas than the other types of magma.

   (C) It emerges only from volcanoes that are fewer than 300 meters high.

   (D) It is formed underground in something called a volcanic field.

6. In paragraph 3, the author uses "a high stratovolcano" as an example of

   (A) something produced by an eruption of andesitic magma

   (B) what causes very much pumice rock and ash to fall in an eruption

   (C) another name for a large field of volcanic stones

   (D) the reason that andesitic magma may erupt violently

7. In paragraph 3, the author's description of andesitic magma mentions which of the following?

   (A) The reason that it can come out of scoria cones

   (B) Its temperature in comparison to rhyolite magma

   (C) The variety in intensity of the eruptions it causes

   (D) What can be found in it in high amounts

8 According to paragraph 4, rhyolite magma is explosive because

    Ⓐ of its fairly high viscosity

    Ⓑ it does not have much iron, magnesium, and calcium

    Ⓒ of the amounts of the gases that it contains

    Ⓓ it expels a lot of pumice rock and ash

9 Look at the four squares [■] that indicate where the following sentence could be added to the passage.

For instance, the 1883 eruption of Krakatoa in Indonesia was so violent that it practically destroyed an entire island.

Where would the sentence best fit?

Click on a square [■] to add the sentence to the passage.

10 *Directions:* Select the appropriate statements from the answer choices and match them to the type of magma to which they relate. TWO of the answer choices will NOT be used. *This question is worth 4 points.*

Drag your answer choices to the spaces where they belong.
To remove an answer choice, click on it. To review the passage, click on **View Text**.

Answer Choices	TYPE OF MAGMA
① Contains high levels of iron and calcium	**Basalt Magma**
② May cause a pyroclastic flow to occur	•
③ Often has pumice rock and ash within it	•
④ Can result in the production of cinder cones	•
⑤ Sometimes produces a stratovolcano afterward	**Andesitic Magma**
⑥ May be as hot as 1,200 degrees Celsius	•
⑦ Is the most common type of magma	•
⑧ Has the highest viscosity of the three types	**Rhyolite Magma**
⑨ Can cause slow-moving or violent eruptions	•
	•

Star Performer Subject Topics | Physical Sciences

1 **Earthquakes**

The Earth's crust is comprised of several tectonic plates. Some are huge while others are much smaller. Occasionally, these plates either move apart from one another or collide with each other. The result is an earthquake. During an earthquake, the ground begins to shake. In some places, it may even crack open. Some earthquakes last for just a few seconds. Others may last for a minute or even longer. In addition, earthquakes vary in their intensity. People can barely feel the vast majority of them, yet some may cause widespread damage and kill thousands of people.

2 **Lightning**

During some rainstorms, it is common to see brilliant streaks of light in the air. This light is called lightning. In thunderclouds, there are millions of small ice particles. The constant bumping of these ice particles against one another creates an electrical charge. After the cloud builds up enough electrical charges, it begins to seek an object with an opposite charge for it to strike. Typically, this is a high object such as a tree or building. The result is a lightning strike. Due to lightning's intense heat, the air around it explodes, which creates the sound known as thunder.

3 **Pangaea**

The tectonic plates that comprise the Earth's crust are in constant motion. However, they move quite slowly—perhaps only a few centimeters a year or decade. Over time, however, these movements can become noticeable. In fact, in the past, the Earth's surface looked nothing like it does today. Around 200 million years ago, there were not seven continents like there are now. Instead, there was one enormous supercontinent. Geologists have named it Pangaea, which is Greek for "all earth." Eventually, Pangaea broke apart into two separate continents. From these, the Earth's landmasses eventually formed into their present-day shapes.

4 **Gas Giants**

There are eight planets in the solar system. The four largest are Jupiter, Saturn, Uranus, and Neptune. All four are farther from the sun than the solar system's other four planets. These large planets are called gas giants, or Jovian planets. They share several characteristics in addition to their large sizes. First, they are comprised primarily of gases such as hydrogen and helium. At each planet's center is a small rocky core, but they are mostly large balls of gas. Gas giants are surrounded by rings of ice crystals. Saturn's are the largest, but the other three have them, too.

5 **Comets**

There are many objects in outer space. Among them are comets. Most comets are 100 meters to forty kilometers in diameter. A comet is a loose collection of ice, dust, and small rocky particles. Some are also comprised of frozen gases, carbon dioxide, ammonia, and methane. These are located in the comet's nucleus. Comets typically have elongated orbits. Many times, their orbits take them into the solar system. As they approach the sun, its heat causes the comets to begin melting. The result is the creation of a tail that can stretch millions of kilometers behind it.

6 **Antoine Lavoisier**

During the eighteenth century, Antoine Lavoisier, a Frenchman, conducted many experiments in chemistry. During his lifetime, he made several notable accomplishments. He determined that air was made primarily of two gases—oxygen and nitrogen. He devised the theory on the conservation of mass, which states that the combined weight of the substances in a reaction must equal the weight of the final result. He also conducted experiments on combustion and oxidation and wrote what many people call the first chemistry textbook. Thanks to his work, he is often referred to as the father of modern chemistry.

7 ▸ Earth's Lithosphere

The Earth has three distinct layers: the crust, the mantle, and the core. However, within these three layers are other divisions. One is the lithosphere, which basically comprises the solid outer part of the planet. This includes the entire crust and part of the mantle. The mantle, which is the largest of the Earth's layers, is solid in some places yet liquid in others. The upper mantle is where the rocks remain solid. The lithosphere reaches around 100 kilometers below the Earth's surface. That deep below ground, the high levels of heat and pressure begin to melt rocks and minerals.

8 ▸ The Compass

Sailors, campers, and other travelers often cannot do without a crucial piece of equipment: the compass. This is a tool that enables people to determine which direction they are facing. The Earth has magnetic poles. These are near—but not at—the North and South poles. The locations of these magnetic poles can be detected by a magnet, which is essentially what a compass is. A compass has a magnetized needle that rests in a container of fluid. No matter which direction a person turns, the needle always points northward. This has enabled generations of travelers to avoid getting lost.

9 ▸ Black Holes

Eventually, all stars die. They typically expend all of their fuel, which causes them to die. However, some huge stars—ones with at least three times the mass of the sun—collapse on themselves as they die. The result may be the creation of a black hole. Little is known about black holes because they cannot be seen. The reason is that their gravity is so strong that nothing—not even light—can escape their pull. Some astronomers believe there is a giant black hole in the center of the Milky Way Galaxy, but that has yet to be confirmed.

10 ▸ The Earth in Its Infancy

The Earth was created approximately 4.5 billion years ago. However, the planet at that time in no way resembled the way it looks now. In the beginning, the Earth was extremely unstable. There were likely enormous volcanic eruptions all over the planet. In addition, since the planet was still cooling after its formation, the temperatures on the surface were high. While the Earth likely had an atmosphere then, it was primarily hydrogen, helium, methane, and ammonia. There was little free-standing oxygen at first. It was only later, once plants began creating oxygen through photosynthesis, that the atmosphere became breathable to living organisms.

11 ▸ The Sun

The sun is a star and the center of the solar system. It provides both heat and light for the Earth. Without the sun, it would be impossible for life to exist anywhere. The sun is more than 100 times the size of the Earth. As for its composition, it is around ninety-four percent hydrogen and almost six percent helium. The remainder includes oxygen, carbon, nitrogen, and traces of other elements. The sun creates energy from nuclear fusion in its core, which is in its center. The sun has several other layers, including the radiative zone, the convective zone, and the photosphere.

12 ▸ Dating Methods

Geologists and other scientists are often interested in determining the ages of rocks and other objects. To do so, they utilize a number of dating methods. The most reliable methods involve measuring the radioactive decay of certain elements in an object. Carbon-14 dating is one well-known yet limited method. It is limited because it can only test objects with carbon back to around 60,000 years ago. Most geologists require tests on objects millions or billions of years old. So they use methods such as potassium-argon dating or uranium-lead dating, which are accurate to billions of years in the past.

- **ash** (n) the residue left from something that has burned
- **atmosphere** (n) the air
- **bacterium** (n) a one-celled organism that may often cause diseases
- **ban** (v) to prohibit; to forbid
- **basin** (n) a natural area that contains water
- **blame** (v) to accuse
- **boundary** (n) something that indicates a line or limit
- **bubble** (v) to boil; to flow while making a gurgling sound
- **burn** (v) to catch on fire
- **caldera** (n) a large depression that is the result of an explosive volcanic eruption
- **canal** (n) an artificial waterway connecting two bodies of water
- **category** (n) a classification
- **class** (n) a group; a category; a classification
- **collide** (v) to run into; to crash into
- **composition** (n) the makeup or contents of something
- **content** (n) material; a substance
- **contribute** (v) to add to
- **control** (v) to run; to operate
- **controversial** (adj) divisive
- **crater** (n) an impression or hole formed by the impact of something
- **crust** (n) the upper layer of the Earth
- **dating method** (n) a way to determine how old something is
- **descend** (v) to go down; to decline
- **determine** (v) to figure out
- **disastrous** (adj) catastrophic; terrible; awful
- **display** (v) to show; to exhibit
- **disrupt** (v) to upset; to change the way that something works or operates
- **distortion** (n) the act of being deformed or altered in some way
- **divide** (v) to split; to put into smaller groups
- **dominate** (v) to control; to rule over
- **eon** (n) a very long period of time in the Earth's history
- **era** (n) a distinct period of time
- **eruption** (n) an explosion
- **estimate** (v) to guess
- **expand** (v) to become greater in size or amount
- **exposed** (adj) open to the air; able to be seen
- **factor** (n) an aspect; a reason

- **fail** (v) not to do something; not to succeed
- **feature** (n) a characteristic; an aspect
- **field** (n) an area of land that has been cleared for farming
- **flea** (n) a small bloodsucking insect
- **geologist** (n) a person who studies the Earth
- **hit** (v) to strike; to impact
- **influence** (v) to have a great effect on
- **ingredient** (n) a component
- **lens** (n) a curved transparent substance often used to look more closely at something
- **mature** (adj) adult
- **means** (n) a method; a way
- **mine** (n) a place in the ground where ores or minerals are removed
- **modified** (adj) changed; altered
- **orbit** (v) to go around in a circle; to revolve around
- **outward** (adj) external
- **pest** (n) an organism that is bothersome to others
- **pesticide** (n) a compound that kills pests
- **present** (v) to show; to provide
- **pressure** (n) the exertion of force on an object
- **prevent** (v) to stop; to halt
- **primary** (adj) main; major
- **principle** (n) a tenet; a theory; an idea
- **pumice** (n) a porous type of volcanic stone
- **reach** (v) to attain; to get to; to arrive at
- **release** (v) to let go; to emit
- **remote** (adj) far off; distant
- **repeat** (v) to do again
- **rubbery** (adj) having the characteristics of rubber; tough; hard
- **slope** (n) an inclination; a rising side of a mountain
- **spray** (v) to spew
- **subclass** (n) a small group or category within a larger one
- **suffer** (v) to endure
- **surface** (n) the uppermost layer of something; the part of the Earth touching the atmosphere
- **telescope** (n) a device that allows one to view faraway objects in detail
- **transfer** (v) to move from one place to another
- **uplift** (n) an elevation; the act of lifting or raising something
- **wind** (n) the natural movement of air

Choose the word or phrase closest in meaning to the highlighted part of the sentence.

1 The atmosphere consists of five primary layers: the troposphere, the stratosphere, the mesosphere, the thermosphere, and the exosphere.
   (A) exhibits
   (B) appears in
   (C) contains
   (D) reveals

2 Thus they were made when asteroids, meteorites, and possibly even comets struck the moon's surface.
   (A) hit
   (B) assaulted
   (C) passed by
   (D) destroyed

3 He concluded that the fossils in each layer were plants and animals from that age.
   (A) researched
   (B) assumed
   (C) determined
   (D) foretold

4 Telescopes are instruments that allow observers to view distant objects more clearly.
   (A) weapons
   (B) devices
   (C) materials
   (D) ingredients

5 In that relatively small amount of space, the PBL can be divided into three individual layers.
   (A) apparently
   (B) considerably
   (C) visibly
   (D) fairly

6 On account of its high level of gases, rhyolite magma is highly explosive and may cause massive eruptions.
   (A) volatile
   (B) liquid
   (C) viscous
   (D) orderly

7 These impacts can result in widespread geological disruption on the moon and may seriously alter the satellite's appearance.
   (A) estimate
   (B) cause
   (C) discourage
   (D) erode

8 It can prevent flea and mosquito larvae from becoming mature insects.
   (A) encourage
   (B) stop
   (C) demand
   (D) find

9 His detailed maps laid the foundation for many future studies of geology.
   (A) expanding
   (B) massive
   (C) basic
   (D) thorough

10 While the mirrors in reflecting telescopes do not distort images, they still cannot provide perfect images.
   (A) create
   (B) increase
   (C) entice
   (D) deform

11 DDT, while banned in the U.S. and other nations, is widely sprayed in tropical regions.

(A) prohibited
(B) manufactured
(C) utilized
(D) invented

12 This magma causes the world's most disastrous volcanic eruptions.

(A) memorable
(B) impressive
(C) terrible
(D) dramatic

13 Under the Earth's crust, intense heat and pressure create magma by melting rocks and minerals.

(A) vicious
(B) powerful
(C) stressful
(D) constant

14 Orbiting the planet, this telescope with a 2.4-meter lens has produced the best images of distant space.

(A) Trailing
(B) Abandoning
(C) Following
(D) Revolving

15 These plants have been genetically modified.

(A) altered
(B) considered
(C) examined
(D) strengthened

16 This warm air goes up yet cools as it ascends into the atmosphere.

(A) condenses
(B) forms
(C) rises
(D) appears

17 Due to its low silica content, basalt magma has a low viscosity.

(A) substance
(B) ingredient
(C) value
(D) crystal

18 They then disappeared around sixty-five million years ago.

(A) evolved
(B) migrated
(C) transformed
(D) vanished

19 Despite being highly effective, the usage of some pesticides is controversial since many are made from chemicals some experts believe may harm humans and other animals.

(A) injure
(B) annoy
(C) reinforce
(D) revolt

20 Over time, Smith realized that this layered pattern repeated itself throughout the country.

(A) estimated
(B) recognized
(C) agreed
(D) predicted

Part B

Chapter 08 Environmental Sciences

Environmental sciences are concerned with the study of the environment. The people who practice it often have knowledge in many fields. These include biology, geology, physics, and meteorology. Researchers look at the environment as a whole and at smaller ecosystems. They are often concerned with the environment's effects on the organisms that live in it. They also look at how the organisms living in it can affect the environment. Some individuals are concerned with preserving the environment while others are more focused on the climate. They study both global warming and cooling. Essentially, environmental scientists study the Earth, the things living on it, and the things affecting it.

Mastering **the Question Types**

☑ Vocabulary   ☐ Fill in a Table   ☐ Factual Information   ☐ Negative Factual Information   ☑ Prose Summary
☐ Insert Text   ☐ Reference   ☑ Rhetorical Purpose   ☐ Sentence Simplification   ☐ Inference

Lake Water Layers and the Seasons

Deep lakes have three water layers. The **topmost**, called the epilimnion layer, extends around twenty feet below the lake's surface. It contains oxygen-rich circulating warm water. Next is the thermocline layer. It is quite thin and has lower oxygen levels and cooler temperatures. Finally, underneath the thermocline layer is the hypolimnion layer, which extends to the lake's bottom. It is the coldest layer and has the least amount of oxygen.

In warmer weather, when a lake has no surface ice, the wind pushes the surface water from one side of the lake to the other. This action causes the water to circulate. As the water moves around, some of it is forced downward. When this water is pushed down, it displaces other water in the epilimnion layer. This water, in turn, frequently moves upward, where it replaces the water being pushed by the wind.

[3]→ In summer, this circulation does not extend to the bottom two layers. So the warmer water in the upper layer fails to mix with the colder water below. However, when fall arrives, cold winds, combined with less sunlight, decrease the water's surface temperature. Gradually, the epilimnion layer becomes colder. Soon, it mixes with the other two layers. Then, the entire lake becomes one large mass of circulating water. In fact, distinct layers cease to exist at this time. This is referred to as the fall turnover. The primary benefit of the fall turnover is that it allows the lower layers of water to circulate freely. In doing so, all of the water in the lake can **replenish** its oxygen supply, which is vital for the organisms living in it. Slowly, however, as temperatures rise in spring, the three layers are reestablished in what is called the spring turnover.

Glossary
topmost: upper; highest
replenish: to renew

1   The word "displaces" in the passage is closest in meaning to

  (A) removes

  (B) shifts

  (C) flows

  (D) evaporates

2   In paragraph 3, why does the author mention "the fall turnover"?

  (A) To compare it with the spring turnover

  (B) To indicate the season when it happens

  (C) To state how its effects can benefit lakes

  (D) To explain why lakes have different layers

3   *Directions:* An introductory sentence for a brief summary of the passage is provided below. Complete the summary by selecting the THREE answer choices that express the most important ideas of the passage. Some sentences do not belong because they express ideas that are not presented in the passage or are minor ideas in the passage. *This question is worth 2 points.*

Depending on the temperature, deep water lakes may or may not have different layers in their water.

Answer Choices

1 The deepness of a lake's waters determines whether or not it actually has any layers.

2 When the spring turnover occurs as the weather warms, the three layers of deep lakes form again.

3 Cold wind and less sunlight can cause the temperature of a lake to decrease, which makes its layers vanish.

4 The epilimnion layer of a lake is the one that is on top while the thermocline is beneath it.

5 During the fall turnover, all three of a lake's layers disappear because of the cold weather.

6 The layer of water that is at the bottom of a lake has the least amount of oxygen within it.

Summarizing   Complete the summary by using the words or phrases given in the box.

it circulates	the hypolimnion	the oxygen level	the fall turnover

Deep lakes have three layers: the epilimnion, the thermocline, and the hypolimnion. The epilimnion has the most oxygen while _____ has the least. As the wind blows the water on top of the lake, _____ . The lower two layers do not circulate. When the weather becomes colder, the layers all disappear. This is _____ . Then, water circulates through the entire lake. This replenishes _____ of all of the lake's regions. As the temperature gets warmer, the layers return. This is the spring turnover.

Mastering **the Question Types**

☐ Vocabulary   ☑ Fill in a Table   ☐ Factual Information   ☑ Negative Factual Information   ☐ Prose Summary
☐ Insert Text   ☐ Reference   ☐ Rhetorical Purpose   ☐ Sentence Simplification   ☑ Inference

Geothermal Energy

Geothermal energy comes from heat created by forces within the planet. This heat can melt rock and turn it into magma. In certain locations, such as Iceland, the magma and its heat are close enough to the surface to be useful to people. There are two main ways that geothermal energy is utilized. It is used in the creation of electricity and in heating.

²➜ To create electricity, the steam from water produced by underground heat is used to turn **turbines** in electric plants. This creates energy that is cheap, clean, and reusable. As for heating, the hot water is pumped from surface springs or from underground. Then, it is passed through heating pipes and **radiator** systems in homes and other buildings. Sometimes pipes are even driven underground, and surface water is run through the pipes. Once underground, the heat turns the water hot, and it is then piped back up to the surface.

³➜ Unfortunately, geothermal power only accounts for a small part of the world's energy needs. At present, less than one percent of the world's electricity is produced by geothermal methods. Its primary drawback is that it is only useful in places where it is located. Unlike oil, natural gas, or coal, heated water cannot be transported long distances. Secondly, places that have access to geothermal energy are sitting on top of magma that could one day erupt through a volcano. For example, Iceland, which uses a great deal of geothermal energy, is an island with many volcanoes. Not all are dormant as some have erupted in the recent past. This fact makes using geothermal power a risky proposition.

Glossary
turbine: a machine with a rotor that is able to turn
radiator: a heating device

1   In paragraph 2, the author implies that geothermal energy

     Ⓐ requires a lot of expensive facilities

     Ⓑ is not available all throughout the day

     Ⓒ involves advanced technology

     Ⓓ does not create any pollution

2   According to paragraph 3, which of the following is NOT true of present-day geothermal energy usage?

     Ⓐ It cannot be transported the way oil can.

     Ⓑ It has several major disadvantages.

     Ⓒ It is a minor source of energy for most people.

     Ⓓ Those living in Iceland use it a lot.

3   *Directions:* Select the appropriate statements from the answer choices and match them to the advantages and disadvantages of geothermal energy to which they relate. TWO of the answer choices will NOT be used. **This question is worth 3 points.**

Answer Choices	GEOTHERMAL ENERGY
① May have to be accessed in dangerous areas	**Advantage**
② Is a renewable form of energy	•
③ Must be used where it is created	•
④ Does not cost a lot of money	•
⑤ Is only available for use in Iceland	**Disadvantage**
⑥ Is a clean source of energy	•
⑦ Has many technological difficulties	•

Summarizing   Complete the summary by using the words or phrases given in the box.

> be dangerous   reusable form   piping water   to other places

Geothermal energy uses heat from inside the Earth. People use it to make electricity and to heat buildings and homes. It makes a cheap, clean, and _____ of electricity. For heating, it involves _____ underground to heat it and then sending the water back aboveground. Geothermal energy is not used much nowadays. It cannot be transported _____, and it is not accessible in all places. Since it is available for use near volcanoes, it can also _____ to access.

Mastering **the Question Types**

☐ Vocabulary   ☐ Fill in a Table   ☑ Factual Information   ☐ Negative Factual Information   ☐ Prose Summary
☑ Insert Text   ☑ Reference   ☐ Rhetorical Purpose   ☑ Sentence Simplification   ☐ Inference

Irrigation and the Environment

    Irrigation refers to the movement of water from one place to another for a specific purpose. The most common is to water crops on farms. Irrigation may also be practiced to provide water for yards and other types of landscapes. The most obvious effect of irrigation is that it enables plants to grow. It also has other less apparent effects on the environment.

    The primary effect is that irrigation redirects water from its original location and then takes it to another place. In most cases, the water used comes from rivers, lakes, streams, or underground sources. These sources all suffer from the depletion of their water supplies. This can result in less water moving downriver. This loss of water can have tremendous negative effects on animals, especially fish, that rely on the water in these rivers, lakes, and streams. And when water is extracted from underground sources, **groundwater** supplies may become exhausted. **1** As for the places where the water is transported to, groundwater levels often increase. **2** This happens since so much water soaks into the ground. **3** More water in irrigated areas also evaporates. **4** This can produce a greater amount of rainfall in those places. Higher levels of **humidity** may occur, too.

    ³➙ Another negative effect is that soil salinization may occur in places that water is taken from. When water levels are reduced, the soil may have salt levels that are higher than normal. Most plants are unable to grow well in soil which is too salty. As for the irrigated areas, they can become waterlogged. This happens when there is too much water in the soil. One immediate effect of this is that roots become saturated with water. They can be harmed over time, so plants often die as a result. In this regard, too much water can be lethal to vegetation.

Glossary

groundwater: water from the surface that has seeped into the ground
humidity: the amount of moisture that is in the air

1   Which of the sentences below best expresses the essential information in the highlighted sentence in the passage? *Incorrect* answer choices change the meaning in important ways or leave out essential information.

       Ⓐ It is not possible for many fish to live in rivers, lakes, and streams when too much water is lost.

       Ⓑ Too much water is being lost from rivers, lakes, and streams due to the effects of irrigation.

       Ⓒ A large number of animals, including fish, rely upon the water that is found in certain places.

       Ⓓ Fish and other animals can be harmed when water in various natural sources is removed.

2   The word "They" in the passage refers to

       Ⓐ salt levels

       Ⓑ irrigated areas

       Ⓒ roots

       Ⓓ plants

3   According to paragraph 3, one effect of salinization on the soil is that

       Ⓐ the roots of plants get harmed over time

       Ⓑ fewer crops are produced in salty soil

       Ⓒ plants are unable to grow well in the soil

       Ⓓ water is depleted from that soil more rapidly

4   Look at the four squares [■] that indicate where the following sentence could be added to the passage.

It can take years for them to recover.

Where would the sentence best fit?

Summarizing Complete the summary by using the words or phrases given in the box.

harm animals	soil salinization	support crops	groundwater supplies

One effect of irrigation is that water is moved from one place to another to _____, yards, or other landscapes. There are also some negative effects. For instance, water is removed from sources such as rivers, lakes, and streams. This can _____ such as fish. _____ may also be depleted. The weather in the irrigated areas can become rainier, too. _____ and waterlogging can take place as well. These both can cause problems for vegetation growing in some areas.

Mastering **the Subject**

The Characteristics of Soil

Soil is the uppermost layer of the crust. The eroding of rock into tiny particles forms it. Soil formation is a complex process dependent on several factors. These include the type of rock that makes it, the topography—or shape—of the land, the climate of the area, the actions of vegetation, bacteria, and fungi on the rocks, and the passage of time. Because of these factors, soil is not identical everywhere. It differs in color, texture, and chemical and organic composition. As a result, some soils are excellent for growing crops and other vegetation while others are not. Additionally, soil conditions are not constant but change due to natural forces and the actions of humans.

2➜ Soil consists of four basic <u>components</u>: minerals, water, air, and organic matter. About forty-five percent of a soil sample is mineral. Air and water make up about twenty-five percent each. And organic matter comprises between two and five percent. There are three main types of soil texture: sand, silt, and clay. Sand particles are the largest. Composed mostly of minerals such as quartz, sand does not retain water well. Thus sandy soils are ill suited for growing vegetation. Silt is the next largest. It has more water-retaining abilities than sand but is still not the best soil for plant growth. Clay is the smallest particle of soil. Soils with higher percentages of clay are more densely packed so are better able to resist erosion. They also retain water and nutrients well, which makes them ideal for growing plants.

Some soils are dark black, some are shades of brown, and others are reddish, yellow, or whitish. A soil's color depends primarily on its formation and composition. Every mineral produces different-colored soil. Sand and silt soils are typically light colored. Those with more clay are usually darker. **1** The amount of organic material present also affects the color. **2** Soil with a high organic material content can be quite dark. **3** Darker soil is typically the most fertile of all. **4**

Soil is vulnerable to change in several ways. One is through overuse by humans. The continuous growing of one type of crop on a plot of land will <u>expend</u> all of the soil's nutrients. Extensive use of fertilizers and pesticides can result in their chemicals damaging the soil. The cutting down of trees to clear areas for farmland can lead to accelerated soil erosion. Finally, nature can change a soil's composition. In hot climates or during long periods of drought, water may evaporate from the soil. This can increase its salinity, which, in turn, reduces the soil's fertility.

NOTE

Over time, soil can change from being very fertile to being infertile. Likewise, infertile soil can, after a certain amount of time, become fertile and be able to grow crops and vegetation.

Very little vegetation is able to grow in sandy soil, such as on beaches or in deserts.

Many places in the South and Midwest in the United States have dark, fertile soil. This makes them ideal locations for farming.

Desertification is another way that soil may change. When this occurs, the soil loses its fertility and becomes very sandy. This is a problem that is occurring in numerous places around the world, such as in China and Russia.

Glossary
component: a part of something larger
expend: to use entirely; to exhaust

1   The word "retain" in the passage is closest in meaning to

  Ⓐ keep
  Ⓑ utilize
  Ⓒ protect
  Ⓓ provide

2   According to paragraph 2, which of the following is true of clay?

  Ⓐ It often gets eroded by the wind.
  Ⓑ Sandy soil is smaller than it is.
  Ⓒ It is the most common type of soil.
  Ⓓ It is the best soil for raising crops.

3   Look at the four squares [■] that indicate where the following sentence could be added to the passage.

It is in these areas that farmers prefer to grow their crops.

Where would the sentence best fit?

4   ***Directions:*** An introductory sentence for a brief summary of the passage is provided below. Complete the summary by selecting the THREE answer choices that express the most important ideas of the passage. Some sentences do not belong because they express ideas that are not presented in the passage or are minor ideas in the passage. ***This question is worth 2 points.***

While the components that make up soil determine how fertile it is, every kind of soil can change due to natural or manmade reasons.

Answer Choices

> 1 Water is one of the most powerful forces in nature, and it can cause soil to erode as it washes away valuable topsoil.
>
> 2 Soil changes its color depending upon what it is made of, so it can be light, dark, or any shade in between.
>
> 3 Minerals, water, air, and organic material all combine in different amounts to make various kinds of soil.

> 4 People who use an excessive amount of fertilizers on their soil can cause it to lose its nutrients and become less fertile.
>
> 5 It takes a long time for soil to be made, and there are many factors that determine what kind of soil rock will become after it changes.
>
> 6 Because clay is so densely packed, soil with large quantities of it has many characteristics that make it fertile.

Summarizing   Complete the summary by filling in the blanks.

There are many factors involved in _____. Because of this, some soils become fertile while others do not. There are four basic components in soil: minerals, water, air, and organic matter. There are three main types of _____ : sand, silt, and clay. Sand is _____.
Clay is the most fertile. Soil can also be different colors depending on its content. In general, dark soil is _____. Fertilizers, pesticides, and a lack of rain can all harm the soil.

Water Purification

Water is a necessity for almost all living things. Yet most of the Earth's water has too much salt to make it suitable for consumption. And non-salty water often has impurities that can make those who drink it ill. Some impurities are natural while others are manmade. Some examples are bacteria, viruses, parasites, algae, suspended particles of dirt, and toxic chemicals. No matter what the impurity is, the demand for clean water means that ways must be found to purify it. There are three basic methods to do this: the addition of chemicals, filtration, and irradiation.

Most water in the public drinking water systems of developed countries is purified by using a combination of two or three of these methods. For instance, water is pumped from its source to a water purification plant. First, it gets filtered through screens. These screens capture large objects that may **contaminate** the water. Then, chemicals are added to purify the water. Chlorine, which kills many impurities, is the most common of these. Sometimes, other chemicals or treatments are used if the water is too acidic or alkaline. Once chemicals are added, more processes are utilized to give the water a clear, colorless appearance. Next, the water is filtered again. Some plants also use irradiation purification by exposing the water to ultraviolet light. Finally, the water is ready to be released.

³→ Despite all of these treatments, many people are convinced that the water is not pure enough because of the chemicals that are used during the filtration process. So home water purification systems have become more common. For example, a filter may be attached directly to the pump that brings water into a home. Other people opt to install filters on their kitchen taps. These are typically carbon-based filters that can remove impurities. A third process some use is reverse osmosis. This involves forcing water through a membrane at high pressure. In doing that, the membrane filters out any impurities.

Not everyone has access to purified drinking water. Estimates are that more than one billion people lack a clean source of drinking water. Thus many people fall ill to waterborne diseases such as cholera. Even more serious is the number of people who suffer from diarrhea after drinking bad water. Around two million people die from diarrhea-related illnesses every year. Many who **succumb** are children and the elderly. A majority live in developing countries. Yet there are some instances where people in developed countries drink water that has been improperly purified. This often results in their becoming ill. On rare occasions, the end result is death.

NOTE

Due to the nature of many impurities, it is virtually impossible to see many of the most dangerous impurities in water. This includes bacteria, viruses, and parasites.

Sometimes fluorine is added to drinking water as well. It is often used to help improve the health of people's teeth.

Nowadays, there are numerous water filters available for people to purchase. This indicates both the interest in having clean water and the lack of trust many people have in their public drinking systems.

Many places in Africa lack clean water. However, there are many ongoing charitable efforts to improve the condition of the water that people there drink.

Glossary
contaminate: to pollute with something impure or poisonous
succumb: to fall victim to; to die

1 The word "these" in the passage refers to

(A) these screens

(B) large objects

(C) chemicals

(D) impurities

2 Which of the sentences below best expresses the essential information in the highlighted sentence in the passage? *Incorrect* answer choices change the meaning in important ways or leave out essential information.

(A) The filtration process fails to use enough chemicals to convince many people that it is clean.

(B) Some people believe the chemicals used while the water is being filtered result in it not being pure.

(C) The only way to get the water clean enough is to use treatments with chemicals during the filtration process.

(D) During the filtration process, the chemicals used make the water seem pure enough for most people.

3 In paragraph 3, why does the author mention "reverse osmosis"?

(A) To discuss why people choose to use that filtration method

(B) To compare it with the use of carbon-based filters

(C) To stress that it is the most effective filtration method

(D) To explain one method of filtering water at home

4 *Directions:* Select the appropriate statements from the answer choices and match them to what happens to water in the stages of the purification process to which they relate. TWO of the answer choices will NOT be used. **This question is worth 3 points.**

Answer Choices	PURIFICATION PROCESS
1 Is given chemicals to make it have no color	**During**
2 Is filtered by some people in their homes	•
3 Is pumped from its source to the treatment center	•
4 Is run through screens to capture impurities	•
5 Makes many people sick in developing countries	**After**
6 Is often treated with chemicals such as chlorine	•
7 Is released into the public drinking system	•

Summarizing   Complete the summary by filling in the blanks.

People need clean water in order to survive. So the water must be purified at a plant. There are several steps. Water _____ and is treated with various chemicals. These make the water _____. Once it is released, people can access it in their homes. But some people further purify their water by _____ in their homes. Many people around the world get sick from drinking unpurified water. Some even die because of _____ that harm them.

Mastering **the Subject**

The Impact of Changes in the Environment

The environment affects all living things. The amount of rainfall and sunlight, the temperature, and the soil conditions can all determine where people live. If one of them changes, the lives of countless numbers of people can be disrupted. Throughout history, large groups of people have frequently died because of changes in the environment. In other less severe cases, people have been merely forced to move to more hospitable locations.

Since the discovery of agriculture, most humans have depended on farming to provide them with much of their food. But crops only grow upon receiving proper amounts of rainfall and sunlight. They also need for the temperature to be neither too cold nor too hot. Should the growing conditions not be perfect, the crops could fail. This could result in famine and, ultimately, disaster. This was the fate of the Anasazi people. They lived in what is today the southwestern United States around a thousand years ago. At one time, the Anasazi's land received plenty of rainfall, and they led comfortable lives. Then, conditions changed. For some reason, rain began falling less often. The Anasazi's crops died, and they were forced to depart their ancestral homelands.

3→ More recently, a serious drought—one that lasted for years—in the Great Plains of North America occurred in the 1930s. The rain stopped falling, the land dried up, and the once-fertile topsoil was blown away by the wind. This became known as the Dust Bowl. Tens of thousands of farmers and their families were forced to seek better homes in what became an enormous mass migration. This cycle of drought, topsoil erosion, and migration has not been limited to areas in North America. It has occurred all around the world throughout history.

4→ There are other ways that the environment can change. Some experts believe the world's ocean levels could rise in the future because of melting ice. According to studies, if the entire Greenland icecap melted—an unlikely, yet possible, event—the world's water levels could rise significantly. Those individuals living on islands might be forced to move. Coastal towns and cities might find themselves underwater. Millions of people worldwide would find their lives seriously disrupted. In addition to melting ice, floods, tropical storms, and even wildfires can all spark changes in the environment. When and where these natural disasters will occur is unknown. Yet it is highly likely that, one day in the future, Mother Nature's actions will force large groups of people to move.

NOTE

These changes in the environment can be sudden or can manifest over a period of years or even decades.

The Anasazi were not the only tribe in the Americas that was affected by changes in the environment. Many experts believe the Maya Empire declined because of changes in the environment, particularly in the land they farmed.

The Dust Bowl occurred during the Great Depression in the United States. This made its effects even more severe than they would have been had it happened during good economic times.

Around a quarter of the land in the Netherlands has been reclaimed from the sea. Should the ocean levels begin to rise, much of this land could once again be flooded.

Glossary
hospitable: welcoming; pleasant
spark: to result in; to cause

1   The word "They" in the passage refers to

(A) Humans

(B) Crops

(C) Proper amounts of rainfall and sunlight

(D) The growing conditions

2   What can be inferred about the Anasazi?

(A) They were responsible for the soil in their land becoming poor.

(B) They no longer reside in the southwestern United States.

(C) Many of them died in a severe famine.

(D) They both raised crops and hunted animals for food.

3   In paragraphs 3 and 4, which of the following is NOT mentioned as a reason that people were forced to migrate in the past?

(A) Drought

(B) Famine

(C) Topsoil erosion

(D) Melting ice

4   ***Directions:*** An introductory sentence for a brief summary of the passage is provided below. Complete the summary by selecting the THREE answer choices that express the most important ideas of the passage. Some sentences do not belong because they express ideas that are not presented in the passage or are minor ideas in the passage. ***This question is worth 2 points.***

Many times in the past, changes in the environment have forced people to move from the lands that they were living on, and similar events are likely to occur in the future.

Answer Choices

[1] The land the Anasazi lived on received much less rain, so their crops failed, which forced them to move away.

[2] The North American Great Plains frequently endure long periods of time when little or no rain falls on them.

[3] When the environment changes, it might cause famines that result in large numbers of people starving to death.

[4] The Dust Bowl saw valuable topsoil eroded, so farmers had to leave the land and take their families elsewhere.

[5] If the icecap on Greenland melts, it is probable that the levels of the oceans will rise a significant amount.

[6] Some people fear that melting ice could drastically affect the coast and upset millions of people's lives.

Summarizing   **Complete the summary by filling in the blanks.**

The environment can often change. This can disrupt the lives of people and sometimes force them to move to other lands. When _____, it can negatively affect farming. This happened to the Anasazi people. Their once-fertile land received less rain. _____ died, so they moved away. In the 1930s, _____ in North America ruined the land, so farmers and their families moved. Some people fear that melting ice could _____. This would greatly disrupt lives all around the world.

El Nino

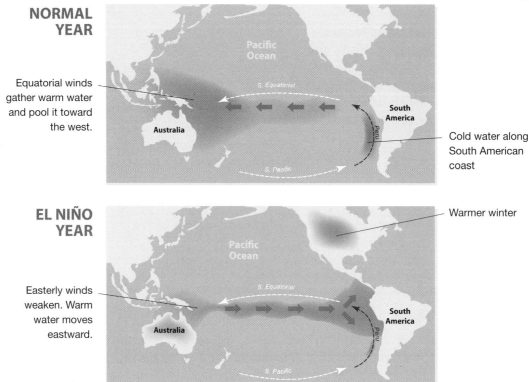

NORMAL YEAR

Equatorial winds gather warm water and pool it toward the west.

Cold water along South American coast

EL NIÑO YEAR

Warmer winter

Easterly winds weaken. Warm water moves eastward.

Wind circulation patterns over the Pacific Ocean

¹→ El Nino is the unusual warming of the water in the Pacific Ocean south of the equator. It is not a constant phenomenon. It occurs at **intervals** of between two and seven years. It sometimes lasts for only a few months. Other times, its consequences may be felt for a year or longer. El Nino has many wide-ranging effects on ocean life. It also alters weather patterns on land. It has been blamed for numerous problems. These include the reduction of fish stocks in the eastern Pacific, heavy rainfall in South America, and droughts in Australia.

²→ In normal years, the southwestern Pacific is warmer than the southeastern region by as many as eight degrees Celsius. Trade winds mainly account for this. The winds originate in the south-central Pacific and usually blow in a westerly direction. This pushes warm water toward the southwestern Pacific. In comparison, the water in the southeastern Pacific is cooler. One reason is that a cold ocean current—the Humboldt Current—runs along the Pacific coast of South America. The Humboldt Current is nutrient rich, thereby making it a prime place for ocean life.

³→ On occasion, the trade winds stop blowing. This keeps warm water in the south-central Pacific. After enough warm water mingles with the cold water, El Nino conditions can occur. Scientists know about this since they are able to measure changes in the water due to a system of buoys with temperature gauges that has been placed in that part of the Pacific. During El Nino conditions, the buoys show that the water in the southeastern Pacific is warmer. The difference may be as little as half a degree Celsius. Other times, the

temperature is higher than that. As the water warms, its nutrient levels fall. This can cause a decrease in the number of fish there. Accordingly, during El Nino, the fisheries of South America suffer major losses.

⁴→ El Nino can also alter the weather. In the cold water of the Humboldt Current, there is little evaporation. As a result, the western coast of South America receives **scanty** amounts of rain. **1** However, during El Nino, the warmer water results in more evaporation. In turn, more rain falls on the land. **2** Floods in Peru and other countries in western South America then become common. **3** In the southwestern Pacific, the cooler water means there is less rainfall. **4** Droughts in Indonesia and Australia may happen. North American winters may be warmer and drier. Even some parts of Africa may endure droughts while other regions there receive heavy rainfall. One positive aspect is that fewer typhoons strike northeastern Asia. These changes in weather patterns do not occur simultaneously. They manifest over a period of twelve to eighteen months after El Nino conditions first occur.

⁵→ El Nino usually begins in the fall and lasts into the next year. Its conditions lessen as the south-central Pacific trade winds strengthen and start to push warmer water toward the southwestern Pacific. Meteorologists refer to this as La Nina. During this time, weather conditions return to normal. In recent decades, there has been a greater incidence of severe El Nino conditions, and more are predicted for the near future.

Glossary
interval: the space between two periods of time
scanty: little; sparse

1 According to paragraph 1, which of the following is NOT true of El Nino?

(A) It can change the weather in faraway places.

(B) It begins in the waters of the Pacific Ocean.

(C) It may last for two to seven years at a time.

(D) It can cause changes in the water and on the land.

2 In paragraph 2, why does the author mention "the Humboldt Current"?

(A) To declare that there are many nutrients in its waters

(B) To explain why part of the Pacific Ocean's waters are cold

(C) To state that it is a prime fishing ground for sailors

(D) To make a note of its location in the Pacific Ocean

3 In paragraph 2, the author implies that the Pacific trade winds

(A) occasionally begin blowing from the north

(B) may cease blowing for years at a time

(C) begin to blow harder during a typhoon

(D) make sailing west easier than sailing east

4 The word "mingles" in the passage is closest in meaning to

(A) transforms

(B) condenses

(C) overlaps

(D) mixes

5 Which of the sentences below best expresses the essential information in the highlighted sentence in the passage? *Incorrect* answer choices change the meaning in important ways or leave out essential information.

(A) Thermometers in the Pacific Ocean enable scientists to know how the water temperature is changing.

(B) Scientists are placing buoys throughout the Pacific so that they can measure the water temperature in the future.

(C) The water is constantly changing temperature, so scientists have placed buoys in the ocean to measure these changes.

(D) Temperature gauges in the Pacific alerted scientists to the fact that the ocean conditions were undergoing changes.

6 According to paragraph 3, South American fisheries lose money during El Nino because

(A) the cold water makes the fish swim deeper

(B) the heavy rains ruin the fishing conditions

(C) they are unable to sail as often as they want

(D) there are fewer fish for them to catch

7 According to paragraph 4, which of the following is true of El Nino's effects on the weather?

(A) It may increase the frequency of Pacific Ocean typhoons.

(B) It may cause some places to get greater amounts or rain.

(C) It can make the Humboldt Current's waters colder.

(D) It can result in droughts occurring in South America.

8 In paragraph 5, the author's description of La Nina mentions which of the following?

(A) The severity of its effects in relation to El Nino

(B) What happens to weather conditions during it

(C) The length of time its effects may last

(D) What happens to trade winds during it

9 Look at the four squares [■] that indicate where the following sentence could be added to the passage.

But El Nino's influence is not limited only to the area around South America.

Where would the sentence best fit?

Click on a square [■] to add the sentence to the passage.

10 *Directions:* Select the appropriate sentences from the answer choices and match them to the cause and effect of El Nino to which they relate. TWO of the answer choices will NOT be used. ***This question is worth 3 points.***

Drag your answer choices to the spaces where they belong.
To remove an answer choice, click on it. To review the passage, click on **View Text**.

Answer Choices

1 The Humboldt Current runs adjacent to western South America.

2 Severe weather conditions are expected in the future.

3 South Pacific trade winds stop blowing.

4 Fewer fish are in the water off South America.

5 Water in the southeastern Pacific begins to warm.

6 More rain than normal falls in western South America.

7 Places far from South America experience changing weather.

EL NINO

Cause

•

•

Effect

•

•

•

1 ▸ Renewable Energy Resources

Much of the Earth's energy needs are provided by fossil fuels. Examples of these are coal, natural gas, and oil. However, these resources are nonrenewable. Once they are expended, they cannot be replaced. So people are trying to switch to renewable energy sources. These are sources of energy that do not run out. People today utilize solar, wind, hydroelectric, and geothermal power. These energy sources are all promising but have limitations. The limits are mostly technological, especially with regard to solar power. In the future, it is likely that renewable energy sources will provide a greater percentage of the Earth's energy.

2 ▸ Ice Ages

The Earth is currently in a state of relative warmth. Yet, in the past, the Earth was often much cooler than the present. During these occasions, the Earth is said to be in an ice age. There have been several major ice ages and numerous mini ice ages in the Earth's past. In an ice age, temperatures plunge, and large regions are covered in ice. Over one quarter of the planet was covered in ice during parts of the Great Ice Age. It began around two million years ago and ended around 11,000 years ago. Ice ages are inhospitable to life and may cause the extinction of numerous species.

3 ▸ Endangered Species

There are millions of species of plants and animals. However, they all exist in different numbers. Some are plentiful while others are rare. In some cases, plants or animals become endangered species. When this occurs, it means that their numbers are so low that they are in danger of becoming extinct. Species become endangered for many reasons. They may suffer from diseases or be hunted by predators. Man's actions—through hunting as well as changing and polluting the environment—have caused many species to become endangered. Currently, there are about 40,000 species around the world that are endangered.

4 ▸ Ecosystems

Ecosystems exist everywhere on the Earth. They are geographical areas that are comprised of both the living organisms and the nonliving materials in these regions. The living organisms include plants and animals. The nonliving materials include soil, rocks, water, and air. They exist on both land and in the water. Mountains, jungles, deserts, forests, and prairies are all land ecosystems. Lakes, rivers, seas, and oceans are all water ecosystems. Ecosystems are complex in that the living organisms and nonliving materials all interact with one another. They can be enormous areas or incredibly tiny microecosystems.

5 ▸ Erosion

Erosion is the constant wearing away of the Earth's surface. Most notable are water, wind, and ice erosion. Water typically erodes the surface slowly. For instance, it took the Colorado River millions of years to carve out the Grand Canyon in Arizona, USA. Even today, erosion is still ongoing there. Wind erosion often takes place in desert areas where the topsoil is not anchored to the ground. And ice erosion is actually a very swift form of erosion. Water seeps into cracks in rocks and subsequently freezes. When it turns to ice, it expands. As a result, the rock often shatters into small pieces.

6 ▸ Glacier Movements

In areas that are cold all year around, glaciers often form. These are huge sheets of compressed snow and ice. They can be up to several hundred kilometers long. Due to their immense size and weight, glaciers actually move. Some move a few centimeters a year while others can move several meters a day. Glaciers may move forward or backward. When they move, they often alter the surface. They are so heavy and powerful that they can reduce mountains to flatlands. This is why the Great Plains exists in North America. Receding glaciers altered the planet's surface, leaving nothing but flat land behind them.

7 ▸ Paleogeology

There are several subfields in geology. One of them is paleogeology. This is the study of the geological history of an area. Paleogeologists often research layers of rocks to learn more about the Earth. This field also encompasses the study of plate tectonics and the movements of the continents. It is paleogeologists who research faults between various plates, which can often cause earthquakes when they shift. Finally, these scientists are often useful in the search for deposits of oil, natural gas, and valuable minerals.

8 ▸ Rainforests

Many regions near the equator are covered in dense tropical forests. These are called rainforests. Rainforests are filled with dense vegetation—including very tall trees—and receive a large amount of rainfall each year. They are usually, but not always, found in tropical regions. The largest is the Amazon Rainforest, which is found by the Amazon River in South America. Rainforests are the planet's most diverse ecosystems. They are home to enormous numbers of plants and animals. It is estimated that millions of insect species, thousands of other animal species, and tens of thousands of plant species live in the Amazon Rainforest alone.

9 ▸ Forest Fires

On occasion, large areas in a forest catch fire and burn. These forest fires may start because of arson. More frequently, though, they are caused by lightning strikes during the forest's dry season. Forest fires can burn down huge areas of land. Yet they are not necessarily detrimental to the forest. The fires rarely kill many animals since most are able to escape. The fires also clear brush from the forest and burn down old and dead trees. The resulting ash acts to fertilize the land. This enables new growth to arise very quickly. Forest fires are a seasonal event in many places.

10 ▸ Fertilizers

Most soil has nutrients in it. These nutrients are used by plants when they grow in the soil. However, plants can eventually exhaust the soil of its nutrients, making the soil worthless for growing anything. That is why people use fertilizers. Fertilizers are natural or artificial materials that replenish the soil with nutrients. This allows plants to grow much better. Manure from animals is one common natural fertilizer. Many of the fertilizers used today are artificial. Too much fertilizer can harm the soil, so people must find a balance between using too much and too little.

11 ▸ Causes of Extinction

The plant and animal species on the Earth are constantly changing. Old species die while new ones arise. When a species dies, it is said to be extinct. Species might become extinct for many reasons. They may be outcompeted by other animals. They may fail to adapt to a changing environment. They could be hunted to extinction by predators as well. This happened to the dodo bird, passenger pigeon, and numerous other species. Or in the case of the dinosaurs, a global catastrophe could be the cause of extinction. Most scientists believe an asteroid strike severely altered the planet's climate and killed all of the dinosaurs.

12 ▸ Floods

Sometimes the water level of a body of water such as a lake or river may rise above its banks. When this occurs, the water begins to flood the local area. Floods can cause great damage to the land. They wash away valuable topsoil, making land worthless for farming. They can also alter the geography of an area. This is particularly true when rivers, with their fast-flowing waters, flood. Some floods devastate human settlements. They can destroy homes and buildings, wash away roads and bridges, and cause the loss of human and animal life.

- **accelerate** (v) to increase the speed of
- **benefit** (n) an advantage
- **buoy** (n) something that floats in the water and is often used to mark location or to make signals
- **capture** (v) to catch; to seize
- **circulate** (v) to flow; to move
- **coastal** (adj) near an area where the land meets the water
- **comprise** (v) to make up; to constitute
- **consumption** (n) the act of eating or drinking a substance
- **convince** (v) to convince a person to believe something
- **current** (n) a moving flow of water within a larger body of water
- **cycle** (n) a recurring sequence or series
- **declining** (adj) decreasing
- **dependent** (adj) needy; reliant
- **dinosaur** (n) a large reptilian creature that lived millions of years ago
- **disrupt** (v) to upset; to change; to alter
- **drive** (v) to impel; to force one to do something
- **drought** (n) a period during which there is little or no rainfall in an area
- **dust** (n) a fine, powdery substance
- **endure** (v) to last; to survive
- **equator** (n) the imaginary line that runs around the center of the Earth at zero degrees latitude
- **evaporate** (v) to turn into a gas; to dry up
- **exhausted** (adj) completely empty or used up
- **extract** (v) to remove; to take out or away
- **fertile** (adj) productive
- **fertilizer** (n) a substance that increases the ability of the soil to grow vegetation
- **filtration** (n) the act of filtering something
- **fishery** (n) an area in the ocean where many fish may be caught
- **gauge** (n) a device that can measure something
- **geothermal** (adj) relating to the heat that is produced by the Earth
- **gradually** (adv) slowly
- **growth** (n) an increase in size or development
- **icecap** (n) a thick cover of ice above an area
- **ill-suited** (adj) inappropriate; unsuitable
- **impurity** (n) a contaminant; something that contaminates another substance
- **incidence** (n) an occurrence
- **install** (v) to put in; to equip; to set up
- **irradiation** (n) the act of subjecting something to radiation

- **landscape** (n) a section or area of outdoor scenery
- **manifest** (v) to form; to appear; to occur
- **meteorologist** (n) a person who studies the weather
- **migration** (n) the moving of people or animals from one place to another
- **mix** (v) to combine
- **natural** (adj) occurring in nature; not manmade
- **nutrient** (n) something that provides nutrition
- **opt** (v) to choose; to select
- **organic** (adj) natural; wholesome
- **originate** (v) to come from; to form; to arise
- **overuse** (n) the extensive use of something
- **packed** (adj) crammed
- **pipe** (v) to move through a pipe
- **process** (n) a method; a way
- **proposition** (n) an offer; a plan; a proposal
- **pump** (v) to drive or force a liquid to go somewhere
- **purify** (v) to make clean or pure
- **replace** (v) to take the place of; to substitute
- **resist** (v) to fight against
- **reusable** (adj) able to be used again
- **roots** (n) the underground parts of plants that remove water and nutrients from the soil
- **salinity** (n) the amount of salt in something
- **salinization** (n) the process through which soil becomes salty
- **saturated** (adj) completely filled
- **shade** (n) a tint; a degree in color
- **soak** (v) to go into completely, as in water going into the ground
- **steam** (n) water in its gaseous form
- **stock** (n) an amount of something
- **sunlight** (n) the light that is produced by the sun
- **texture** (n) a feel; a touch
- **topography** (n) the geographical features of an area
- **topsoil** (n) the fertile soil found on the top of the ground
- **tropical** (adj) relating to the tropics
- **typhoon** (n) a tropical storm that is similar to a hurricane
- **upward** (adj) toward the surface
- **vegetation** (n) any kind of plant life
- **waterborne** (adj) carried by water; found in water
- **waterlogged** (adj) completely filled with water; having too much water
- **wildfire** (n) a forest fire

Vocabulary Review

Choose the word or phrase closest in meaning to the highlighted part of the sentence.

1 In this regard, too much water can be lethal to vegetation.
   - (A) apparent
   - (B) helpful
   - (C) risky
   - (D) deadly

2 Additionally, soil conditions are not constant but change due to natural forces and the actions of humans.
   - (A) steady
   - (B) fertile
   - (C) normal
   - (D) monitored

3 This creates energy that is cheap, clean, and reusable.
   - (A) inexhaustible
   - (B) inflexible
   - (C) inexpensive
   - (D) insolent

4 These include the reduction of fish stocks in the eastern Pacific, heavy rainfall in South America, and droughts in Australia.
   - (A) expanding
   - (B) lessening
   - (C) controlling
   - (D) researching

5 No matter what the impurity is, the demand for clean water means that ways must be found to purify it.
   - (A) consume
   - (B) cleanse
   - (C) obtain
   - (D) preserve

6 In doing so, all of the water in the lake can replenish its oxygen supply, which is vital for the organisms living in it.
   - (A) necessary
   - (B) considerate
   - (C) focused
   - (D) important

7 This action causes the water to circulate.
   - (A) flow
   - (B) sink
   - (C) condense
   - (D) evaporate

8 In other less severe cases, people have been merely forced to move to more hospitable locations.
   - (A) well-known
   - (B) long-lasting
   - (C) serious
   - (D) offensive

9 Accordingly, during El Nino, the fisheries of South America suffer major losses.
   - (A) endure
   - (B) accept
   - (C) account for
   - (D) avoid

10 These include the type of rock that makes it, the topography—or shape—of the land, the climate of the area, the actions of vegetation, bacteria, and fungi on the rocks, and the passage of time.
   - (A) elapsing
   - (B) consideration
   - (C) keeping
   - (D) eroding

11 This pushes warm water toward the southwestern Pacific.

   (A) keeps
   (B) forces
   (C) pulls
   (D) circulates

12 Other people opt to install filters on their kitchen taps.

   (A) want
   (B) ask
   (C) attempt
   (D) choose

13 The primary effect is that irrigation redirects water from its original location and then takes it to another place.

   (A) transports
   (B) abandons
   (C) replaces
   (D) refills

14 Tens of thousands of farmers and their families were forced to seek better homes in what became an enormous mass migration.

   (A) population
   (B) catastrophe
   (C) movement
   (D) environment

15 Soil is vulnerable to change in several ways.

   (A) susceptible
   (B) required
   (C) forced
   (D) weak

16 At one time, the Anasazi's land received plenty of rainfall, and they led comfortable lives.

   (A) some
   (B) ample
   (C) little
   (D) constant

17 Its primary drawback is that it is only useful in places where it is located.

   (A) initial
   (B) main
   (C) bothersome
   (D) detracting

18 These sources all suffer from the depletion of their water supplies.

   (A) destruction
   (B) stealing
   (C) reduction
   (D) abandoning

19 Yet there are some instances where people in developed countries drink water that has been improperly purified.

   (A) theories
   (B) beliefs
   (C) occasions
   (D) demands

20 The primary benefit of the fall turnover is that it allows the lower layers of water to circulate freely.

   (A) hope
   (B) purpose
   (C) requirement
   (D) advantage

Part C

Experiencing the TOEFL iBT Actual Tests

CONTINUE

Reading Section Directions

This section measures your ability to understand academic passages in English. You will have **72 minutes** to read and answer questions about **4 passages**. A clock at the top of the screen will show you how much time is remaining.

Most questions are worth 1 point but the last question for each passage is worth more than 1 point. The directions for the last question indicate how many points you may receive.

Some passages include a word or phrase that is **underlined** in blue. Click on the word or phrase to see a definition or an explanation.

When you want to move to the next question, click on **Next**. You may skip questions and go back to them later. If you want to return to previous questions, click on **Back**. You can click on **Review** at any time, and the review screen will show you which questions you have answered and which you have not answered. From this review screen, you may go directly to any question you have already seen in the Reading section.

Click on **Continue** to go on.

Deep-Sea Organisms

An anglerfish deep beneath the ocean

The waters deep beneath the world's oceans are perhaps the most inhospitable places on the Earth. Crushing pressure, cold temperatures, and a lack of food and oxygen make it impossible for most life forms to survive at these depths. Yet life still manages to exist there in many varied and unique forms. Most of these life forms have had to adapt to their surroundings, so the organisms found in the ocean depths often have unique characteristics that are not found anywhere else.

Most life forms cannot survive without some source of food and oxygen. These exist at the bottoms of the deepest oceans but are not present in large quantities. Oxygen is present in ocean water. It is richest at the surface and not very abundant as it goes deeper. But some oxygen manages to filter down to the deepest levels. Food may also be found there. Some of it comes in the guise of marine snow. This is the remains of dead fish and marine plants from the surface that have sunk to the bottom of the ocean. Other food is found in the life forms that occupy these areas. Some deep-sea creatures are predators. Therefore, they attack and feed on other organisms living in their area.

Something else that helps some deep-sea creatures survive is the vents that can be found on the ocean floors. These are places where hot gases—and sometimes molten rock—burst out of the Earth. These warm places attract life. Tubeworms, a type of invertebrate, live near the vents. They survive by using a process called <u>chemosynthesis</u>. The tubeworms take bacteria near the vents and convert it into organic material, which they then consume.

The bodies of deep-sea creatures have also adapted to their particular ecosystems. Most of the fish living deep below the surface are small. They are typically less than half a meter in length. This means they require much less food and oxygen than do larger fish. In addition, many deep-sea life forms process food slowly since finding nourishment is often a chore. For example, the coelacanth, a fish, can go for long periods of time without eating. Most deep-sea creatures have different bodies than creatures living closer to the surface. For instance, most sea animals rely on internal gases to maintain buoyancy. This enables them to float in the water. Yet using such gases is not possible at great depths. The water pressure that far deep would crush those fish. Nor would bony skeletons survive the overwhelming pressure. Instead, most deep-sea fish have gelatinous bodies with non-rigid skeletal structures. This enables them to float yet avoid being crushed by the ocean pressure.

Seeing is difficult in the total darkness of the ocean depths since the sun's light cannot penetrate that deep. Thus several deep-sea creatures rely on <u>bioluminescence</u> to create their own light. Many deep-sea fish have large eyes to help them with their sight. Some have feelers, which they use to find prey or to attract a mate. The anglerfish, for instance, has a long feeler emerging from its forehead and hanging in front of its mouth. It emits a bluish-green bioluminescent light at its end. This attracts other fish, which the anglerfish then attacks and eats. It also has a wide jaw that can stretch to let it swallow prey twice its size. Anglerfish are further noted for the bizarre way in which they reproduce. When a male matures, it becomes unable to digest food. So it finds a female and bites her. An enzyme fuses his mouth to her body. From then on, in a parasitic manner, he gets his nourishment from her. In return, the female is assured that a male will be nearby to fertilize her eggs when she is ready to reproduce.

These are but a few examples of the ways that life has adapted to the ocean depths. Undoubtedly, researchers will discover more unique creatures in the future. The deepest parts of the oceans are still mostly unexplored. So scientists, as they investigate these unknown areas, will surely be surprised by the ways that other organisms have managed to evolve to survive deep below the surface.

Glossary

chemosynthesis: a form of synthesis some simple organisms can perform that lets them provide their own food sources
bioluminescence: the ability of some organisms to create their own light

Deep-Sea Organisms

The waters deep beneath the world's oceans are perhaps the most inhospitable places on the Earth. Crushing pressure, cold temperatures, and a lack of food and oxygen make it impossible for most life forms to survive at these depths. Yet life still manages to exist there in many varied and unique forms. Most of these life forms have had to adapt to their surroundings, so the organisms found in the ocean depths often have unique characteristics that are not found anywhere else.

[2]→Most life forms cannot survive without some source of food and oxygen. These exist at the bottoms of the deepest oceans but are not present in large quantities. Oxygen is present in ocean water. It is richest at the surface and not very abundant as it goes deeper. But some oxygen manages to filter down to the deepest levels. Food may also be found there. Some of it comes in the guise of marine snow. This is the remains of dead fish and marine plants from the surface that have sunk to the bottom of the ocean. Other food is found in the life forms that occupy these areas. Some deep-sea creatures are predators. Therefore, they attack and feed on other organisms living in their area.

1   Which of the sentences below best expresses the essential information in the highlighted sentence in the passage? *Incorrect* answer choices change the meaning in important ways or leave out essential information.

   Ⓐ The water deep in the ocean is dangerous, so organisms have to evolve in order to survive down there.

   Ⓑ Thanks to their unique characteristics, many creatures are sometimes able to swim down to the ocean floor.

   Ⓒ Many organisms have not gotten used to the ocean depths, so they still lack unique characteristics.

   Ⓓ Organisms that live deep in the ocean have unique adaptations that are found in no other animals.

2   According to paragraph 2, which of the following is true of life forms that live at the bottom of the ocean?

   Ⓐ They have to find places with abundant amounts of oxygen.

   Ⓑ They may feed on other organisms living there.

   Ⓒ Oxygen is not necessary for them to live.

   Ⓓ The majority of them are prey animals.

3 The author discusses "Tubeworms" in paragraph 3 in order to

   Ⓐ show how that species survives deep under the water

   Ⓑ name the most abundant species in the deep ocean

   Ⓒ describe the process of chemosynthesis

   Ⓓ compare them with other deep-sea invertebrates

4 In stating that finding nourishment is often a "chore," the author means that locating food

   Ⓐ is a full-time obligation

   Ⓑ is a job

   Ⓒ requires much energy

   Ⓓ can be difficult

5 Which of the following can be inferred from paragraph 4 about deep-sea creatures?

   Ⓐ They must eat regularly in order to live there.

   Ⓑ Smaller ones tend to have an easier time surviving.

   Ⓒ Their bones are usually harder than those of other creatures.

   Ⓓ Some species have been alive since prehistoric times.

6 According to paragraph 4, deep-sea creatures avoid being crushed by water pressure because

   Ⓐ their bodies are more gelatinous than rigid

   Ⓑ they rely upon internal gases to balance themselves

   Ⓒ they have strong enough skeletal structures

   Ⓓ they can find enough food to strengthen their bodies

³➜ Something else that helps some deep-sea creatures survive is the vents that can be found on the ocean floors. These are places where hot gases—and sometimes molten rock—burst out of the Earth. These warm places attract life. Tubeworms, a type of invertebrate, live near the vents. They survive by using a process called chemosynthesis. The tubeworms take bacteria near the vents and convert it into organic material, which they then consume.

⁴➜ The bodies of deep-sea creatures have also adapted to their particular ecosystems. Most of the fish living deep below the surface are small. They are typically less than half a meter in length. This means they require much less food and oxygen than do larger fish. In addition, many deep-sea life forms process food slowly since finding nourishment is often a chore. For example, the coelacanth, a fish, can go for long periods of time without eating. Most deep-sea creatures have different bodies than creatures living closer to the surface. For instance, most sea animals rely on internal gases to maintain buoyancy. This enables them to float in the water. Yet using such gases is not possible at great depths. The water pressure that far deep would crush those fish. Nor would bony skeletons survive the overwhelming pressure. Instead, most deep-sea fish have gelatinous bodies with non-rigid skeletal structures. This enables them to float yet avoid being crushed by the ocean pressure.

Glossary

chemosynthesis: a form of synthesis some simple organisms can perform that lets them provide their own food sources

7 According to paragraph 5, which of the following is NOT true of how deep-sea fish see underwater?

(A) They create their own light.

(B) They have enlarged eyes.

(C) They rely on the sun's rays.

(D) They have feelers to help them see.

8 The word "Undoubtedly" in the passage is closest in meaning to

(A) Surely

(B) Respectfully

(C) Individually

(D) Probably

9 Look at the four squares [■] that indicate where the following sentence could be added to the passage.

The aptly named lanternfish is one such species that can create its own light.

Where would the sentence best fit?

> Click on a square [■] to add the sentence to the passage.

⁵➡ Seeing is difficult in the total darkness of the ocean depths since the sun's light cannot penetrate that deep. **1** Thus several deep-sea creatures rely on <u>bioluminescence</u> to create their own light. **2** Many deep-sea fish have large eyes to help them with their sight. **3** Some have feelers, which they use to find prey or to attract a mate. **4** The anglerfish, for instance, has a long feeler emerging from its forehead and hanging in front of its mouth. It emits a bluish-green bioluminescent light at its end. This attracts other fish, which the anglerfish then attacks and eats. It also has a wide jaw that can stretch to let it swallow prey twice its size. Anglerfish are further noted for the bizarre way in which they reproduce. When a male matures, it becomes unable to digest food. So it finds a female and bites her. An enzyme fuses his mouth to her body. From then on, in a parasitic manner, he gets his nourishment from her. In return, the female is assured that a male will be nearby to fertilize her eggs when she is ready to reproduce.

These are but a few examples of the ways that life has adapted to the ocean depths. Undoubtedly, researchers will discover more unique creatures in the future. The deepest parts of the oceans are still mostly unexplored. So scientists, as they investigate these unknown areas, will surely be surprised by the ways that other organisms have managed to evolve to survive deep below the surface.

Glossary

bioluminescence: the ability of some organisms to create their own light

10 *Directions:* An introductory sentence for a brief summary of the passage is provided below. Complete the summary by selecting the THREE answer choices that express the most important ideas of the passage. Some sentences do not belong because they express ideas that are not presented in the passage or are minor ideas in the passage. *This question is worth 2 points.*

> Drag your answer choices to the spaces where they belong.
> To remove an answer choice, click on it. To review the passage, click **View Text**.

Creatures that live deep beneath the surface of the ocean have adapted their bodies to enable them to survive that far underwater.

-
-
-

Answer Choices

1. Both oxygen and food are found deep under the water, but they are not available in large quantities.

2. Since seeing in complete darkness is virtually impossible, some fish, such as the anglerfish, use bioluminescence to create light.

3. The coelacanth and the anglerfish are two of the many fish that call the deep ocean their home.

4. Scientists hope that they will discover more unique creatures as they continue to explore the ocean depths.

5. Many fish have developed bodies that are jellylike, which prevents them from being crushed by the water pressure.

6. Some organisms live near underwater vents that provide heat and other forms of nourishment for them.

The Revolutions of 1848

In 1848, a series of revolutions broke out across Europe. These events occurred mostly in Southern, Central, and Western Europe. They barely affected Russia, Scandinavia, and England. They were sparked by several factors. Among these issues were the unresolved feelings of nationalism left over from the French Revolution, the large gap between the ruling classes and the masses of people they dominated, and a series of economic failures and bad harvests in the 1840s. While the revolutions were quelled by the ruling classes, they achieved a few changes. Some monarchs were quickly replaced. Reforms were also enacted. Over the long term, feelings of nationalism intensified. This caused many minority populations to start demanding their own countries.

A major **legacy** of the French Revolution of the late 1800s was nationalism. Nationalism—the feeling of belonging to a nation and having pride in it—motivated the French armies under Napoleon as they rampaged across Europe. Nationalist feelings spread from France and had become powerful forces by the mid-1800s. Many of the major countries and empires in Europe had minority populations. These people were inspired by nationalist feelings. They desired either more autonomy within their parent country or total independence in the form of their own nation. These feelings built up until they burst forth in 1848.

Monarchies ruled most of Europe in 1848. A few old and established families, such as the Austrian Hapsburgs, dominated millions of people. Some nations, most notably England, had already granted their citizens limited rights. This was not true for most European countries though. In these places, the masses had little or no say in how their country was run. But the masses began asking for reforms. They wanted a role in the government as well as constitutions that granted them specific rights and freedoms. These people suffered from abject poverty, which also contributed to the revolutions. During the 1840s, many countries experienced economic troubles and bad harvests, which added to sentiments of unrest among the populace. Countless urban dwellers had no jobs. In the countryside, farmers were near starvation. The time was ripe for a period of upheaval.

The troubles began in Sicily in 1848. It was ruled by Naples, an Italian city-state. But Sicily's people revolted against their faraway rulers. Once the revolt began and news of it spread, a chain reaction occurred. Why and how this happened is still a matter of debate. In all likelihood, others saw the Sicilian rebellion as a sign it was time for a change. Quickly, revolts began in Paris, Vienna, Berlin, and Prague. At first, the ruling classes sought to appease the revolutionaries. The French king abdicated, and a new republican government was declared. In Berlin, the Prussian rulers enacted a constitution. In the Austrian Empire, the Hungarians—the empire's largest minority—were granted some measure of autonomy.

These steps pleased some, particularly the middle classes, but they did not satisfy everyone. The lower classes—peasants and out-of-work city dwellers—wanted much more. They desired changes that would vastly improve their lives. For instance, in Hungary, the people demanded independence from Austria. Fighting began there, and, soon, the major cities of Europe saw blood being shed in their streets. The ruling classes, with the support of the middle class, who feared a peasant uprising, crushed the rebellions. The fighting in Austria continued until 1849. It finally ended when Russian troops arrived to put down the Hungarian revolt. The other revolts failed as well. They did not succeed since there was no center to the revolutions nor were there any strong, charismatic leaders.

The short-term results of the revolutions were many. France became a republic. Louis Napoleon, a nephew of Napoleon Bonaparte, was chosen to be its president. The Hungarians received more autonomy. Naples gave the Sicilians a constitution. Many German states did the same for their own people. As for long-term effects, the primary one was the unleashing of **pent-up** feelings of nationalism. Nationalist movements began all over Europe. By the 1870s, the German and Italian states had united to form the modern nations of Germany and Italy. Yet many minorities were still not satisfied. Their nationalist feelings and desires for independence would eventually help cause World War I, which began in 1914.

Glossary
legacy: a bequest; an inheritance; a result
pent-up: confined; locked up

The Revolutions of 1848

In 1848, a series of revolutions broke out across Europe. These events occurred mostly in Southern, Central, and Western Europe. They barely affected Russia, Scandinavia, and England. They were sparked by several factors. Among these issues were the unresolved feelings of nationalism left over from the French Revolution, the large gap between the ruling classes and the masses of people they dominated, and a series of economic failures and bad harvests in the 1840s. While the revolutions were quelled by the ruling classes, they achieved a few changes. Some monarchs were quickly replaced. Reforms were also enacted. Over the long term, feelings of nationalism intensified. This caused many minority populations to start demanding their own countries.

²➜ A major **legacy** of the French Revolution of the late 1800s was nationalism. Nationalism—the feeling of belonging to a nation and having pride in it—motivated the French armies under Napoleon as they rampaged across Europe. Nationalist feelings spread from France and had become powerful forces by the mid-1800s. Many of the major countries and empires in Europe had minority populations. These people were inspired by nationalist feelings. They desired either more autonomy within their parent country or total independence in the form of their own nation. These feelings built up until they burst forth in 1848.

11 Which of the sentences below best expresses the essential information in the highlighted sentence in the passage? *Incorrect* answer choices change the meaning in important ways or leave out essential information.

Ⓐ Economic problems and bad harvests created problems between the people and their rulers, and this caused feelings of nationalism to increase.

Ⓑ Nationalist sentiments, problems between the ruling classes and the people they ruled, and economic and farming issues were some of the problems that existed.

Ⓒ The issue of nationalism had never been settled, and this caused the masses to resent their rulers, especially when the economy and crops both failed.

Ⓓ The 1840s saw a number of problems, which included nationalist feelings, restructured governments, and bad economies due to farming problems.

12 In paragraph 2, which of the following can be inferred about Napoleon?

Ⓐ He was a leader during the French Revolution.

Ⓑ He became the most powerful man in Europe.

Ⓒ He led his armies to victory throughout Europe.

Ⓓ He was disliked by most of the French people.

13 According to paragraph 2, which of the following is true of nationalist feelings in Europe?

Ⓐ They had their origins in France.

Ⓑ Napoleon tried to silence them.

Ⓒ They were ignored by minority populations.

Ⓓ They helped the Europeans defeat the French.

Glossary
legacy: a bequest; an inheritance; a result

14 In paragraph 3, all of the following questions are answered EXCEPT:

Ⓐ Which country in Europe granted its people some limited rights?

Ⓑ What did the masses want from their rulers?

Ⓒ What were some problems that countries experienced in the 1840s?

Ⓓ Who were some of the families that ruled most of the countries in Europe?

15 Why does the author mention "Sicily" in paragraph 4?

Ⓐ To claim that the revolutions' leaders came from there

Ⓑ To explain its relationship with the city-state of Naples

Ⓒ To name the place where the revolutions of 1848 began

Ⓓ To compare the fighting there with that in other parts of Europe

16 The word "abdicated" in the passage is closest in meaning to

Ⓐ stepped down

Ⓑ died

Ⓒ went into exile

Ⓓ fled

³→ Monarchies ruled most of Europe in 1848. A few old and established families, such as the Austrian Hapsburgs, dominated millions of people. Some nations, most notably England, had already granted their citizens limited rights. This was not true for most European countries though. In these places, the masses had little or no say in how their country was run. But the masses began asking for reforms. They wanted a role in the government as well as constitutions that granted them specific rights and freedoms. These people suffered from abject poverty, which also contributed to the revolutions. During the 1840s, many countries experienced economic troubles and bad harvests, which added to sentiments of unrest among the populace. Countless urban dwellers had no jobs. In the countryside, farmers were near starvation. The time was ripe for a period of upheaval.

⁴→ The troubles began in Sicily in 1848. It was ruled by Naples, an Italian city-state. But Sicily's people revolted against their faraway rulers. Once the revolt began and news of it spread, a chain reaction occurred. Why and how this happened is still a matter of debate. In all likelihood, others saw the Sicilian rebellion as a sign it was time for a change. Quickly, revolts began in Paris, Vienna, Berlin, and Prague. At first, the ruling classes sought to appease the revolutionaries. The French king abdicated, and a new republican government was declared. In Berlin, the Prussian rulers enacted a constitution. In the Austrian Empire, the Hungarians—the empire's largest minority—were granted some measure of autonomy.

17 The word "uprising" in the passage is closest in meaning to

Ⓐ government

Ⓑ withdrawal

Ⓒ mob

Ⓓ revolt

18 According to paragraph 6, World War I later occurred because

Ⓐ some countries' people were still demanding a constitution

Ⓑ many European people had a desire to be free

Ⓒ Germany and Italy were affected by nationalism

Ⓓ Hungarian autonomy led to a desire for more independence

These steps pleased some, particularly the middle classes, but they did not satisfy everyone. The lower classes—peasants and out-of-work city dwellers—wanted much more. They desired changes that would vastly improve their lives. For instance, in Hungary, the people demanded independence from Austria. Fighting began there, and, soon, the major cities of Europe saw blood being shed in their streets. The ruling classes, with the support of the middle class, who feared a peasant uprising, crushed the rebellions. The fighting in Austria continued until 1849. It finally ended when Russian troops arrived to put down the Hungarian revolt. The other revolts failed as well. They did not succeed since there was no center to the revolutions nor were there any strong, charismatic leaders.

6 ➔ The short-term results of the revolutions were many. France became a republic. Louis Napoleon, a nephew of Napoleon Bonaparte, was chosen to be its president. The Hungarians received more autonomy. Naples gave the Sicilians a constitution. Many German states did the same for their own people. As for long-term effects, the primary one was the unleashing of **pent-up** feelings of nationalism. Nationalist movements began all over Europe. By the 1870s, the German and Italian states had united to form the modern nations of Germany and Italy. Yet many minorities were still not satisfied. Their nationalist feelings and desires for independence would eventually help cause World War I, which began in 1914.

Glossary

pent-up: confined; locked up

19 Look at the four squares [■] that indicate where the following sentence could be added to the passage.

Many were inspired by the American Revolution and the independence the American people had gotten from it.

Where would the sentence best fit?

> Click on a square [■] to add the sentence to the passage.

Monarchies ruled most of Europe in 1848. A few old and established families, such as the Austrian Hapsburgs, dominated millions of people. Some nations, most notably England, had already granted their citizens limited rights. This was not true for most European countries though. In these places, the masses had little or no say in how their country was run. But the masses began asking for reforms. They wanted a role in the government as well as constitutions that granted them specific rights and freedoms. **1** These people suffered from abject poverty, which also contributed to the revolutions. **2** During the 1840s, many countries experienced economic troubles and bad harvests, which added to sentiments of unrest among the populace. **3** Countless urban dwellers had no jobs. **4** In the countryside, farmers were near starvation. The time was ripe for a period of upheaval.

20 *Directions:* Select the appropriate sentences from the answer choices and match them to the causes and effects of the revolutions of 1848. TWO of the answer choices will NOT be used. *This question is worth 3 points.*

> Drag your answer choices to the spaces where they belong.
> To remove an answer choice, click on it. To review the passage, click **View Text**.

Answer Choices	THE REVOLUTIONS OF 1848
1 The British people had more rights than other Europeans.	**Cause**
2 Constitutions were written for people in some places.	•
3 Common people endured economic suffering.	•
4 Minorities desired to have more autonomy.	•
5 Napoleon Bonaparte led his troops through Europe.	**Effect**
6 The French underwent a change in their government.	•
7 The lower classes wanted to help run their countries.	•

Space Stations in the 1970s and 1980s

The *Mir* space station in orbit around the Earth

In the 1800s, scientists began proposing space stations that could orbit the Earth. At that time, the technology that existed did not even allow for space travel, so the ideas were unfeasible. In the 1950s, however, the Space Race between the <u>Soviet Union</u> and the United States began. Once manned space travel was achieved, engineers started to develop space stations. The objective was to have a permanent presence in outer space and to use space stations for future trips to the moon, Mars, and other planetary bodies. In the 1970s and 1980s, several space stations went into orbit: the *Salyut* series, *Skylab*, and *Mir*.

The Soviet Union was the first to send both a satellite and a human into space, so it should come as no surprise that the Soviets also orbited the first space station. On April 19, 1971, *Salyut 1*, the world's first space station, was launched. It was a single module that required only one launch to put it into orbit. The Soviets had hoped that *Salyut 1* would remain in orbit perpetually. However, it only stayed in orbit for around six months before it plummeted to the Earth. The Soviets were not deterred by this and launched several more *Salyut* space stations, putting a total of seven into orbit. The last one, *Salyut 7*, managed to remain in orbit from April 1982 to February 1991.

The Soviets used their space stations for several purposes. They wanted to see how long <u>cosmonauts</u> could live in space. They conducted a variety of scientific experiments. They also used some space stations, particularly *Salyut 3* and *Salyut 5*, for military purposes. Many *Salyut* crews spent two or more months in space, proving that long-term stays in space were possible. There were some failures though. A three-member crew that had stayed on *Salyut 1* was killed during reentry. In addition, a couple of space stations were never crewed and subsequently fell to the Earth. Yet overall, the *Salyut* program was a tremendous success.

The Americans also launched their own space station in the 1970s. *Skylab* was sent into low-Earth orbit in May 1973. There were three separate crews that lived and worked there in 1973 and 1974. The purpose of *Skylab* was mainly scientific. Its astronauts performed a wide variety of experiments, including learning how the human body reacted to being in space for a long time. Among them were also doing research on the sun as well as the comet Kohoutek. One advantage of *Skylab* was that it was much larger than the *Salyut* stations. It was more than thirty meters long and 6.7 meters wide, and it weighed a massive 75,000 kilograms. Due to its larger size, astronauts had more living room and space for conducting experiments. After its third crew left, *Skylab* remained uninhabited for years. There were plans to use the space shuttle to boost it into a higher orbit around the Earth. Before that happened though, its orbit degraded, and it fell to the Earth in 1979.

Using the information they had learned from the *Salyut* series, in 1986, the Soviets launched *Mir*, a new space station. It would go on to be a spectacular success. When first launched, *Mir* was a single module. However, it contained several docking ports, so additional modules were launched into space and connected to it. These modules contained equipment for studying the Earth, for conducting astrophysics, and for doing materials-science work. *Mir* was originally designed to last for five years, but it greatly exceeded expectations. It remained in orbit until 2001 and was continually occupied for nearly ten years at one point. More than 100 individuals from a dozen countries, including the United States, spent time on it. One cosmonaut stayed more than fourteen continuous months in space, setting a longevity record at the time.

The space stations operated by the Soviet Union and the United States contributed tremendously to mankind's knowledge of space and living conditions there. This knowledge, combined with an agreement to work together by Russia and the United States, would help lead to the establishment of the *International Space Station*. First launched in 1998, it has remained in service until the present day.

Glossary

Soviet Union: a union of Russia and several other countries that was under communist rule and lasted until 1991
cosmonaut: a Soviet or Russian astronaut

Space Stations in the 1970s and 1980s

In the 1800s, scientists began proposing space stations that could orbit the Earth. At that time, the technology that existed did not even allow for space travel, so the ideas were unfeasible. In the 1950s, however, the Space Race between the <u>Soviet Union</u> and the United States began. Once manned space travel was achieved, engineers started to develop space stations. The objective was to have a permanent presence in outer space and to use space stations for future trips to the moon, Mars, and other planetary bodies. In the 1970s and 1980s, several space stations went into orbit: the *Salyut* series, *Skylab*, and *Mir*.

² → The Soviet Union was the first to send both a satellite and a human into space, so it should come as no surprise that the Soviets also orbited the first space station. On April 19, 1971, *Salyut 1*, the world's first space station, was launched. It was a single module that required only one launch to put it into orbit. The Soviets had hoped that *Salyut 1* would remain in orbit perpetually. However, it only stayed in orbit for around six months before it plummeted to the Earth. The Soviets were not deterred by this and launched several more *Salyut* space stations, putting a total of seven into orbit. The last one, *Salyut 7*, managed to remain in orbit from April 1982 to February 1991.

21 The word "unfeasible" in the passage is closest in meaning to

Ⓐ unclear

Ⓑ unprofitable

Ⓒ undesirable

Ⓓ unworkable

22 Which of the sentences below best expresses the essential information in the highlighted sentence in the passage? *Incorrect* answer choices change the meaning in important ways or leave out essential information.

Ⓐ Unsurprisingly, the Soviet Union launched the first space station just as it sent the first person and satellite into space.

Ⓑ While it failed to send the first satellite or human into space, the Soviet Union was able to launch the world's first space station.

Ⓒ The Soviets managed to send a satellite and humans into space before they put a space station into orbit.

Ⓓ It was not a surprise that launching a space station was more difficult for the Soviet Union than putting a man and a satellite into space.

23 According to paragraph 2, which of the following is true of the *Salyut* space stations?

Ⓐ Some of them were comprised of two or more modules.

Ⓑ All of the ones that were launched were considered successes.

Ⓒ The first one launched remained in orbit for half a year.

Ⓓ They were intended to help send cosmonauts to the moon.

> **Glossary**
> **Soviet Union:** a union of Russia and several other countries that was under communist rule and lasted until 1991

24 In paragraph 3, the author uses "*Salyut 3* and *Salyut 5*" as examples of

Ⓐ space stations whose crews made long-term stays in space

Ⓑ space stations that failed to make orbit around the Earth

Ⓒ space stations whose crews did not return to the Earth alive

Ⓓ space stations that did not have civilian purposes

25 According to paragraph 4, which of the following can be inferred about *Skylab*?

Ⓐ It had been designed to last for more than ten years.

Ⓑ Some of its crew members had long-term stays in space.

Ⓒ A lack of funding caused the Americans to abandon it.

Ⓓ It was considered a failure by most people in the space industry.

26 In paragraph 4, all of the following questions are answered EXCEPT:

Ⓐ How was the large size of *Skylab* beneficial to the astronauts onboard?

Ⓑ What caused *Skylab* to fall out of orbit and return to the Earth?

Ⓒ What kind of research did the astronauts on *Skylab* conduct?

Ⓓ Why did the Americans abandon *Skylab* for a period of several years?

³➡ The Soviets used their space stations for several purposes. They wanted to see how long **cosmonauts** could live in space. They conducted a variety of scientific experiments. They also used some space stations, particularly *Salyut 3* and *Salyut 5*, for military purposes. Many *Salyut* crews spent two or more months in space, proving that long-term stays in space were possible. There were some failures though. A three-member crew that had stayed on *Salyut 1* was killed during reentry. In addition, a couple of space stations were never crewed and subsequently fell to the Earth. Yet overall, the *Salyut* program was a tremendous success.

⁴➡ The Americans also launched their own space station in the 1970s. *Skylab* was sent into low-Earth orbit in May 1973. There were three separate crews that lived and worked there in 1973 and 1974. The purpose of *Skylab* was mainly scientific. Its astronauts performed a wide variety of experiments, including learning how the human body reacted to being in space for a long time. Among them were also doing research on the sun as well as the comet Kohoutek. One advantage of *Skylab* was that it was much larger than the *Salyut* stations. It was more than thirty meters long and 6.7 meters wide, and it weighed a massive 75,000 kilograms. Due to its larger size, astronauts had more living room and space for conducting experiments. After its third crew left, *Skylab* remained uninhabited for years. There were plans to use the space shuttle to boost it into a higher orbit around the Earth. Before that happened though, its orbit degraded, and it fell to the Earth in 1979.

Glossary

cosmonaut: a Soviet or Russian astronaut

27 According to paragraph 5, the Soviets used the docking ports on *Mir* to

Ⓐ connect additional modules that served various purposes

Ⓑ dock several rockets from the Earth at the same time

Ⓒ store fuel so that the height of *Mir*'s orbit could be altered

Ⓓ add telescopes that could be used to survey the galaxy

28 The word "it" in the passage refers to

Ⓐ an agreement

Ⓑ Russia

Ⓒ the United States

Ⓓ the *International Space Station*

5→ Using the information they had learned from the *Salyut* series, in 1986, the Soviets launched *Mir*, a new space station. It would go on to be a spectacular success. When first launched, *Mir* was a single module. However, it contained several docking ports, so additional modules were launched into space and connected to it. These modules contained equipment for studying the Earth, for conducting astrophysics, and for doing materials-science work. *Mir* was originally designed to last for five years, but it greatly exceeded expectations. It remained in orbit until 2001 and was continually occupied for nearly ten years at one point. More than 100 individuals from a dozen countries, including the United States, spent time on it. One cosmonaut stayed more than fourteen continuous months in space, setting a longevity record at the time.

The space stations operated by the Soviet Union and the United States contributed tremendously to mankind's knowledge of space and living conditions there. This knowledge, combined with an agreement to work together by Russia and the United States, would help lead to the establishment of the *International Space Station*. First launched in 1998, it has remained in service until the present day.

29 Look at the four squares [■] that indicate where the following sentence could be added to the passage.

In comparison, the Soviet modules were only around 18,000 kilograms in weight.

Where would the sentence best fit?

Click on a square [■] to add the sentence to the passage.

The Americans also launched their own space station in the 1970s. *Skylab* was sent into low-Earth orbit in May 1973. There were three separate crews that lived and worked there in 1973 and 1974. The purpose of *Skylab* was mainly scientific. Its astronauts performed a wide variety of experiments, including learning how the human body reacted to being in space for a long time. Among them were also doing research on the sun as well as the comet Kohoutek. One advantage of *Skylab* was that it was much larger than the *Salyut* stations. **1** It was more than thirty meters long and 6.7 meters wide, and it weighed a massive 75,000 kilograms. **2** Due to its larger size, astronauts had more living room and space for conducting experiments. **3** After its third crew left, *Skylab* remained uninhabited for years. **4** There were plans to use the space shuttle to boost it into a higher orbit around the Earth. Before that happened though, its orbit degraded, and it fell to the Earth in 1979.

30 ***Directions:*** An introductory sentence for a brief summary of the passage is provided below. Complete the summary by selecting the THREE answer choices that express the most important ideas of the passage. Some sentences do not belong because they express ideas that are not presented in the passage or are minor ideas in the passage. ***This question is worth 2 points***.

> Drag your answer choices to the spaces where they belong.
> To remove an answer choice, click on it. To review the passage, click **View Text**.

In the 1970s and the 1980s, both the Soviet Union and the United States successfully put space stations into orbit.

-
-
-

Answer Choices

1. *Skylab* fell to the Earth in 1979 after it had been without any crew members for a period of several years.

2. *Mir* was comprised of several modules for doing various experiments, and it remained in space for fifteen years.

3. The *International Space Station* was launched in 1998 and is still orbiting the Earth at the present time.

4. The Soviets successfully put seven *Salyut* space stations into orbit, and they conducted a number of different missions.

5. Some of the *Salyut* space stations never made it into orbit, and there were also some deaths involved in the program.

6. The American *Skylab* had several crews that did many experiments, including on effects of long-term stays in space.

The Effects of an Ice Age

An ice age happens when temperatures become lower and large sheets of ice advance from northern polar regions and mountain ranges. The Earth has experienced many ice ages. The most recent one began 100,000 years ago and did not end until about 10,000 years ago. The ice reached its maximum **extent** approximately 18,000 to 20,000 years ago. When this ice age took place, two major things occurred that have impacted the Earth's history and geography. First, land bridges appeared between large land formations. These allowed people to travel to places they could not access prior to the ice age. Second, the land itself was carved up by moving sheets of ice, which altered the surface of the planet.

During an ice age, large amounts of seawater freeze. This causes ocean levels to drop. In the last ice age, the ocean level was about 120 meters lower than it is today. This exposed large areas of shallow coastal waters. It also created land bridges between landmasses normally divided by water. The seafloor was exposed in certain places, so people could walk across it to other lands. Research suggests that two such places where this occurred were between New Guinea and Australia and between Asia and North America. Prior to the last ice age, both Australia and the Americas were unpopulated. Then, around 40,000 years ago, people began moving to Australia. There were only two ways to get there: by boat or by crossing a land bridge. The latter seems more likely. The distance between New Guinea and Australia is considerable, and there is little evidence of any sea voyages between the two lands. However, the debate on this issue is ongoing.

Archaeologists accept that people walked from Asia to the Americas. There is no archaeological evidence for people living in the Americas until about 12,000 to 13,000 years ago. The most logical explanation is that they came across a land bridge. Some have suggested that people may have gone there by sea, but there is a lack of evidence for this. The people who left Asia were hunter–gatherers that were following herds of animals. They had no knowledge of ships or sailing. In all likelihood, they found a valley through the melting fields of ice. After crossing the Bering Strait to go from the land in modern-day Russia to Alaska, they emerged in a pristine land filled with animals that had no fear of humans. Within a thousand years, descendants of these first arrivals had migrated to the southern tip of South America. By the time Europeans arrived 12,000 years later, people were living across the Americas and had established their own civilizations.

Ice ages have also made dramatic impacts on the landscape. The massive sheets of ice moving southward—and, later, northward as they melted—cut and carved the land. The most obvious changes were the thousands of lakes that currently dot the Northern Hemisphere. The ice sheets gouged huge holes, which were subsequently filled by water when the sheets melted and retreated. Another sign of ice sheet movement is the long, low ridges called terminal moraines. Their presence indicates where ice sheets stopped. These ridges were formed as ice sheets pushed earth forward while they moved. Rounded hills called drumlins are another sign of ice sheet movement. These hills were probably formed when earth was lodged against some rocks that the ice could not **dislodge**. Some drumlins are tiny while others may be more than sixty meters high and several kilometers long. Large boulders pushed from their original locations to far-off lands are another result of ice ages. For example, rocks that formed in parts of Scandinavia are today found in England, Ireland, Germany, and Poland.

Past ice ages helped shape the modern world. By creating land bridges, they permitted humans to migrate from their homelands to entirely new places. This has had a major impact on lands that were formerly empty of humans. Perhaps history might have been quite different had the Europeans found Australia and the Americas empty when they discovered them. Even so, the ice sheets have definitely changed the face of the world. Lakes, hills, ridges, and large rocks in areas that ice sheets once covered are the lasting legacy they left.

Glossary
extent: coverage; an amount
dislodge: to move; to dislocate

31 According to paragraph 1, which of the following is true of the last ice age?

    (A) It lasted for around twenty thousand years.

    (B) It connected some landmasses to one another.

    (C) It spread ice as far south as the equator.

    (D) It prevented the spread of human civilization.

32 According to paragraph 2, during an ice age, the water level becomes lower because

    (A) land bridges rise above the water

    (B) the height of the land increases

    (C) very much ocean water freezes

    (D) there are more glaciers formed

33 In paragraph 2, which of the following can be inferred about the first humans on Australia?

    (A) They likely sailed there on crude ships.

    (B) They arrived there before Europe was discovered.

    (C) Remains of their civilization have been unearthed.

    (D) Their manner of arrival is not known for sure.

The Effects of an Ice Age

1 → An ice age happens when temperatures become lower and large sheets of ice advance from northern polar regions and mountain ranges. The Earth has experienced many ice ages. The most recent one began 100,000 years ago and did not end until about 10,000 years ago. The ice reached its maximum <u>extent</u> approximately 18,000 to 20,000 years ago. When this ice age took place, two major things occurred that have impacted the Earth's history and geography. First, land bridges appeared between large land formations. These allowed people to travel to places they could not access prior to the ice age. Second, the land itself was carved up by moving sheets of ice, which altered the surface of the planet.

2 → During an ice age, large amounts of seawater freeze. This causes ocean levels to drop. In the last ice age, the ocean level was about 120 meters lower than it is today. This exposed large areas of shallow coastal waters. It also created land bridges between landmasses normally divided by water. The seafloor was exposed in certain places, so people could walk across it to other lands. Research suggests that two such places where this occurred were between New Guinea and Australia and between Asia and North America. Prior to the last ice age, both Australia and the Americas were unpopulated. Then, around 40,000 years ago, people began moving to Australia. There were only two ways to get there: by boat or by crossing a land bridge. The latter seems more likely. The distance between New Guinea and Australia is considerable, and there is little evidence of any sea voyages between the two lands. However, the debate on this issue is ongoing.

Glossary

extent: coverage; an amount

34 The word "pristine" in the passage is closest in meaning to

Ⓐ beautiful

Ⓑ arable

Ⓒ unique

Ⓓ untouched

Archaeologists accept that people walked from Asia to the Americas. There is no archaeological evidence for people living in the Americas until about 12,000 to 13,000 years ago. The most logical explanation is that they came across a land bridge. Some have suggested that people may have gone there by sea, but there is a lack of evidence for this. The people who left Asia were hunter–gatherers that were following herds of animals. They had no knowledge of ships or sailing. In all likelihood, they found a valley through the melting fields of ice. After crossing the Bering Strait to go from the land in modern-day Russia to Alaska, they emerged in a pristine land filled with animals that had no fear of humans. Within a thousand years, descendants of these first arrivals had migrated to the southern tip of South America. By the time Europeans arrived 12,000 years later, people were living across the Americas and had established their own civilizations.

35 In paragraph 4, why does the author mention "terminal moraines"?

    Ⓐ To contrast their sizes with those of drumlins

    Ⓑ To describe where they can be found

    Ⓒ To explain what their significance is

    Ⓓ To name one of the world's largest ones

36 According to paragraph 4, which of the following is true of how ice ages have an impact on the landscape?

    Ⓐ They create small bodies of water.

    Ⓑ They cover the oceans with ice.

    Ⓒ They gouge out areas to make seas.

    Ⓓ They transform large boulders into soil.

37 According to paragraph 4, which of the following is NOT true of drumlins?

    Ⓐ They are found mostly in Scandinavia.

    Ⓑ They were formed by ice sheets.

    Ⓒ They can vary in size.

    Ⓓ They resemble hills in appearance.

38 The word "they" in the passage refers to

    Ⓐ Australia and the Americas

    Ⓑ lakes, hills, ridges, and large rocks

    Ⓒ areas

    Ⓓ ice sheets

⁴→ Ice ages have also made dramatic impacts on the landscape. The massive sheets of ice moving southward—and, later, northward as they melted—cut and carved the land. The most obvious changes were the thousands of lakes that currently dot the Northern Hemisphere. The ice sheets gouged huge holes, which were subsequently filled by water when the sheets melted and retreated. Another sign of ice sheet movement is the long, low ridges called terminal moraines. Their presence indicates where ice sheets stopped. These ridges were formed as ice sheets pushed earth forward while they moved. Rounded hills called drumlins are another sign of ice sheet movement. These hills were probably formed when earth was lodged against some rocks that the ice could not **dislodge**. Some drumlins are tiny while others may be more than sixty meters high and several kilometers long. Large boulders pushed from their original locations to far-off lands are another result of ice ages. For example, rocks that formed in parts of Scandinavia are today found in England, Ireland, Germany, and Poland.

Past ice ages helped shape the modern world. By creating land bridges, they permitted humans to migrate from their homelands to entirely new places. This has had a major impact on lands that were formerly empty of humans. Perhaps history might have been quite different had the Europeans found Australia and the Americas empty when they discovered them. Even so, the ice sheets have definitely changed the face of the world. Lakes, hills, ridges, and large rocks in areas that ice sheets once covered are the lasting legacy they left.

Glossary

dislodge: to move; to dislocate

39 Look at the four squares [■] that indicate where the following sentence could be added to the passage.

They had also divided into numerous tribes that were independent of one another.

Where would the sentence best fit?

Click on a square [■] to add the sentence to the passage.

Archaeologists accept that people walked from Asia to the Americas. There is no archaeological evidence for people living in the Americas until about 12,000 to 13,000 years ago. The most logical explanation is that they came across a land bridge. Some have suggested that people may have gone there by sea, but there is a lack of evidence for this. The people who left Asia were hunter–gatherers that were following herds of animals. They had no knowledge of ships or sailing. In all likelihood, they found a valley through the melting fields of ice. After crossing the Bering Strait to go from the land in modern-day Russia to Alaska, they emerged in a pristine land filled with animals that had no fear of humans. Within a thousand years, descendants of these first arrivals had migrated to the southern tip of South America. By the time Europeans arrived 12,000 years later, people were living across the Americas and had established their own civilizations.

40 *Directions:* An introductory sentence for a brief summary of the passage is provided below. Complete the summary by selecting the THREE answer choices that express the most important ideas of the passage. Some sentences do not belong because they express ideas that are not presented in the passage or are minor ideas in the passage. *This question is worth 2 points.*

> Drag your answer choices to the spaces where they belong.
> To remove an answer choice, click on it. To review the passage, click **View Text**.

The last major ice age both created land bridges between some landmasses and also changed the landscape of the planet.

-
-
-

Answer Choices

1. Drumlins and terminal moraines are two ways in which huge ice sheets can alter the way the Earth looks.

2. Australia likely would have been unpopulated if not for a land bridge connecting it with New Guinea during an ice age.

3. Ice ages can cause the levels of the oceans to decrease and also spread ice to many places on the planet.

4. The last ice age that had a big effect on the Earth ended approximately 10,000 years in the past.

5. It took humans around one thousand years to travel from the top of North America to the bottom of South America.

6. A land bridge that an ice age opened between Asia and America enabled people to populate the Americas.

CONTINUE

Reading Section Directions

This section measures your ability to understand academic passages in English. You will have **54 minutes** to read and answer questions about **3 passages**. A clock at the top of the screen will show you how much time is remaining.

Most questions are worth 1 point but the last question for each passage is worth more than 1 point. The directions for the last question indicate how many points you may receive.

Some passages include a word or phrase that is **underlined** in blue. Click on the word or phrase to see a definition or an explanation.

When you want to move to the next question, click on **Next**. You may skip questions and go back to them later. If you want to return to previous questions, click on **Back**. You can click on **Review** at any time, and the review screen will show you which questions you have answered and which you have not answered. From this review screen, you may go directly to any question you have already seen in the Reading section.

Click on **Continue** to go on.

The Development of Northern European Agriculture

Agriculture in Northern Europe arrived there from Southern Europe approximately 5,000 years ago and then slowly developed over the course of numerous centuries. As people migrated northward, they brought their farming methods along with them. For thousands of years, small-scale **subsistence farming** was the norm as farmers raised a variety of crops. Later, the Romans introduced large-scale farming on their extensive estates, but the dissolution of the Roman Empire in the fifth century resulted in a return to subsistence farming. It was not until the rise of feudal kingdoms centuries later that more advances were made in Northern European agriculture.

Under **feudalism**, most European farmers—often referred to as serfs by historians—were bound to the land and owed allegiance to their feudal lord. The main type of farm was the manor, which was where the lord and his family lived. As for the serfs, they dwelled in a central village, which typically had a church and a priest. The surrounding land, which may have comprised thousands of acres, was filled with fields planted with crops. Feudal manors utilized the open-field system without hedges or fences between plots. Serfs planted crops in long rows called furrows, which had small ridges between them. Typical crops were wheat, barley, oats, rye, and legumes, which included beans, peas, and lentils. Each season, some of the land was left fallow to rebuild the nutrient levels in it.

The serfs worked the lord's land and usually had individual plots of their own. They often had narrows strips of land in different locations, which meant that part of their day was wasted moving from strip to strip. Most families also had their own small vegetable gardens. Everything they grew was taxed by the lord. A percentage—a tenth of all produce, called a tithe—also went to the church. Most animals were held in common and foraged on communal grounds. There were more teams of oxen than horses, and serfs used both to plow the heavy soil of Northern Europe. Chickens, pigs, cows, and sheep were typically raised by serfs and provided milk, meat, and wool.

This state of affairs continued in Northern Europe with little change for hundreds of years. Crop yields were perhaps five times less than in modern times, and famine was a constant danger. It was very slowly that changes came. After 1000 A.D., the introduction of improvements in plows made it easier to turn over the soil, which reduced the amount of labor during the planting season. Two other improvements were the horse collar and the horseshoe. Horses were more expensive than oxen and could do less work, but horses were faster than slow-moving oxen. With the advent of the horse collar, the horse's neck and shoulders were better protected from strain, so it could pull a heavy plow through thick soil. The use of metal shoes on both oxen and horses protected their hoofs from wear and tear and made them more efficient. At first, they were bronze while later ones were iron. While it is uncertain exactly when they were invented, horse collars and animal shoes became common after 1000 A.D.

Sometime during the late feudal period, farmers introduced the three-crop system—a form of crop rotation—which played an important part in increasing crop yields. Northern Europe's somewhat mild climate meant that crops could be planted both in fall and spring. In one area each autumn, farmers planted winter wheat and rye, and in spring, oats and barley were planted in the same place. In a second area, they planted beans, lentils, or peas. These were planted in spring and harvested in late summer. A third section was left fallow to allow the land to recover some of its nutrient levels. Legumes such as beans and peas also played a role by adding nitrogen to the soil. Each season, the crops planted were changed, or rotated, between different fields, so each field had the opportunity to recover from the previous plantings. Another advantage of planting crops at different times of the year was that it was a hedge against famine. If one crop failed, the serfs did not have to wait an entire year to plant a new one.

Glossary

subsistence farming: the act of farming enough to provide food for one's family with almost nothing left over to sell

feudalism: the political system in medieval Europe based on the holding of fiefs and obligations between lords and vassals

The Development of Northern European Agriculture

1→ Agriculture in Northern Europe arrived there from Southern Europe approximately 5,000 years ago and then slowly developed over the course of numerous centuries. As people migrated northward, they brought their farming methods along with them. For thousands of years, small-scale **subsistence farming** was the norm as farmers raised a variety of crops. Later, the Romans introduced large-scale farming on their extensive estates, but the dissolution of the Roman Empire in the fifth century resulted in a return to subsistence farming. It was not until the rise of feudal kingdoms centuries later that more advances were made in Northern European agriculture.

2→ Under **feudalism**, most European farmers— often referred to as serfs by historians—were bound to the land and owed allegiance to their feudal lord. The main type of farm was the manor, which was where the lord and his family lived. As for the serfs, they dwelled in a central village, which typically had a church and a priest. The surrounding land, which may have comprised thousands of acres, was filled with fields planted with crops. Feudal manors utilized the open-field system without hedges or fences between plots. Serfs planted crops in long rows called furrows, which had small ridges between them. Typical crops were wheat, barley, oats, rye, and legumes, which included beans, peas, and lentils. Each season, some of the land was left fallow to rebuild the nutrient levels in it.

Glossary

subsistence farming: the act of farming enough to provide food for one's family with almost nothing left over to sell

feudalism: the political system in medieval Europe based on the holding of fiefs and obligations between lords and vassals

---

1 Which of the sentences below best expresses the essential information in the highlighted sentence in the passage? *Incorrect* answer choices change the meaning in important ways or leave out essential information.

- Ⓐ The Northern Europeans introduced farming to Southern Europe more than 5,000 years in the past.

- Ⓑ It took more than 5,000 years for agriculture to develop in both Northern and Southern Europe.

- Ⓒ Agriculture progressed slowly over time in Northern Europe after arriving 5,000 years ago from Southern Europe.

- Ⓓ Because agriculture developed in Southern Europe 5,000 years ago, the Northern Europeans learned to farm in just a few centuries.

2 The author discusses "the Romans" in paragraph 1 in order to

- Ⓐ stress that their farming methods were advanced for the time

- Ⓑ claim that they developed farming before Northern Europeans did

- Ⓒ question the importance of farming during the Roman Empire

- Ⓓ focus on how they influenced farming in parts of Europe

3 Select the TWO answer choices from paragraphs 2 and 3 that identify how serfs farmed under feudalism. *To receive credit, you must select TWO answers.*

- Ⓐ They lived in manors and farmed the land immediately around their homes.

- Ⓑ They planted crops such as wheat and barley in long rows.

- Ⓒ They farmed their own crops on large plots of land.

- Ⓓ They shared animals with others and raised chickens and cows for food.

4 The word "foraged" in the passage is closest in meaning to

   Ⓐ grazed

   Ⓑ slept

   Ⓒ hunted

   Ⓓ worked

5 In paragraph 3, the author's description of serfs mentions all of the following EXCEPT:

   Ⓐ An institute that they had to pay taxes to

   Ⓑ The reasons that they raised certain animals

   Ⓒ The shape and the locations of their plots of land

   Ⓓ The amount of crops they harvested yearly

6 The word "they" in the passage refers to

   Ⓐ metal shoes

   Ⓑ both oxen and horses

   Ⓒ their hooves

   Ⓓ wear and tear

7 In paragraph 4, the author implies that crops

   Ⓐ started growing better after the inventing of the horse collar and horseshoes

   Ⓑ could not grow well in the thick soil in Northern Europe

   Ⓒ often produced poor harvests that resulted in people starving

   Ⓓ were easily killed by cold weather during the spring and fall months

³➜ The serfs worked the lord's land and usually had individual plots of their own. They often had narrows strips of land in different locations, which meant that part of their day was wasted moving from strip to strip. Most families also had their own small vegetable gardens. Everything they grew was taxed by the lord. A percentage—a tenth of all produce, called a tithe—also went to the church. Most animals were held in common and foraged on communal grounds. There were more teams of oxen than horses, and serfs used both to plow the heavy soil of Northern Europe. Chickens, pigs, cows, and sheep were typically raised by serfs and provided milk, meat, and wool.

⁴➜ This state of affairs continued in Northern Europe with little change for hundreds of years. Crop yields were perhaps five times less than in modern times, and famine was a constant danger. It was very slowly that changes came. After 1000 A.D., the introduction of improvements in plows made it easier to turn over the soil, which reduced the amount of labor during the planting season. Two other improvements were the horse collar and the horseshoe. Horses were more expensive than oxen and could do less work, but horses were faster than slow-moving oxen. With the advent of the horse collar, the horse's neck and shoulders were better protected from strain, so it could pull a heavy plow through thick soil. The use of metal shoes on both oxen and horses protected their hoofs from wear and tear and made them more efficient. At first, they were bronze while later ones were iron. While it is uncertain exactly when they were invented, horse collars and animal shoes became common after 1000 A.D.

8 According to paragraph 5, the three-crop system was used because

    Ⓐ there were only three main crops the Europeans grew

    Ⓑ it enabled the soil to avoid losing nutrients

    Ⓒ this was the only method that let Europeans plant crops twice a year

    Ⓓ farmers lacked the ability to plant crops in all their fields

9 Look at the four squares [■] that indicate where the following sentence could be added to the passage.

These enabled a valuable nutrient to enter the soil, where it could be used by other crops later.

Where would the sentence best fit?

> Click on a square [■] to add the sentence to the passage.

---

⁵➡ Sometime during the late feudal period, farmers introduced the three-crop system—a form of crop rotation—which played an important part in increasing crop yields. Northern Europe's somewhat mild climate meant that crops could be planted both in fall and spring. In one area each autumn, farmers planted winter wheat and rye, and in spring, oats and barley were planted in the same place. In a second area, they planted beans, lentils, or peas. These were planted in spring and harvested in late summer. A third section was left fallow to allow the land to recover some of its nutrient levels. Legumes such as beans and peas also played a role by adding nitrogen to the soil. **1** Each season, the crops planted were changed, or rotated, between different fields, so each field had the opportunity to recover from the previous plantings. **2** Another advantage of planting crops at different times of the year was that it was a hedge against famine. **3** If one crop failed, the serfs did not have to wait an entire year to plant a new one. **4**

10 *Directions:* An introductory sentence for a brief summary of the passage is provided below. Complete the summary by selecting the THREE answer choices that express the most important ideas of the passage. Some sentences do not belong because they express ideas that are not presented in the passage or are minor ideas in the passage. *This question is worth 2 points.*

> Drag your answer choices to the spaces where they belong.
> To remove an answer choice, click on it. To review the passage, click **View Text**.

Northern Europeans used a number of different farming methods during feudal times.

-
-
-

Answer Choices

1. The three-crop system was used to improve crop yields by ensuring that farmers' fields had enough nutrients.

2. Both lords and churches taxed serfs so much that they were unable to profit from the crops they harvested.

3. Virtually all of the farmers in Northern Europe were subsistence farmers who only grew enough food for their families.

4. The development of the horse collar and the horseshoe made it easier to use horses to plow fields in Northern Europe.

5. Serfs planted a wide variety of crops for themselves and their lords and also raised several kinds of livestock.

6. The Romans introduced a large number of farming innovations that were lost over time after the Roman Empire fell.

Animal Hunting Methods

A crocodile attacking its prey

Animals can be divided into predators and prey. Predators are the carnivorous hunters of the animal kingdom. Some well-known predators are lions, wolves, tigers, crocodiles, eagles, and sharks. Predators employ a wide variety of methods to find, track, and kill their prey. Their sharp senses enable them to locate prey to hunt. Their speed gives them an additional advantage when they are pursuing fleeing animals. Stealth, the art of moving silently, is a great advantage for some predators, particularly those that prefer to wait, hide, and then ambush their prey when it comes near. The bodies of predators have also evolved to transform them into efficient killing machines. Finally, many work together in groups to ensure success while hunting.

Most predators have developed **acute** senses. For instance, wolves and other canines have extremely good senses of smell. Sharks can detect a single drop of blood in a vast area of the ocean. Eagles and hawks have exceptional eyesight. This enables them to detect small animals while flying at great heights. The eyes of most predators are in the front of each one's head. This gives them binocular vision and depth perception. They can see animals directly in front of them and from far away, and predators can judge the distance to these animals. These senses all contribute to a predator's ability to find prey and then to track it.

Stealth and speed are two other major advantages for predators. Most members of the cat family can walk softly and quietly. Birds of prey, such as hawks and eagles, can swoop down silently on unsuspecting victims. Sharks often strike prey animals from below. This lets them hit their target out of its line of sight. Sharks are also fast swimmers, which gives them an additional advantage. The cheetah is the world's fastest land animal, so it can easily run down fleeing prey. Other predators have no need for speed but instead rely on stealth. Crocodiles and alligators use this method. They lie in shallow water with just the tips of their noses and their eyes above water. When an animal comes to drink, it cannot see the waiting hunter. The crocodile or alligator then strikes swiftly and drags the unsuspecting animal into the water, where it holds the animal underwater to drown it before consuming it.

Crocodiles and alligators have powerful jaws, which permit them to hunt this way. Strong muscles and jaws and sharp teeth and claws are common to predators. These weapons enable them to overcome their prey when running it down. Sometimes, however, a prey animal is so swift, strong, or big that it requires more than one predator to hunt it. For instance, many African **game animals** can run swiftly. The same is true of numerous small forest animals, including rabbits, squirrels, and mice. To counter this, lions and wolves, among others, hunt in packs to ensure success. The more predators there are attacking, the greater their chance of success. Afterward, the hunters share the kill. Lions have even been known to attack baby elephants. In a display of teamwork, some lions hold the young animals down while others kill it. Similarly, some species of sharks swim in schools and then attack together. Once blood is drawn, the sharks go into a feeding frenzy and attack and eat whatever they can.

Prey animals are not helpless victims without any defenses of their own. Many set guards to warn of approaching predators. Once a predator is sighted, the animals all scatter or find a hiding place such as an underground lair. Most prey animals also have enhanced senses, allowing them to notice approaching predators more quickly. In addition, many prey animals have their eyes on the sides of their heads, not in front of them. This gives the animals a greater ability to see predators trying to sneak up on them. Some species of herd animals, including water buffaloes, place their babies in the center of a moving herd. This offers their young some measure of protection from predators. However, despite these defenses, some prey animals eventually fall victim to predators. Nature gives prey animals the ability to avoid death, but it gives predators the ability to find, track, and run them down as well.

Glossary
acute: sharp; keen
game animal: an animal that is often hunted by others

11 The word "carnivorous" in the passage is closest in meaning to

Ⓐ meat-eating

Ⓑ ferocious

Ⓒ deadly

Ⓓ stealthy

12 According to paragraph 1, which of the following is true of predators?

Ⓐ They have various skills that let them succeed at hunting.

Ⓑ They need to hunt together in order to be successful.

Ⓒ They sometimes hunt other predators to eat them.

Ⓓ They are all able to outrun the prey they are chasing.

13 In paragraph 2, why does the author mention "binocular vision"?

Ⓐ To compare its usefulness with depth perception

Ⓑ To note that sharks are able to use it very effectively

Ⓒ To explain how it helps some predators hunt better

Ⓓ To list some animals that possess this characteristic

Animal Hunting Methods

¹→ Animals can be divided into predators and prey. Predators are the carnivorous hunters of the animal kingdom. Some well-known predators are lions, wolves, tigers, crocodiles, eagles, and sharks. Predators employ a wide variety of methods to find, track, and kill their prey. Their sharp senses enable them to locate prey to hunt. Their speed gives them an additional advantage when they are pursuing fleeing animals. Stealth, the art of moving silently, is a great advantage for some predators, particularly those that prefer to wait, hide, and then ambush their prey when it comes near. The bodies of predators have also evolved to transform them into efficient killing machines. Finally, many work together in groups to ensure success while hunting.

²→ Most predators have developed **acute** senses. For instance, wolves and other canines have extremely good senses of smell. Sharks can detect a single drop of blood in a vast area of the ocean. Eagles and hawks have exceptional eyesight. This enables them to detect small animals while flying at great heights. The eyes of most predators are in the front of each one's head. This gives them binocular vision and depth perception. They can see animals directly in front of them and from far away, and predators can judge the distance to these animals. These senses all contribute to a predator's ability to find prey and then to track it.

Glossary
acute: sharp; keen

14 Which of the sentences below best expresses the essential information in the highlighted sentence in the passage? *Incorrect* answer choices change the meaning in important ways or leave out essential information.

(A) The animal then grabs the alligator or crocodile, drowns it, and eats it.

(B) Some animals are unaware that they are being drowned by the predator.

(C) If it holds its prey underwater long enough, then the animal will eventually succumb and die.

(D) The predator tends to sneak up, grab a victim, and then drown it prior to eating it.

15 In paragraph 4, the author's description of animals' weapons mentions all of the following EXCEPT:

(A) Their teeth

(B) Their claws

(C) Their tusks

(D) Their jaws

16 Which of the following can be inferred from paragraph 4 about lions?

(A) They prefer hunting very large animals.

(B) They traditionally hunt by themselves.

(C) They will not attack a full-grown elephant.

(D) They will take hours to stalk and hunt their prey.

Stealth and speed are two other major advantages for predators. Most members of the cat family can walk softly and quietly. Birds of prey, such as hawks and eagles, can swoop down silently on unsuspecting victims. Sharks often strike prey animals from below. This lets them hit their target out of its line of sight. Sharks are also fast swimmers, which gives them an additional advantage. The cheetah is the world's fastest land animal, so it can easily run down fleeing prey. Other predators have no need for speed but instead rely on stealth. Crocodiles and alligators use this method. They lie in shallow water with just the tips of their noses and their eyes above water. When an animal comes to drink, it cannot see the waiting hunter. The crocodile or alligator then strikes swiftly and drags the unsuspecting animal into the water, where it holds the animal underwater to drown it before consuming it.

⁴→ Crocodiles and alligators have powerful jaws, which permit them to hunt this way. Strong muscles and jaws and sharp teeth and claws are common to predators. These weapons enable them to overcome their prey when running it down. Sometimes, however, a prey animal is so swift, strong, or big that it requires more than one predator to hunt it. For instance, many African **game animals** can run swiftly. The same is true of numerous small forest animals, including rabbits, squirrels, and mice. To counter this, lions and wolves, among others, hunt in packs to ensure success. The more predators there are attacking, the greater their chance of success. Afterward, the hunters share the kill. Lions have even been known to attack baby elephants. In a display of teamwork, some lions hold the young animals down while others kill it. Similarly, some species of sharks swim in schools and then attack together. Once blood is drawn, the sharks go into a feeding frenzy and attack and eat whatever they can.

Glossary

game animal: an animal that is often hunted by others

17 The word "enhanced" in the passage is closest in meaning to

Ⓐ muted

Ⓑ extra

Ⓒ heightened

Ⓓ advanced

18 According to paragraph 5, which of the following is true of prey animals?

Ⓐ They are completely defenseless against predators.

Ⓑ They try to fight some smaller predators.

Ⓒ They may use herds as defense methods.

Ⓓ They have claws of their own to fight with.

⁵→ Prey animals are not helpless victims without any defenses of their own. Many set guards to warn of approaching predators. Once a predator is sighted, the animals all scatter or find a hiding place such as an underground lair. Most prey animals also have enhanced senses, allowing them to notice approaching predators more quickly. In addition, many prey animals have their eyes on the sides of their heads, not in front of them. This gives the animals a greater ability to see predators trying to sneak up on them. Some species of herd animals, including water buffaloes, place their babies in the center of a moving herd. This offers their young some measure of protection from predators. However, despite these defenses, some prey animals eventually fall victim to predators. Nature gives prey animals the ability to avoid death, but it gives predators the ability to find, track, and run them down as well.

19 Look at the four squares [■] that indicate where the following sentence could be added to the passage.

Fish fleeing them are simply not able to get away and wind up getting devoured.

Where would the sentence best fit?

> Click on a square [■] to add the sentence to the passage.

Stealth and speed are two other major advantages for predators. Most members of the cat family can walk softly and quietly. Birds of prey, such as hawks and eagles, can swoop down silently on unsuspecting victims. **1** Sharks often strike prey animals from below. **2** This lets them hit their target out of its line of sight. **3** Sharks are also fast swimmers, which gives them an additional advantage. **4** The cheetah is the world's fastest land animal, so it can easily run down fleeing prey. Other predators have no need for speed but instead rely on stealth. Crocodiles and alligators use this method. They lie in shallow water with just the tips of their noses and their eyes above water. When an animal comes to drink, it cannot see the waiting hunter. The crocodile or alligator then strikes swiftly and drags the unsuspecting animal into the water, where it holds the animal underwater to drown it before consuming it.

20 *Directions:* Select the appropriate sentences from the answer choices and match them to the type of hunting method to which they relate. TWO of the answer choices will NOT be used. *This question is worth 4 points.*

Drag your answer choices to the spaces where they belong.
To remove an answer choice, click on it. To review the passage, click **View Text**.

Answer Choices	**HUNTING METHOD**
1 Eagles have exceptional vision to locate animals with.	**Senses**
	•
2 Cheetahs can run down the animals that are fleeing them.	•
	•
3 Sharks are able to swim very fast in the water.	
4 Some animals escape to underground dens when under attack.	**Stealth**
	•
5 Lions sometimes hunt in groups to attack baby elephants.	•
	Speed
6 Hawks and eagles swoop down on their victims.	•
	•
7 Sharks can detect small amounts of blood in the water.	
8 Alligators hide in the water before attacking animals.	
9 Some predators can make use of depth perception.	

The Aztecs

When Christopher Columbus discovered the Americas in 1492, there were three large empires in Central and South America. They were the Aztec, Maya, and Inca empires. Among the three, the Aztecs were the most powerful. They ruled the area in modern-day central Mexico. The Aztecs relied upon religion and warfare to maintain rule in the land. Ultimately, however, they were crushed by Spanish invaders, who ended the Aztecs' rule.

The Aztec Empire was based on a coalition of three tribes living in the Valley of Mexico. This central valley—where Mexico City sits today—was comprised of lakes and islands. One tribe, the Mexica, immigrated to the valley from the north during the 1300s. Later, in 1427, the Mexica people joined two other tribes to create the Aztec Alliance, which soon became the Aztec Empire. In the valley, the Aztecs constructed a city on an island in a large lake called Lake Texcoco. They named their city Tenochtitlan. The Aztecs were mainly farmers, yet there were kings, other nobles, priests, and warriors at the top of the hierarchy. Leadership roles were passed down according to heredity. The Aztecs even had their own written language. It was made up of pictograms, which could be placed together to form sentences.

While the Aztecs had some measure of civilization, they were warriors at heart. They spread and enforced their control of their territory by warfare. Many tribes living in the Aztec's vicinity were organized in what could be considered city-states. There was a central location with temples and the homes of the ruling class, and it was surrounded by farmland. The Aztecs conquered many of these city-states. They were usually smaller and had fewer warriors who were not as skilled in battle as the Aztecs. That made them easy to defeat. Once a city-state had lost, it often became allied with the Aztecs. In some cases, the Aztecs left soldiers behind to ensure the city-state's loyalty. The garrisoning of soldiers was not, however, always necessary since most city-states were too weak to rebel after their armies had been defeated by the Aztecs.

The Aztecs tried to capture as many enemy soldiers as possible during battle. These captives were used as human sacrifices. The Aztecs believed certain gods controlled human fate. These gods could only be appeased by human sacrifices. To guarantee a steady supply of captives, the Aztecs constantly waged war. Many wars were not for conquest but for the capturing of enemies. The Aztecs referred to these events as flower wars. Some historians believe flower wars also enabled the Aztecs to train their warriors in combat and to allow members of the lower classes to advance to higher ones by showing bravery in battle.

While the Aztecs built a vast, powerful empire, it was not long lived as far as empires are concerned. The Aztecs themselves were conquered in the early 1500s. This was barely a century after their own empire had been founded. Their conquerors were the Spanish, who were under the command of conquistador Hernan Cortez. Cortez arrived in Aztec territory in 1519, where he was first greeted warmly. Montezuma, the Aztec ruler, sent him gifts of gold. Yet Cortez was not so easily bought off and was determined to conquer the land. After overcoming some initial challenges, Cortez and his men began making headway. They were joined by many tribes, whose people despised their Aztec overlords. The Spanish captured Montezuma early in the war. He pleaded with his people to make peace with the Spanish. They refused and replaced Montezuma with his brother.

After two years of fighting, Cortez defeated the Aztecs in 1521. Despite the small size of his army, he and his men had several advantages which enabled them to win. These included having horses, gunpowder weapons, and metal weapons and armor. The Aztecs had none of these. After their defeat to Cortez, many Aztecs soon lost their lives. The Spanish had unknowingly brought diseases with them. Outbreaks of smallpox and typhus killed off most of the people. The Aztecs and other tribes lacked natural defenses to these illnesses. By the start of the 1600s, most Aztecs had died from disease. The remainder was absorbed by the increasing number of Spaniards. Soon, the Aztecs were no more.

Glossary

hierarchy: a chain of command; an order of people according to their rank or importance

enforce: to make someone follow orders or the law

The Aztecs

[1]→ When Christopher Columbus discovered the Americas in 1492, there were three large empires in Central and South America. They were the Aztec, Maya, and Inca empires. Among the three, the Aztecs were the most powerful. They ruled the area in modern-day central Mexico. The Aztecs relied upon religion and warfare to maintain rule in the land. Ultimately, however, they were crushed by Spanish invaders, who ended the Aztecs' rule.

[2]→ The Aztec Empire was based on a coalition of three tribes living in the Valley of Mexico. This central valley—where Mexico City sits today—was comprised of lakes and islands. One tribe, the Mexica, immigrated to the valley from the north during the 1300s. Later, in 1427, the Mexica people joined two other tribes to create the Aztec Alliance, which soon became the Aztec Empire. In the valley, the Aztecs constructed a city on an island in a large lake called Lake Texcoco. They named their city Tenochtitlan. The Aztecs were mainly farmers, yet there were kings, other nobles, priests, and warriors at the top of the hierarchy. Leadership roles were passed down according to heredity. The Aztecs even had their own written language. It was made up of pictograms, which could be placed together to form sentences.

21 According to paragraph 1, which of the following can be inferred about the Inca Empire?

- Ⓐ Most of its people lived high in the mountains.
- Ⓑ It was not as strong as the Aztec Empire.
- Ⓒ It was located in South America.
- Ⓓ Its people were defeated by the Spanish.

22 According to paragraph 2, which of the following is true of the Mexica?

- Ⓐ They were originally from the Valley of Mexico.
- Ⓑ Lake Texcoco was the site of their homeland.
- Ⓒ They were the strongest of the tribes in the Aztec Alliance.
- Ⓓ They helped form the Aztec Empire.

Glossary

hierarchy: a chain of command; an order of people according to their rank or importance

23 The word "vicinity" in the passage is closest in meaning to

- Ⓐ region
- Ⓑ control
- Ⓒ influence
- Ⓓ tribe

24 Which of the sentences below best expresses the essential information in the highlighted sentence in the passage? *Incorrect* answer choices change the meaning in important ways or leave out essential information.

- Ⓐ Since many city-states rebelled, the Aztecs kept soldiers in all of the lands that they had conquered.
- Ⓑ The Aztecs often did not have to keep soldiers in conquered lands since those places were no longer a threat to them.
- Ⓒ When the Aztecs had to garrison soldiers somewhere, the Aztecs weakened the conquered city-states so much that they could not fight.
- Ⓓ Defeated city-states wanted to rebel against the Aztecs, but soldiers remaining in their lands prevented them from doing so.

25 Which of the following can be inferred from paragraph 3 about the Aztecs?

- Ⓐ Their empire was structured similarly to other city-states.
- Ⓑ They never lost any of the wars they fought.
- Ⓒ Many of them enjoyed fighting in battles.
- Ⓓ They brought civilization to conquered tribes.

26 The author discusses "flower wars" in paragraph 4 in order to

- Ⓐ explain their purpose
- Ⓑ criticize their usage
- Ⓒ describe a religious ceremony
- Ⓓ mention human sacrifices

³➜ While the Aztecs had some measure of civilization, they were warriors at heart. They spread and **enforced** their control of their territory by warfare. Many tribes living in the Aztec's vicinity were organized in what could be considered city-states. There was a central location with temples and the homes of the ruling class, and it was surrounded by farmland. The Aztecs conquered many of these city-states. They were usually smaller and had fewer warriors who were not as skilled in battle as the Aztecs. That made them easy to defeat. Once a city-state had lost, it often became allied with the Aztecs. In some cases, the Aztecs left soldiers behind to ensure the city-state's loyalty. The garrisoning of soldiers was not, however, always necessary since most city-states were too weak to rebel after their armies had been defeated by the Aztecs.

⁴➜ The Aztecs tried to capture as many enemy soldiers as possible during battle. These captives were used as human sacrifices. The Aztecs believed certain gods controlled human fate. These gods could only be appeased by human sacrifices. To guarantee a steady supply of captives, the Aztecs constantly waged war. Many wars were not for conquest but for the capturing of enemies. The Aztecs referred to these events as flower wars. Some historians believe flower wars also enabled the Aztecs to train their warriors in combat and to allow members of the lower classes to advance to higher ones by showing bravery in battle.

Glossary

enforce: to make someone follow orders or the law

27 According to paragraph 5, some tribes joined with Hernan Cortez against the Aztecs because

(A) he became the Aztec's new emperor

(B) he had overwhelming numbers of men in his army

(C) they disliked the Aztecs a great deal

(D) they were frightened of Cortez and his men

28 According to paragraph 6, many Aztecs died because

(A) the Spanish killed them while fighting in several battles

(B) they starved to death in a famine caused by the Spanish

(C) they were infected by diseases brought by the Spanish

(D) they were killed by natural disasters that suddenly happened

29 Look at the four squares [■] that indicate where the following sentence could be added to the passage.

This lack of modern weaponry proved to be the decisive factor in their defeat.

Where would the sentence best fit?

> Click on a square [■] to add the sentence to the passage.

⁵→ While the Aztecs built a vast, powerful empire, it was not long lived as far as empires are concerned. The Aztecs themselves were conquered in the early 1500s. This was barely a century after their own empire had been founded. Their conquerors were the Spanish, who were under the command of conquistador Hernan Cortez. Cortez arrived in Aztec territory in 1519, where he was first greeted warmly. Montezuma, the Aztec ruler, sent him gifts of gold. Yet Cortez was not so easily bought off and was determined to conquer the land. After overcoming some initial challenges, Cortez and his men began making headway. They were joined by many tribes, whose people despised their Aztec overlords. The Spanish captured Montezuma early in the war. He pleaded with his people to make peace with the Spanish. They refused and replaced Montezuma with his brother.

⁶→ After two years of fighting, Cortez defeated the Aztecs in 1521. Despite the small size of his army, he and his men had several advantages which enabled them to win. These included having horses, gunpowder weapons, and metal weapons and armor. ■1 The Aztecs had none of these. ■2 After their defeat to Cortez, many Aztecs soon lost their lives. ■3 The Spanish had unknowingly brought diseases with them. ■4 Outbreaks of smallpox and typhus killed off most of the people. The Aztecs and other tribes lacked natural defenses to these illnesses. By the start of the 1600s, most Aztecs had died from disease. The remainder was absorbed by the increasing number of Spaniards. Soon, the Aztecs were no more.

30 *Directions:* An introductory sentence for a brief summary of the passage is provided below. Complete the summary by selecting the THREE answer choices that express the most important ideas of the passage. Some sentences do not belong because they express ideas that are not presented in the passage or are minor ideas in the passage. ***This question is worth 2 points.***

Drag your answer choices to the spaces where they belong.
To remove an answer choice, click on it. To review the passage, click **View Text**.

The Aztec Empire in modern-day central Mexico became powerful and dominated its territory, but it was soon conquered by the Spaniards.

-
-
-

Answer Choices

1 The Aztecs made war on neighboring city-states and defeated most of these places in the battles they fought.

2 Hernan Cortez's adventures in Mexico began in 1519 and ended a couple of years later in 1521.

3 In creating their empire, the Aztecs developed a hierarchy complete with a strong warrior class.

4 One unusual aspect of the Aztecs' beliefs was that they were convinced that their gods required human sacrifices.

5 The Spanish used their superior technology to overcome their lack of numbers as they defeated the Aztecs.

6 The Spanish brought diseases with them, and the Aztecs and members of other tribes often fell ill to them.

TOEFL® MAP

MAP New TOEFL® Edition

Reading

Intermediate

Answers and Explanations

TOEFL® MAP Reading

New TOEFL® Edition

Reading

Intermediate

Answers and Explanations

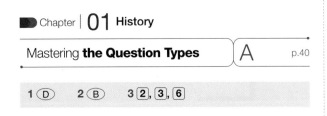

Part **B**

Building Background Knowledge of TOEFL Topics

■▶ Chapter | **01** History

Mastering **the Question Types** — A — p.40

1 Ⓓ   2 Ⓑ   3 ②, ③, ⑥

1 [Rhetorical Purpose Question]

The author writes, "There was little central leadership until Charlemagne founded the Holy Roman Empire in 800 A.D."

2 [Vocabulary Question]

Essentials are the basic practices or theories behind something. These practices and theories are known as fundamentals.

3 [Prose Summary Question]

According to the passage, the king's vassals were ranked differently in terms of land ownership. In addition, the vassals received fiefs from their lords in return for their loyalty. Finally, vassals were expected to fight for their lords in battle as well.

Summarizing

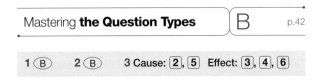

After Rome fell, there was little centralized leadership in Western Europe for centuries. Following Charlemagne though, the system of feudalism was formed. It focused on land ownership and loyalty bonds. Nobles owned the land, but they needed subjects to help them. So they gave their vassals fiefs of land and peasants. In return, the vassals fought for their lords. In the feudal system, the king ruled while peasants were at the bottom. Feudalism eventually disappeared and gave way to the nation-state.

Mastering **the Question Types** — B — p.42

1 Ⓑ   2 Ⓑ   3 Cause: ②, ⑤   Effect: ③, ④, ⑥

1 [Negative Factual Question]

The author mentions that the fire was extinguished, but there is no mention in the passage of how it was put out by the people of London.

2 [Inference Question]

The author writes, "The reconstruction effort took years. For instance, St. Paul's Cathedral was rebuilt." Since the cathedral had to be rebuilt, it is implied that it was destroyed by the Great Fire of London.

3 [Fill in a Table Question]

According to the passage, two causes of the Great Fire of London were that the weather had been very hot and dry and that many homes in the city were constructed of wood. As for the effects, most of the city burned down, some buildings took decades to reconstruct, and London was made better overall.

Summarizing

Large fires were problems in the past because many homes were made of wood. On September 2, 1666, a fire broke out in London. It spread out of control due to the wind and hot, dry weather. Firebreaks and gunpowder failed to stop the fire, and even the king helped try to extinguish it. The fire was finally put out on September 6, but thousands of buildings were destroyed, and hundreds of thousands of people lost their lives. Rebuilding London took a long time, but the city was improved afterward.

Mastering **the Question Types** — C — p.44

1 Ⓑ   2 Ⓐ   3 Ⓐ   4 **4**

1 [Sentence Simplification Question]

The highlighted sentence mentions Alexander's decade of war in Persia and the fact that his army almost always won in battle while going all the way to India. These facts are best described by answer choice Ⓑ.

2 [Reference Question]

The "it" that brought the language, customs, and ideals of Greece eastward was the Macedonian army.

3 [Factual Question]

The author writes, "Even today, many signs of Hellenism are evident in the Middle East."

4 [Insert Text Question]

The sentence to be inserted begins with "These facts." This indicates that the sentence to be inserted is referring to multiple subjects and should therefore come after all of the facts have been listed.

Summarizing

Philip of Macedonia conquered Greece in 338 B.C. but was killed two years later. His son Alexander then took over the Macedonians. His goal was to defeat the Persian Empire. It took him ten years, but he was successful. Then, Alexander died in 323 B.C. Alexander was greatly influenced by Greek culture. His army spread the Greek language, customs, and ideals throughout the lands it conquered. This was called Hellenism. Even after Alexander died, Hellenism remained influential in the Middle East.

Mastering the Subject · A · p.46

1 ⒷB   2 ⒷB   3 ❶   4 Northern Colonies: ⑴, ⑹, ⑺ Southern Colonies: ⑵, ⑸

1 [Reference Question]

The "it" that people abandoned for other pursuits was farming.

2 [Factual Question]

About plantations, the author writes, "The plantations relied upon tobacco and cotton as their major cash crops."

3 [Insert Text Question]

The sentence before the first square notes that the land was "rocky and hilly." The sentence to be inserted notes that the farmers had to "clear the land of stones and rocks while they were tilling their fields."

4 [Fill in a Table Question]

According to the passage, the northern colonies had farmers that grew enough food only for their families, imported machines from abroad, and had excellent harbors. The southern colonies employed most of their people in agriculture and had land that was fairly level.

Summarizing

Almost all early Americans farmed and fished, but the American colonies developed different types of economies. Geography was a primary reason for this. The northern colonies were into shipping and fishing because of their good harbors. But their rocky, hilly land made farming difficult. Thus, the North developed more industries. The South, however, had good land for farming, so large plantations arose there. When the Civil War began, the two regions were very different. The North used its industrial advantage to defeat the agrarian South.

Mastering the Subject · B · p.48

1 Ⓓ   2 Ⓒ   3 Ⓒ   4 ⑴, ⑶, ⑸

1 [Sentence Simplification Question]

The highlighted sentence notes that the Greeks could unite against outside powers such as the Persians but also spent time fighting against one another. These two ideas are best described in answer choice Ⓓ.

2 [Rhetorical Purpose Question]

About the Greek dark ages, the author writes, "City-states in Greece originated at the end of the period called the Greek dark ages. They lasted from around 1200 B.C. to 800 B.C."

3 [Vocabulary Question]

When warfare flares up, it occurs or happens.

4 [Prose Summary Question]

According to the passage, the Greeks founded the city-states to provide protection for the people. In addition, some city-states, such as Athens, gained their wealth from maritime trade, and all city-states shared some similarities yet had distinct customs and practices.

Summarizing

City-states dominated ancient Greece. Each city-state had its own laws, customs, economy, and culture. The first ones arose when the Greek dark ages ended. Most were founded to protect their people. The governments of city-states were often democracies or oligarchies. Some, such as Athens, became wealthy through trade. Others, such as Sparta, became powerful thanks to their land. City-states sometimes battled each other in wars. After Alexander the Great conquered them, city-states disappeared in Greece. Yet they later appeared in medieval and Renaissance Italy.

Mastering the Subject · C · p.50

1 Ⓐ   2 Ⓒ   3 Ⓒ   4 ⑵, ⑶, ⑸

1 [Negative Factual Question]

Many Fujiwara family members assisted the emperors, but they never "served as emperors" during the Heian period.

2 [Factual Question]

The author notes that the samurai were used "to rebel

against the Fujiwara" at the end of the Heian period.

3 [Inference Question]

When the author mentions, "This resulted in an outpouring of high-quality Japanese literature," it is implied that there was more literature produced in the Heian period than in previous times.

4 [Prose Summary Question]

According to the passage, the sons of many Fujiwara women became emperors. There was also an emphasis on literature and art during this time of peace. And the Fujiwara used samurai armies to maintain the peace.

Summarizing

The Heian period in Japan lasted from 794 to 1185. Heian became the capital of Japan in 794. The Fujiwara were the strongest of many prominent families during this age. They became interrelated with the imperial family, which increased their power. Members of the Fujiwara often made imperial decisions. They maintained armies of samurais to help prevent wars. During this peaceful age, literature and art in Japan developed. The Fujiwara eventually lost influence, there were many rebellions, and Japan became controlled by military strongmen.

TOEFL Practice Test   p.52

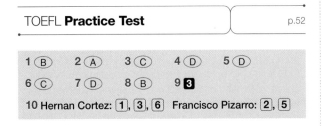

| 1 (B) | 2 (A) | 3 (C) | 4 (D) | 5 (D) |
| 6 (C) | 7 (D) | 8 (B) | 9 **3** | |

10 Hernan Cortez: [1], [3], [6]   Francisco Pizarro: [2], [5]

1 [Factual Question]

The author writes, "Columbus made four trips to the islands in the Caribbean Sea."

2 [Vocabulary Question]

When a person reaps glory, that individual attains it.

3 [Factual Question]

The author writes, "These natives' tribes had often been defeated by the ruthless Aztecs. Thus, they were eager for revenge."

4 [Inference Question]

When the author mentions that the Spanish won "against great numerical odds," it can be inferred that the military force under Cortez was much smaller than the Aztecs' armies.

5 [Reference Question]

The "it" that Pizarro was chosen to find was the Inca Empire.

6 [Negative Factual Question]

The passage mentions that the Spanish executed the Incan emperor. He was not killed in battle.

7 [Factual Question]

It is written, "The natives lacked immunity to European diseases." As a result, millions of them died when the Spanish arrived.

8 [Inference Question]

When writing about the Spanish's efforts in the New World, the author notes that the effects of diseases "made it simpler for rather small bands of Spaniards to conquer the Aztecs and the Incas, which had enormous populations."

9 [Insert Text Question]

When Cortez had his ships burned to stop his men from retreating, it served to motivate his troops.

10 [Fill in a Table Question]

According to the passage, Hernan Cortez lost a few soldiers in battle, recruited soldiers from the natives living there, and destroyed his own ships. Francisco Pizarro failed the first two times he went against the natives and fought natives in South America.

Vocabulary Review   p.59

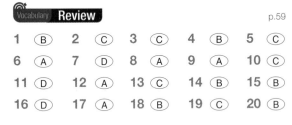

1 (B)	2 (C)	3 (C)	4 (B)	5 (C)
6 (A)	7 (D)	8 (A)	9 (A)	10 (C)
11 (D)	12 (A)	13 (C)	14 (B)	15 (B)
16 (D)	17 (A)	18 (B)	19 (C)	20 (B)

Chapter | 02 The Arts

Mastering the Question Types   **A**   p.62

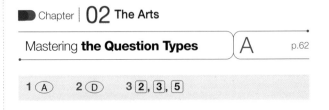

| 1 (A) | 2 (D) | 3 [2], [3], [5] |

1 [Vocabulary Question]

If there are no accompanying instruments, then there are no instruments contributing to the music.

2 [Rhetorical Purpose Question]

About the harpsichord, the author writes, "It was created during the late medieval period, but this keyboard instrument quickly gained popularity. The harpsichord would maintain its popularity even after medieval times as there were numerous works written for it during the Renaissance and the Baroque Period."

3 [Prose Summary Question]

According to the passage, medieval musicians played instruments such as the shawm, the harp, and the sackbut. In addition, the lute was highly influential during medieval times. Finally, there were all kinds of types of musical instruments that were popular during the Middle Ages.

Summarizing

> It is not true that there were few musical instruments in the Middle Ages. There were many, including string, percussion, brass, keyboard, and wind instruments. The lute was the most influential medieval instrument. It—along with the harp—was popular with wandering minstrels. They would pluck the four or five pairs of strings that the lute had. The harpsichord was another instrument that became very popular during the Middle Ages. There were other instruments, such as the shawm, the flute, the pipe, the trumpet, and the sackbut, that medieval musicians played.

Mastering **the Question Types**   B   p.64

1 (B)   **2** (A)   **3** Pre-Impressionist: [5], [7]
Impressionist: [2], [4], [6]

1 [Negative Factual Question]

There is nothing in the passage about Impressionist artists using realism in their works, so that question is not answered.

2 [Inference Question]

The author writes, "The artists often argued amongst themselves as to what constituted Impressionist art. Ultimately, while there was some disagreement, it was generally agreed that the use of bright colors, short brushstrokes, and light in outdoor scenes constituted the main ideals of the movement." So it can be inferred that the Impressionists followed few set standards.

3 [Fill in a Table Question]

According to the passage, in pre-Impressionist times,

artists preferred dark colors and painting realistic-looking pictures. During Impressionist times, artists created abstract art, used a diverse number of styles, and painted topics found in nature.

Summarizing

> Most traditional art was realistic. But in France in the late 1800s, the Impressionist school of art began. Impressionists preferred vivid colors, not dark ones. They also used short brushstrokes, so their paintings were usually abstract. And they painted landscapes and other outdoor scenes. The movement's name came from a painting by Claude Monet. The works of the Impressionists often have only a few similarities. The Impressionists themselves could never agree on what exactly Impressionist art was. This makes the works of these artists quite diverse.

Mastering **the Question Types**   C   p.66

1 (B)   **2** (B)   **3** (D)   **4** **4**

1 [Sentence Simplification Question]

The highlighted sentence mentions that some members of the audience are far from the stage, so without makeup, they would not be able clearly to see the actors' faces. This is best described in answer choice (B).

2 [Reference Question]

The "them" that it is important for the audience to see clearly are "the eyes" of the performers.

3 [Factual Question]

The author notes, "There are several types of makeup that performers use." In the rest of the paragraph, the ways in which different types of cosmetics make performers more easily seen by the audience are described.

4 [Insert Text Question]

The sentence before the fourth square notes that actors can use makeup to make it seem as though they have blood on them. In the sentence to be inserted, "gory" is used to describe the appearance of blood. In addition, an "open wound" implies the appearance of blood.

Summarizing

> Most actors in dramatic productions wear makeup. This lets the audience get a better look at their faces. Actors

use different kinds of cosmetics. Foundation makeup highlights the jaw and facial contours and darkens the skin. Eye makeup and lipstick help actors convey their emotions to the audience. Some actors wear makeup for special reasons. Clowns and vampires need to wear lots of makeup. Actors may need to put scars, bruises, or blood on their bodies, too. These all require the usage of makeup.

Mastering **the Subject** 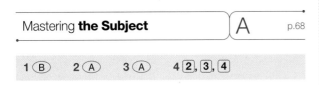 A   p.68

1 Ⓑ   2 Ⓐ   3 Ⓐ   4 ②, ③, ④

1   [Factual Question]

The author writes, "The main purpose of spoken dialogue is to convey information. The audience is able to understand the story from the dialogue as well as from the film's visuals."

2   [Sentence Simplification Question]

The highlighted sentence notes that the director might use music to give the audience a sense of anticipation when the hero is in a dangerous situation. This concept is best described in answer choice Ⓐ.

3   [Vocabulary Question]

Something that is atypical is uncommon or unusual.

4   [Prose Summary Question]

According to the passage, the director chooses the music used depending on the emotions he wants the audience to feel. In addition, movies with sound effects become more realistic. And spoken dialogue lets the audience understand what is going on in the movie.

Summarizing

One important element in movies is sound. The three main types of sound are spoken dialogue, music, and sound effects. Spoken dialogue expresses information to the audience. It lets the viewers know exactly what is happening in the film. Music can set the mood in the film. Different kinds of music are used to create various feelings or emotions. Sound effects make films more realistic. Some are everyday sounds while others are more unusual sounds. Sound effects today are more believable than ones from the past.

Mastering **the Subject**  B   p.70

1 Ⓒ   2 Ⓒ   3 Ⓓ   4 ①, ③, ④

1   [Reference Question]

The "their" whose fame increased when others copied their style were the "masters" such as Leonardo da Vinci, Michelangelo, and Raphael.

2   [Negative Factual Question]

The author writes, "There were some brilliant artists in the Middle Ages. Yet most were not especially talented." This is the exact opposite of answer choice Ⓒ.

3   [Inference Question]

The passage reads, "Paintings that sold for a few hundred pounds or francs in the 1700s garnered tens of thousands of pounds or francs in the 1800s. By the end of the 1900s, some paintings were selling for millions of pounds, francs, and dollars." People can make huge sums of money from art, so it can be inferred that purchasing it can be a good investment.

4   [Prose Summary Question]

According to the passage, Renaissance masters whose styles were copied by others became very famous. In addition, Renaissance artists learned more about painting and used perspective in their works. And many modern-day artists are not anonymous but have become famous even during their lives.

Summarizing

During the Middle Ages, most artists had little skill. They were considered craftsmen and were almost never famous. But during the Renaissance, this changed. Artists began to learn skills such as using perspective and depth. This improved the quality of their work. This brought some artists more fame. Over time, people began collecting art, which caused the prices of some works of art to increase. Today, many artists have achieved a lot of fame, and some paintings sell for millions of dollars.

Mastering **the Subject**  C   p.72

1 Ⓓ   2 Ⓐ   3 **2**   4 Entertainment: ①, ⑥
Inspiration: ④, ⑤, ⑦

1 [Negative Factual Question]

The author writes, "They can listen to it on their stereos or portable electronic devices, the radio, or the Internet." There is no mention in the passage of cassettes.

2 [Rhetorical Purpose Question]

The author mentions, "Minstrels were musicians who traveled the countryside to play their music. They frequently sang songs that were well known to the villagers."

3 [Insert Text Question]

The sentence before the second square notes some types of songs or poems that wandering minstrels often sang. The sentence to be inserted mentions stories about King Arthur and his knights, which are similar to those other poems. It also includes the words "as well," which indicate that the two sentences have a common theme and therefore go together.

4 [Fill in a Table Question]

According to the passage, music meant for entertainment included the singing of epic poems and was often done by wandering minstrels. As for music meant for inspiration, it could help people experience the divine, it was played for soldiers, and it could improve people's spirits.

Summarizing

People usually listen to music because it entertains them. Nowadays, people can listen to music through a wide range of mediums. This was not true in the past. Centuries ago, wandering minstrels often went to villages and played music for the people. But music did not just entertain. Religious music and battle music inspired people. Religious music was played in churches and cathedrals. And soldiers often listened to battle music before they fought. Sometimes the music was even played as they marched into battle.

TOEFL **Practice Test**   p.74

1 (B)   2 (D)   3 (C)   4 (A)   5 (D)
6 (D)   7 (A)   8 (C)   9 **2**
10 First Theory: (3), (7)   Second Theory: (1), (8)   Third Theory: (5), (6), (9)

1 [Rhetorical Purpose Question]

About Chauvet, the author writes, "A cave in Chauvet, France, has paintings estimated to be 32,000 years old.

This makes them among the world's oldest-known cave paintings."

2 [Factual Question]

The author notes, "Cave paintings depict a variety of images. Most are animals, yet there are other images. They include shapes, tracings of hands, and abstract images."

3 [Inference Question]

When the author writes, "It, however, seems the most unlikely," while describing the first theory, it can be inferred that the least number of scholars believe it is accurate.

4 [Negative Factual Question]

The author writes, "It is indisputable that early humans led bleak lives. They surely would have enjoyed anything that would have brightened their days." This is the only plausible reason given for the first theory.

5 [Vocabulary Question]

An illiterate person is someone who cannot read.

6 [Inference Question]

When the author notes that shamans were "religious leaders," it is implied that they were important to prehistoric tribes.

7 [Factual Question]

The author mentions, "Since prehistoric people were illiterate, they have left no writings concerning their beliefs. This makes it impossible to determine what their religious beliefs or practices were. Accordingly, the idea that the paintings were for religious purposes cannot be verified."

8 [Sentence Simplification Question]

The highlighted sentence notes that the idea is similar to the second in that it is possible yet cannot be proven to be true or not. This is best described in answer choice (C).

9 [Insert Text Question]

The sentence prior to the second square mentions that there are three main theories about why cave paintings were made. The sentence to be inserted points out that each of these theories has its own supporters.

10 [Fill in a Table Question]

According to the passage, the first theory considers people's need for decorations and is the least likely theory to be true. The second theory is a religious explanation and explains that the art may have been made by a shaman. The third theory explains why there are animal paintings, shows that the paintings could have been instructions, and notes that the paintings might have been messages from the old to the young.

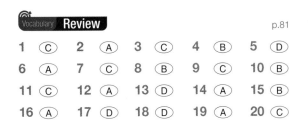

Vocabulary Review

p.81

1	C	2	A	3	C	4	B	5	D
6	A	7	C	8	B	9	C	10	B
11	C	12	A	13	D	14	A	15	B
16	A	17	D	18	D	19	A	20	C

Chapter | 03 Archaeology and Anthropology

Mastering the Question Types   A   p.84

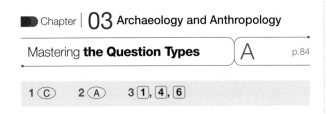

1 C   2 A   3 1, 4, 6

1 [Vocabulary Question]

By converting their dead into mummies, the Egyptians transformed them.

2 [Rhetorical Purpose Question]

The author writes, "There were more than 5,000 relics found in the tomb of King Tutankhamen, which was discovered by Howard Carter in 1922."

3 [Prose Summary Question]

According to the passage, people in Europe and the Mediterranean area buried the dead with valuables. In addition, the Egyptians turned their dead into mummies. And the Greeks buried people with a coin while the Egyptians buried them with food and drinks.

Summarizing

Humans have been burying the dead for around 50,000 years and had unique customs in ancient times. The Egyptians turned people into mummies. But other cultures, such as the Greeks, the Romans, and the Celts, buried their dead. People were often buried with some of their possessions. King Tutankhamen's tomb had more than 5,000 relics, and the Celts buried people with valuable personal items. The Greeks put a coin under the tongue of the deceased. And the Egyptians buried people with food and drinks.

Mastering the Question Types   B   p.86

1 C   2 D   3 Geometric Style: 5, 8   Black-Figure Pottery: 2, 4, 6   Red-Figure Pottery: 1, 7

1 [Negative Factual Question]

The author mentions, "From around 1000 B.C. to 700 B.C., the geometric style of pottery dominated."

2 [Inference Question]

The author mentions, "This style was created in Athens and was found to be much easier to work with than black-figure pottery." It can therefore be inferred that Athens was influential on ancient Greek pottery.

3 [Fill in a Table Question]

According to the passage, the geometric style used triangles and squares and also affected later styles of pottery. Black-figure pottery was popular for a century and a half, made parts of the pots turn red, and was not developed in Athens. Red-figure pottery let artists create more details and was the third major style of pottery.

Summarizing

There were three major styles of pottery in ancient Greece. The first was the geometric style. It used shapes such as triangles and squares to draw animals and people. The second was black-figure pottery. For it, artists made decorations prior to firing the pot in the kiln. This turned the design black and the pot red. Later, red-figure pottery was used. The pot turned black while the designs stayed red. Red-figure pottery was popular because of the level of detail it permitted.

Mastering the Question Types   C   p.88

1 C   2 B   3 B   4 **4**

1 [Sentence Simplification Question]

The highlighted sentence mentions that famine is often the explanation that archaeologists give when a culture suddenly disappears for no apparent reason. This idea is best described in answer choice C.

2 [Factual Question]

The author notes that the Anasazi were "a tribe that started to dominate what is now the southwestern

United States around 900."

3 [Reference Question]

The most famous of "them" in the passage is "other pre-Columbian American cultures."

4 [Insert Text Question]

The sentence prior to the fourth square mentions the "slash-and-burn land-clearing techniques" used by the Mayas. This is the "manner" referred to in the sentence to be inserted.

Summarizing

Vibrant cultures in the past sometimes suddenly disappeared. When there is no evidence for warfare or natural disasters, archaeologists often blame this on famines. In pre-Columbian America, there were many famines. Around 900, the Anasazi dominated a region in the modern-day southwestern United States. But they went into decline and disappeared by 1200. Many believe that drought, which led to famine, caused this. The Maya Empire was similarly affected. It likely experienced years of famine. It did not quickly disappear but went into a slow decline.

Mastering **the Subject**　　A　p.90

1 Ⓓ 　 2 Ⓐ 　 3 **2** 　 4 Middle East: ③, ④
India: ①, ⑤ 　Central America: ②

1 [Rhetorical Purpose Question]

The author writes, "Humans are thought to have developed agriculture first in the Middle East. They did this in the region around the Tigris and Euphrates rivers."

2 [Factual Question]

The author notes, "It is thought that farming first reached India around 9000 B.C. and Egypt by 7000 B.C. Most archaeologists claim that people began farming in southern Europe at the same time they were doing so in Egypt."

3 [Insert Text Question]

The sentence before the second square mentions "potatoes, tomatoes, corn, squash, and beans." They are "some of these crops" that are noted in the sentence to be inserted.

4 [Fill in a Table Question]

According to the passage, in the Middle East, several types of grains were farmed for the first time, and people first learned how to farm there. In India, the people learned to farm rice from the Chinese and needed lots of rain for some of their crops. And Central America was one of the last places that people learned how to farm.

Summarizing

Farming likely developed independently in several places around the world at different times. The first place people learned how to farm was the Middle East. People there discovered agriculture and spread this knowledge elsewhere. They raised wheat and other plants. People in India learned about farming in 9000 B.C., in China around 8000 B.C, and in New Guinea around 7000 B.C. About 5000 B.C., farming was learned in Central Africa and South and Central America. People in the Americas grew a wide variety of crops.

Mastering **the Subject**　　B　p.92

1 Ⓑ 　 2 Ⓑ 　 3 Ⓐ 　 4 ③, ④, ⑤

1 [Sentence Simplification Question]

The highlighted sentence notes that despite living for 1,000 years, the Hohokams were gone by 1600, which was when the Spanish arrived. These facts are best described in answer choice Ⓑ.

2 [Inference Question]

The passage notes, "While the Tucson Basin is mostly desert today, this was not true when the Hohokams lived there. Instead, it received some rainfall, retained water well, and had more vegetation than today." Thus it can be inferred that the land today is not as fertile as it once was.

3 [Vocabulary Question]

When there is an ample amount of water, it means that there is enough of it, so water is plentiful.

4 [Prose Summary Question]

According to the passage, the Hohokams raised corn and cotton for both food and clothing. They used irrigation methods to raise enough crops. And they declined as a culture when they lost touch with the ancestral homeland.

From 300 to 1500, the Hohokam tribe dominated the Tucson Basin, an area that is now in the southwestern United States. It received enough rainfall then, so the land was good for farming. The Hohokams used canals to irrigate their land. They raised crops such as corn, squash, beans, and cotton. They relied heavily on corn but also made great use of cotton. They used cotton for both food and clothing. The Hohokams were assimilated by other tribes over a period of about 400 years.

Mastering **the Subject** C   p.94

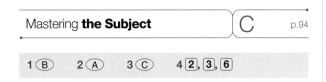

1 [Reference Question]

The "they" that have "provided archaeologists with numerous pictorial views of Minoan life" are frescoes.

2 [Negative Factual Question]

It is written that the Minoans "lacked a powerful navy as they used their sailing vessels for fishing and trading."

3 [Rhetorical Purpose Question]

The author writes that "their civilization suddenly vanished. The reason remains unknown to archaeologists." Then, the author lists several reasons why Minoan civilization might have disappeared.

4 [Prose Summary Question]

According to the passage, the Minoans traded with people all around the Mediterranean Sea. They might have been killed by natural disaster or warfare. And written and artistic sources from their time have shown the lives of luxury that some people lived.

The Minoans lived on the island of Crete from around 2600 to 1100 B.C. Archaeologists have learned about them because of the ruins of their palaces and translations of Linear B, their writing system. The Minoans used ships to trade all over the Mediterranean Sea. They traded metals and other goods, which made them wealthy. Minoan culture suddenly vanished around 1100 B.C. No one is sure what happened. There may have been an earthquake or volcano that destroyed their culture, or they could have been invaded by another people.

TOEFL **Practice Test**   p.96

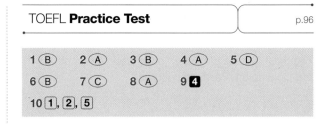

1 [Factual Question]

The author writes, "The primary question facing archaeologists is how the Egyptians managed to shape, move, and place so many large blocks without advanced machines or electrical power."

2 [Rhetorical Purpose Question]

The author mentions, "Granite is much harder, so it required tougher tools. Those were made of dolerite, a hard, volcanic rock."

3 [Negative Factual Question]

According to the author, "To cut the stones out, the workers made holes and drove wooden pegs into them. Then, they poured water into the holes. This made the wooden pegs expand, and the stones subsequently cracked." The pegs were therefore not used to lift the stones out; they were used to make the stones crack.

4 [Vocabulary Question]

Since the Egyptians were ignorant of the wheel, they were unaware of its existence.

5 [Inference Question]

The passage notes, "Stones from quarries far away were brought to the Nile, loaded onto barges, and transported on water." It can be inferred that the Egyptians built the ships—the barges—that they transported the stones on.

6 [Factual Question]

The author writes, "Some believe a single ramp that became progressively higher and wider—to strengthen it—was made. Others claim that a series of ramps spiraled their way up around the pyramid."

7 [Factual Question]

The author writes, "Perhaps 20,000 to 30,000 people simultaneously worked on a single pyramid."

8 [Sentence Simplification Question]

The highlighted sentence notes that pharaohs started to build their own pyramids once they took power because the pyramids took so long to construct and they wanted to be sure they had a tomb when they died. This thought is best described in answer choice Ⓐ.

9 [Insert Text Question]

The sentence before the fourth square notes, "Once construction was complete, the ramps were dismantled." Since the ramps were taken apart, something had to be done with the materials in them. What was done is explained in the sentence to be inserted.

10 [Prose Summary Question]

According to the passage, the Egyptians devised a method using water and wooden pegs to get the stones out of the quarries. They also used huge ramps to get the stones up to the tops of the pyramids. And they dragged the stones on sleds by using either human or animal power.

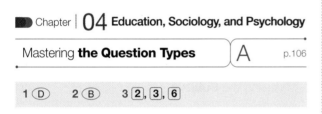

Vocabulary Review   p.103

1	Ⓑ	2	Ⓐ	3	Ⓑ	4	Ⓓ	5	Ⓓ
6	Ⓑ	7	Ⓐ	8	Ⓐ	9	Ⓓ	10	Ⓐ
11	Ⓑ	12	Ⓒ	13	Ⓒ	14	Ⓐ	15	Ⓓ
16	Ⓑ	17	Ⓓ	18	Ⓐ	19	Ⓒ	20	Ⓓ

◗ Chapter │ **04** Education, Sociology, and Psychology

Mastering **the Question Types**   A   p.106

1 Ⓓ   2 Ⓑ   3 ②, ③, ⑥

1 [Rhetorical Purpose Question]

The author notes, "Some ads focus on positive values such as honesty. These ads can encourage children to be truthful to others."

2 [Vocabulary Question]

Stunts are feats that people do which can often be dangerous or risky.

3 [Prose Summary Question]

According to the passage, children may do dangerous activities and get hurt because of ads. In addition, ads for unhealthy foods can help children become overweight. Finally, children can learn about advanced technology thanks to ads.

Summarizing

Businesses focus on advertising to children so much that they may see 40,000 ads a year. Ads can be positive.

Some show positive values such as honesty and introduce advanced technology and new innovations to children. But junk food ads can show healthy, attractive people. Children think those actors use the products, so they try them and then become overweight. Other ads show dangerous behavior such as skateboard stunts. Despite warnings in the ads, children try the stunts and then get hurt and may be hospitalized.

Mastering **the Question Types**   B   p.108

1 Ⓑ   2 Ⓐ   3 Principles: ③, ⑥   Influences on Educators: ①, ②, ⑤

1 [Negative Factual Question]

There is no mention in the passage of how students benefitted from the education system during John Dewey's time.

2 [Inference Question]

The passage reads, "Dewey's ideas on education became popular. They influenced several generations of educators. Even today, people still try to implement his ideas. As a result, several new types of education have been developed." Thus it can be implied that instructors who are influenced by Dewey's teaching philosophy may use several teaching methods.

3 [Fill in a Table Question]

According to the passage, John Dewey's principles on education include students doing hands-on work and students working together with others. As for his influences on educators, they include students spending time outdoors, students doing community work, and the fact that there are many new types of education today.

Summarizing

John Dewey was an American educator. He disliked the state of American education during his life. At that time, teachers lectured, students took notes, and the students took tests. Dewey preferred a hands-on approach to education. He also liked group work and problem solving. Many educators were influenced by Dewey, so they developed new forms of education. These included outdoor education, service learning, and environmental learning. These types of education let students do activities they would not normally get an opportunity to do in the classroom.

1 Ⓐ   2 Ⓒ   3 Ⓓ   4 **2**

1 [Factual Question]

The author writes, "At the start of the Middle Ages, civilization declined. There was a lack of learning, and urban centers began crumbling. Many historians refer to this bleak period as the Dark Ages."

2 [Reference Question]

The "they" who had to pay a part of their earnings to the nobles were "some townsmen."

3 [Sentence Simplification Question]

The highlighted sentence notes that the free townsmen formed guilds, and this enabled them to control business and trade in their region. This is best described in answer choice Ⓓ.

4 [Insert Text Question]

The sentence before the second square is about the importance of the Catholic Church in people's lives. The sentence to be inserted explains just how important the Church was to most people's lives.

Summarizing

After the Roman Empire fell, the Middles Ages began. The first part was called the Dark Ages. This was a time when cities disappeared and people lived in villages. They lived under a system called feudalism. In it, the villagers were under the control of the local noble. They had to provide services for him. However, as the Middle Ages progressed, this changed. Some men became wealthy merchants and craftsmen. They started to form guilds and later established local governments. These men helped end feudalism throughout Europe.

1 Ⓐ   2 Ⓑ   3 Ⓓ   4 Rural Area: ①, ③, ⑦
Urban Area: ②, ④

1 [Inference Question]

The author writes, "In villages and small towns, most people live in private houses," and, "In cities, however, many people live in cramped apartments." It can be inferred, therefore, that homes in cities are smaller than those in rural areas.

2 [Negative Factual Question]

The passage reads, "People in rural areas do not always get along with one another." So answer choice Ⓑ is not a factual statement.

3 [Vocabulary Question]

When a place is sparsely populated, it can be said to be lightly populated.

4 [Fill in a Table Question]

According to the passage, people in rural areas go to social events with their neighbors, often have strong relationships with one another, and usually help one another out. As for people in urban areas, they often rarely interact, and they hardly know their neighbors.

Summarizing

Nowadays, people live in both urban and rural areas. But the relationships between the people in each place are different. People in rural areas often have homes, spend time outside, and get to know their neighbors. People in urban areas frequently live in apartments and rarely see their neighbors. Those in rural areas have strong bonds because they are related and do many activities together. They trust one another more. So people in rural areas are more likely to help others than people in cities.

1 Ⓐ   2 Ⓑ   3 **1**   4 ①, ②, ⑥

1 [Factual Question]

The passage reads, "Jean Piaget, a Swiss philosopher, proposed the most-accepted theory of children's development."

2 [Sentence Simplification Question]

The highlighted sentence notes that people cannot remember memories from before they were two, but they might be able to remember other memories depending upon what they are. These ideas are best described in answer choice Ⓑ.

3 [Insert Text Question]

The sentence before the first square notes that there is little evidence to support the supposed memories of abuse that some people claim to have. The sentence to be inserted explains why some people may have these "memories" from the past.

4 [Prose Summary Question]

According to the passage, most memories from before a person's teen years are of crucial events in that person's life. People may also remember or forget key events from their childhood. And most experts believe people cannot remember anything from before they turned two years old.

Summarizing

People have difficulty remembering anything before they turn three years old. One reason was discovered by Jean Piaget. He learned that children's abilities develop in stages. One is memory. People have no memories from two years of age or younger, and they have only selective memories after that until their teens. In addition, adults may or may not remember traumatic events from their childhood. In some cases, they make fake memories or want to forget something but cannot. Sometimes, though, they can block disturbing memories.

Mastering **the Subject**   C   p.116

1 Ⓒ   2 Ⓑ   3 Ⓐ   4 ③, ④, ⑤

1 [Negative Factual Question]

There is no mention in the passage of where children in farm families attended school.

2 [Rhetorical Purpose Question]

The passage reads, "This made many families follow the practice of primogeniture. So only the oldest son inherited any land. While this ensured that farms remained large, it left nothing for second and third sons." This explains why younger sons left their family farms.

3 [Reference Question]

The "them" that lost contact with their families back in the east were sons.

4 [Prose Summary Question]

According to the passage, young men traveling west helped populate the American frontier. In addition, many American farm families stayed together in the seventeenth and eighteenth centuries. And second and third sons got no land from their fathers, so they left the farms to find land of their own.

Summarizing

In colonial America, families lived on farms and worked hard to support one another. Both sons and daughters were expected to get married and to start their own families. Sons also expected to inherit land. But many Americans practiced primogeniture, so only the oldest son got any land. The younger sons left the farms and headed west. They wanted their own land. These sons helped populate the western part of the United States. They lost contact with their families, but they started new lives of their own.

TOEFL **Practice Test**   p.118

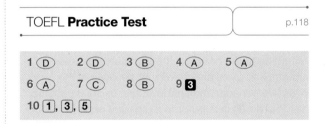

1 Ⓓ   2 Ⓓ   3 Ⓑ   4 Ⓐ   5 Ⓐ
6 Ⓐ   7 Ⓒ   8 Ⓑ   9 ❸
10 ①, ③, ⑤

1 [Factual Question]

About suburbs, the author writes, "They are primarily residential areas, so most of their buildings are homes and apartments."

2 [Sentence Simplification Question]

The highlighted sentence notes that couples with young children often become homeowners in the suburbs because of their many advantages. This fact is best described in answer choice Ⓓ.

3 [Factual Question]

The author notes, "While real estate prices are often outrageously high in metropolitan areas, housing costs in suburbs are much lower."

4 [Inference Question]

The author mentions, "They have no factories spewing pollution," so it can be inferred that there is a lack of manufacturing jobs in the suburbs.

5 [Vocabulary Question]

When referring to the proximity of one place to another, the nearness of the two places is being discussed.

6 [Negative Factual Question]

The author writes, "Making this easier is the fact that many suburbs are linked to metropolitan areas by extensive transportations systems. These include highways, bus and subway lines and commuter trains." Clearly, suburbanites' commutes do not require cars.

7 [Rhetorical Purpose Question]

The passage notes, "Many suburbs have a single shopping mall with a movie theater to serve as the entertainment district."

8 [Factual Question]

It is written, "White families moved to the suburbs while black and Hispanic families remained in the inner cities."

9 [Insert Text Question]

The sentence prior to the third square mentions how small the entertainment district in most suburbs is. The sentence to be inserted focuses on the mall, which is mentioned in the sentence in front of the third square. Thus, the two sentences go together.

10 [Prose Summary Question]

According to the passage, the commutes between suburbs and cities are convenient because of the extensive transportation network that exists. In addition, raising children in suburbs is a pleasant experience for many reasons. And homes are cheaper in the suburbs than they are in big cities.

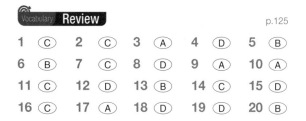

Vocabulary Review

p.125

1	Ⓒ	2	Ⓒ	3	Ⓐ	4	Ⓓ	5	Ⓑ
6	Ⓑ	7	Ⓒ	8	Ⓓ	9	Ⓐ	10	Ⓐ
11	Ⓒ	12	Ⓓ	13	Ⓑ	14	Ⓒ	15	Ⓓ
16	Ⓒ	17	Ⓐ	18	Ⓓ	19	Ⓓ	20	Ⓑ

Chapter | 05 Economics

Mastering **the Question Types** A p.128

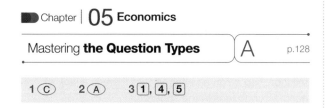

1 Ⓒ   2 Ⓐ   3 ①, ④, ⑤

1 [Rhetorical Purpose Question]

The passage reads, "They wanted to protect their rights, to set standards of skill and payment, to prevent nonmembers from doing business in an area, and to train apprentices."

2 [Vocabulary Question]

When competitors get eliminated, then they are removed from competition.

3 [Prose Summary Question]

According to the passage, guilds protected the rights of their members. In addition, they established monopolies that kept people from stealing their business. And the members of guilds had to follow all of their rules and regulations.

Summarizing

Guilds were associations of craftsmen that formed during the Middle Ages. There were guilds for carpenters, masons, bakers, blacksmiths, and many others. Guilds tried to regulate the way that craftsmen worked. They protected their members and helped them train new apprentices. Guilds formed monopolies, which helped their members. However, these monopolies discouraged innovation. After the Renaissance ended, guilds slowly began losing power. During the Industrial Revolution, they mostly disappeared.

Mastering **the Question Types** B p.130

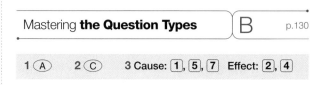

1 Ⓐ   2 Ⓒ   3 Cause: ①, ⑤, ⑦   Effect: ②, ④

1 [Negative Factual Question]

The passage reads, "On top of all this, many British factories utilized child labor."

2 [Inference Question]

When the author writes, "More police patrolled the streets to keep crime under control," it can be inferred that the British government wanted to decrease the amount of crime in the country.

3 [Fill in a Table Question]

According to the passage, the causes of the problems during the Industrial Revolution included factories making air pollution, children being obligated to work in factories, and social issues such as crime and disease occurring. As for the effects on the problems during this period, urban planning led to better-designed cities, and laws were passed requiring children to get educations.

Summarizing

The Industrial Revolution started in Great Britain in the 1700s. It had many negative effects. British cities became overcrowded, which increased crime and disease rates. Factories created air pollution, which made people sick. Workers were hurt or killed in factories, and even children worked in them. The British government acted to solve these problems. It designed cities better and hired more police. Pollution levels were reduced, and factories became safer. And children had to work fewer hours and attend school.

Mastering **the Question Types** C p.132

1 Ⓐ, Ⓓ　　**2** Ⓑ　　**3** Ⓒ　　**4** ❸

1 [Reference Question]

The passage reads, "As the years went by, the sizes of the ships also increased. So the tonnage transported increased from 440,000 tons a year to more than a billion tons annually nowadays. Petroleum, coal, ore, metal, grain, and wood are some of the main items transported."

2 [Sentence Simplification Question]

The highlighted sentence notes that large freighters carry many goods to Europe and Asia, which makes many products available. This is best described in answer choice Ⓑ.

3 [Factual Question]

The "it" that is vital to the global economy is the canal.

4 [Insert Text Question]

The sentence before the third square notes that the Suez Canal had an initial transit time of forty hours. The sentence to be inserted points out that ships can move through the canal in half that amount of time today.

Summarizing

> For centuries, sailors wanted to go from Europe to Asia to trade for various exotic goods. But the journey was long and dangerous. In 1869, the Suez Canal in Egypt opened and made the voyage shorter. Initially, it only took forty hours to transit the canal. Large numbers of ships began passing through the canal daily, and today, more than one billion tons of goods go through it. The canal has made the prices of goods lower, and there are more products available for people to purchase.

Mastering **the Subject** A p.134

1 Ⓓ　　**2** Ⓑ　　**3** Ⓒ　　**4** ①, ②, ⑤

1 [Vocabulary Question]

When people are erecting something, such as a skyscraper, they are building it.

2 [Factual Question]

The passage notes, "The Second Industrial Revolution saw innovations in many fields. There were advances in the electric, steel, chemical, and petroleum industries. Developments in these fields dramatically altered society."

3 [Reference Question]

The "those" that were found far away were raw materials.

4 [Prose Summary Question]

According to the passage, the large amount of raw materials in the U.S. let factories make many finished products. In addition, the large number of immigrants coming to the country were employed these factories. And the steel and petroleum industries advanced very much in the mid-eighteenth century.

Summarizing

> The United States started to industrialize around 1850 when the Second Industrial Revolution began. There were advances in the electric, steel, chemical, and petroleum industries. The discovery of oil in the U.S. let people use it in the internal combustion engine. The U.S. had large amounts of raw materials, including iron, coal, oil, and timber. Factories used them to make finished products. Finally, in the 1800s, millions of immigrants moved to the U.S. Many worked in factories and provided the manpower that helped the country industrialize.

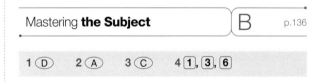

Mastering **the Subject** B p.136

1 Ⓓ　　**2** Ⓐ　　**3** Ⓒ　　**4** ①, ③, ⑥

1 [Sentence Simplification Question]

The highlighted sentence notes that the two countries to which the Industrial Revolution came the fastest were the two that made the most effort to protect the works of inventors. This idea is best described in answer choice Ⓓ.

2 [Rhetorical Purpose Question]

About Eli Whitney, the author writes, "In others, such as the invention of the cotton gin by Eli Whitney, they did not. While Whitney's invention revolutionized the cotton industry, he received virtually no royalties. People simply copied his design without paying him at all."

3 [Negative Factual Question]

The paragraph does not mention anything about people becoming wealthy from the inventions that they made.

4 [Prose Summary Question]

According to the passage, government enforcement of patents made inventors work harder and share their work. In addition, patents were used in Greece and in Renaissance Italy. And the British and American governments began trying to protect inventors' rights.

Summarizing

A patent gives its creator ownership of an invention. Then, the patent holder receives royalties when others use the invention. Patents date back to ancient Greece. However, they were not well protected until Great Britain and the United States began enforcing them during the Industrial Revolution. Still, inventors often received few royalties for their inventions. Governments have many reasons to enforce patents. Patent enforcement encourages inventors to work hard and to share their knowledge with others. It also persuades corporations to spend money on research.

Mastering **the Subject**

C   p.138

1 Ⓑ   2 Ⓐ   3 **2**   4 Population: ⑤, ⑦
History: ①, ②, ④

1 [Inference Question]

About China's size, the author writes, "China is a huge country. This long hampered its economic progress. There were several reasons for this. Due to a lack of infrastructure in terms of roads, waterways, and railways, traveling there was a laborious process. This caused many problems. Communications were inefficient and slow. Transporting goods was even slower. And ruling such a large land was a difficult task." From this, it can be inferred that China's huge size helped divide it.

2 [Vocabulary Question]

When economic progress is hindered by something, it is deterred.

3 [Insert Text Question]

The sentence before the second square notes that fewer people on farms could suddenly produce more

food. The sentence to be inserted reinforces this point, so the two sentences belong together.

4 [Fill in a Table Question]

According to the passage, China's population mostly engaged in subsistence farming, and the lack of technology kept these people from doing work other than farming. As for the country's history, the Japanese influenced China once the Europeans left, there were many Europeans in China in the 1800s, and there were many conflicts and revolutions fought within China itself.

Summarizing

Today, China is a leading world power and was a great country in the past. For many centuries though, it was poor with numerous problems. Its size made communication and transportation throughout the country difficult. Its enormous population was mostly involved in subsistence farming since the country industrialized very late. China's history was troubled. The Europeans and Japanese were both involved in its internal affairs. There was a revolution in China as well. Finally, in 1976, after Mao Zedong died, China's economy began to improve.

TOEFL **Practice Test**

p.140

1 Ⓒ   2 Ⓑ   3 Ⓒ   4 Ⓐ   5 Ⓓ
6 Ⓐ   7 Ⓒ   8 Ⓐ   9 **2**
10 ①, ③, ⑤

1 [Vocabulary Question]

When power is derived, it is attained.

2 [Factual Question]

The author writes, "The Venetians were ruthless as they built their monopoly. They raided cities and destroyed rival salt production centers. Eventually, using their peerless navy, they seized control of the local salt trade."

3 [Negative Factual Question]

There is no mention in the passage of the main reason that people needed salt in the past.

4 [Inference Question]

The author notes, "Salt from mines is generally of a higher quality than sea salt." Thus it can be inferred that the Venetians preferred mined salt to sea salt.

5 [Rhetorical Purpose Question]

The passage notes, "Recognizing the value of salt, the Venetians sought to control the local trade. They tried making their own salt works to evaporate seawater. However, the low-lying areas around the islands Venice is built on are vulnerable to storms. So the rainy weather caused problems for them. For centuries, the Venetians made salt, yet it was never very profitable."

6 [Factual Question]

The passage reads, "They tried making their own salt works to evaporate seawater. However, the low-lying areas around the islands Venice is built on are vulnerable to storms. So the rainy weather caused problems for them."

7 [Factual Question]

It is written, "This initiated a long period of conflict between Venice and Ravenna."

8 [Vocabulary Question]

When a tax is imposed on something or someone, it is levied.

9 [Insert Text Question]

The sentence before the second square notes that the Venetians came to control the entire salt trade in northern Italy. Thus, they had a monopoly. The sentence to be inserted describes one effect that this monopoly had on Venice.

10 [Prose Summary Question]

According to the passage, the Venetians had rivals that they needed to deal with to establish a monopoly in the salt trade. In addition, the Venetians did not get salt from the sea very well but still dominated the salt trade. And the Venetians used violence—like they did against Comacchio—to control the salt trade and to keep others out of it.

Vocabulary Review　　　　　p.147

1	D	2	B	3	B	4	C	5	A
6	C	7	B	8	D	9	A	10	A
11	B	12	C	13	D	14	A	15	B
16	B	17	C	18	C	19	D	20	A

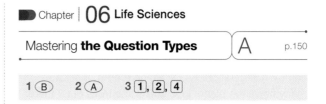

■ Chapter | **06** Life Sciences

Mastering **the Question Types**　　A　p.150

1 (B)　　2 (A)　　3 [1], [2], [4]

1 [Rhetorical Purpose Question]

Much of the first paragraph notes the various ways in which snakes' tongues are forked.

2 [Vocabulary Question]

When snakes perceive differences in chemical compositions, they detect the differences.

3 [Prose Summary Question]

According to the passage, snakes use their tongues to identify the chemical compositions of prey animals. In addition, male snakes use their tongues when searching for females to mate with. And an organ in snakes' bodies analyzes and interprets chemical particles.

Summarizing

All snakes have forked tongues, so they are split in two near the tip. Their tongues are useful because snakes smell with them. Their tongues collect chemical particles from the moisture in the air. Then, the Jacobson's organ analyzes the particles to determine what they are. Snakes use this knowledge to avoid enemies and to find food. Males also use their tongues to find females. They flick their tongues in and out when trying to attract female snakes' attention.

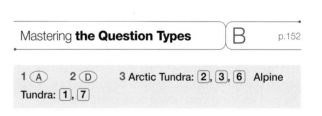

Mastering **the Question Types**　　B　p.152

1 (A)　　2 (D)　　3 Arctic Tundra: [2], [3], [6]　Alpine Tundra: [1], [7]

1 [Negative Factual Question]

There is no mention in the passage about the average depth of the permafrost in arctic tundra.

2 [Inference Question]

About arctic tundra, the author writes, "This combination of factors makes it impossible for trees to grow." And about alpine tundra, it is written, "Some trees actually grow there." It can therefore be inferred that plants grow taller in alpine tundra than in arctic tundra.

3 [Fill in a Table Question]

According to the passage, arctic tundra has ferns and grasses, supports small plants in places with little permafrost, and has mosses and lichens as its most common vegetation. As for alpine tundra, there are many flowering plants in it, and some trees grow there.

Summarizing

Tundra is a biome that features frigid temperatures and permafrost. Arctic tundra is in northern areas near the North Pole. It can have very thick permafrost as well as winters that are very dark. Because of that, trees do not grow there. Mosses, lichens, grasses, and ferns can grow in it though. Alpine tundra is located in mountainous areas with high elevations. Its permafrost is not so thick, and winters are not completely dark. Some dwarf trees grow there as well as flowering plants.

Mastering **the Question Types**   C   p.154

1 Ⓑ   **2** Ⓐ   **3** Ⓐ   **4** 3

1 [Factual Question]

The author writes, "Scientists call this period the Cambrian Explosion. The term Cambrian comes from the geological name of the period. The word 'explosion' refers to the fact that so many organisms appeared in a short time."

2 [Reference Question]

The "some" that believe there was a mass extinction are scientists.

3 [Sentence Simplification Question]

The highlighted sentence notes that some scientists say no pre-Cambrian fossils have been found because the animals living then lacked body parts that could become fossils. This theory is best described in answer choice Ⓐ.

4 [Insert Text Question]

The sentence before the third square describes the possibility of there being a mass extinction of life before the Cambrian Explosion. The sentence to be inserted provides one possible explanation for how a mass extinction could have occurred.

Summarizing

For four billion years, the Earth had few life forms. Then,

during the Cambrian Explosion, large numbers of species suddenly appeared. Scientists have three main theories about this. Some say the Earth's oxygen level increased, so complex life forms appeared. Others say new species evolved because of a mass extinction before this period. And others say there was no explosion of species at all. The problem is the lack of fossil evidence from this period, so scientists know little about it.

Mastering **the Subject**   A   p.156

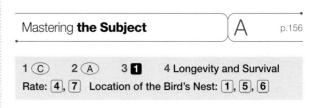

1 Ⓒ   **2** Ⓐ   **3** 1   **4** Longevity and Survival Rate: 4, 7   Location of the Bird's Nest: 1, 5, 6

1 [Rhetorical Purpose Question]

The author writes, "Some birds, such as penguins, albatrosses, and ostriches, live for decades."

2 [Factual Question]

The passage reads, "Some birds, such as woodpeckers, construct nests inside trees. These birds are cavity nesters."

3 [Insert Text Question]

The sentence before the first square notes that birds in North America and Europe often lay more eggs than birds in tropical areas. The sentence to be inserted provides an example of this.

4 [Fill in a Table Question]

According to the passage, birds' longevity and survival rates can affect how well the parents take care of their offspring and can make birds lay many eggs to increase their chances of survival. As for the location of the bird's nest, the closeness of the nest to predators makes birds lay few eggs, cavity nesters may lay many eggs, and birds lay many eggs when they are safe from attack.

Summarizing

All birds lay eggs. However, each species lays varying numbers of eggs. For instance, birds that live a long time, such as penguins, albatrosses, and ostriches, lay one egg; however, short-lived birds lay many eggs at once. Birds in colder places lay many eggs while those in tropical conditions lay fewer eggs. The location of a bird's nest is important, too. Cavity nesters, which have nests in safe places, lay many eggs. Open nesters, whose nests are vulnerable to predators, lay only a few.

Mastering the Subject   B   p.158

1 Ⓓ	2 Ⓑ	3 Ⓒ	4 NREM Sleep: ③, ④, ⑥

REM Sleep: ②, ⑤

1   [Factual Question]

The passage notes, "When a person is in NREM sleep, that individual's breathing is slow, and the body's heart rate and blood pressure are low. Additionally, the person's body remains quite still. Brainwave activity also slows since the amount of blood flowing to the brain is reduced."

2   [Inference Question]

The author writes, "This is the deepest stage of sleep as bodily functions are at their lowest level of activity. If someone manages to awaken a sleeper during this stage, the sleeper will be disoriented and unable to do anything for some time." Thus it can be inferred that it is difficult to awaken someone during this stage.

3   [Reference Question]

The "others" that can last for an hour are dreams.

4   [Fill in a Table Question]

According to the passage, in NREM sleep, it may be difficult to wake up a person, there are three distinct stages, and there is a progression from light to very deep sleep. As for REM sleep, people may dream during it, and it only takes up about a fifth of a person's sleeping time.

Summarizing

People experience four different stages of sleep. Three involve NREM sleep, and the other is REM sleep. NREM sleep occurs when a person goes to sleep. Stage 1 is a light sleep, and Stage 2 is deeper. Stage 3 is a very deep sleep. During NREM sleep, the person's bodily functions slow down. The fourth stage is REM sleep. This is when people dream. The person's breathing rate, heart rate, and brain activity increase. A person often goes through all four stages repeatedly while sleeping.

Mastering the Subject   C   p.160

1 Ⓒ	2 Ⓐ	3 Ⓓ	4 ②, ⑤, ⑥

1   [Sentence Simplification Question]

The highlighted sentence notes that because of changes in the pinyon pine tree and the pinyon jay bird, they are able to use each other to reproduce and to live. This is best described in answer choice Ⓒ.

2   [Negative Factual Question]

There is no mention in the passage of when pinyon pine tree seeds become mature.

3   [Vocabulary Question]

Caches are hidden stores of supplies.

4   [Prose Summary Question]

According to the passage, pinyon jay birds consume large amounts of pinyon pine trees' seeds. In addition, the pinyon pine tree seeds that are hidden and forgotten by the jays often become adult trees. And the color of the trees' seeds lets the jays determine whether they can be eaten or not.

Summarizing

Pinyon pine trees and pinyon jay birds have a mutually beneficial relationship. The jays eat many of the pines' seeds. The seeds have two separate colors. These indicate which ones are ripe and which are not. The jays have beaks that can easily grab the seeds from the cones. The jays then bury the seeds in the ground. In spring, they dig up the seeds to feed their young. But the jays occasionally forget about some seeds. These then germinate and become adult trees.

TOEFL Practice Test   p.162

1 Ⓒ	2 Ⓐ	3 Ⓓ	4 Ⓓ	5 Ⓒ
6 Ⓑ	7 Ⓑ	8 Ⓓ	9 **④**	

10 ①, ②, ⑥

1   [Factual Question]

The author writes, "They may migrate thousands of kilometers from their breeding places to their feeding grounds."

2   [Vocabulary Question]

When sand incubates the eggs, it heats them.

3   [Negative Factual Question]

The passage mentions that baby turtles are eaten by birds, but the birds do not eat the eggs.

4 [Rhetorical Purpose Question]

The author mentions, "Their favorite species is the lion's mane jellyfish, which, weighing around ten pounds, is one of the largest of its kind."

5 [Factual Question]

The passage notes, "However, the turtles have adapted to survive in these conditions. They can maintain body temperatures higher than the surrounding water temperature. Their high metabolic rate enables this."

6 [Vocabulary Question]

When people help revitalize a species, they invigorate it.

7 [Factual Question]

It is written, "Instead, the encroachment of humans on their traditional nesting beaches and their getting caught in fishing nets depleted their numbers."

8 [Inference Question]

The author writes, "Sadly, the Pacific Ocean leatherbacks are in serious decline and may not recover." Thus it can be inferred that the leatherback turtle will soon be extinct in one ocean.

9 [Insert Text Question]

The sentence before the fourth square notes that leatherback turtles could be considered warm-blooded animals because of one of their characteristics. The sentence to be inserted notes that this makes them an exception since they are reptiles.

10 [Prose Summary Question]

According to the passage, leatherback turtles can increase their metabolic rate to stay warm. In addition, they can stay warm since warm blood heats the cold parts of their bodies. And the turtles swim thousands of kilometers from their birthplaces to their feeding grounds.

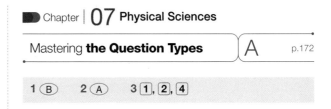

Vocabulary Review   p.169

1	D	2	C	3	A	4	A	5	D
6	B	7	C	8	D	9	D	10	A
11	C	12	A	13	D	14	A	15	C
16	B	17	C	18	A	19	D	20	A

Mastering **the Question Types**   A   p.172

1 (B)   2 (A)   3 [1], [2], [4]

1 [Vocabulary Question]

An extensive eon is very lengthy.

2 [Rhetorical Purpose Question]

The author writes, "The Paleozoic Era began with what scientists call the Cambrian Explosion. For reasons yet unknown, many complex life forms, including small and large plants, insects, and land animals, suddenly developed then."

3 [Prose Summary Question]

According to the passage, the current eon has been divided into three eras. In addition, geologists have used different methods to create the geological time scale. And there was just one supereon, but there were four eons.

Summarizing

The Earth is around 4.5 billion years old. While humanoids have only been alive for about four million years, geologists have learned much about the Earth's past. They have divided the Earth's history into many time periods. The Pre-Cambrian Supereon was the longest one. It has been divided into several eons and eras. During it, small organisms and the Earth's atmosphere developed. More advanced life developed during the Phanerozoic Era. The Cambrian Explosion, dinosaurs, and the rise of humans all occurred during it.

Mastering **the Question Types**   B   p.174

1 (C)   2 (B)   3 Reflecting Telescope: [1], [3], [7]
Refracting Telescope: [4], [5]

1 [Negative Factual Question]

The author writes, "Three Dutchmen invented the first telescope in the early 1600s. It was rapidly improved upon by Galileo and, later, others. Since then, several types have been devised." So there are more than two types of telescopes.

2 [Inference Question]

The lens of the Hubble Space Telescope is 2.4 meters.

Since refracting telescopes are no larger than one meter in diameter, it can be inferred that the Hubble is a reflecting telescope.

3 [Fill in a Table Question]

According to the passage, reflecting telescopes are ideal for looking at distant objects, do not get distorted as they increase in size, and gather light with mirrors. As for refracting telescopes, they are limited in the sizes of their lenses and have several lenses to collect light.

Summarizing

The first telescopes were invented in the 1600s. Since then, many improvements have been made. There are two main types of telescopes: reflecting and refracting telescopes. Reflecting telescopes collect light with mirrors while refracting telescopes use lenses. Reflecting telescopes are good for viewing distant objects and have no size limit on their mirrors. Refracting telescopes return distorted images when their lenses get too large. The best telescope is the Hubble Space Telescope, which orbits the Earth.

Mastering **the Question Types**   C   p.176

1 Ⓑ   **2** Ⓐ   **3** Ⓓ   **4** **2**

1 [Factual Question]

The author writes, "The PBL starts at the surface and rises roughly 1.5 kilometers above the ground. In that relatively small amount of space, the PBL can be divided into three individual layers."

2 [Sentence Simplification Question]

The highlighted sentence notes that the fact that the PBL is so close to the ground means it is influenced by certain things on the ground. This is best described in answer choice Ⓐ.

3 [Reference Question]

The "it" that cools off enough is the air.

4 [Insert Text Question]

The sentence before the fourth square mentions some of the factors that influence the PBL. The sentence to be inserted adds that pollution is another factor that can have an effect on the weather.

Summarizing

The planetary boundary layer is part of the troposphere

and is also the part of the atmosphere closest to the ground. The PBL has three parts, the surface layer, the mixed layer, and the capping inversion layer or entrainment zone. Many aspects of the surface, including temperature, wind, convection, and friction, affect the PBL. The PBL also changes more than any other part of the atmosphere. The PBL changes greatly during the day depending on where the sun is. At times, it even disappears in places.

Mastering **the Subject**   A   p.178

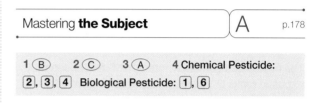

1 Ⓑ   **2** Ⓒ   **3** Ⓐ   **4 Chemical Pesticide:**
2, **3**, **4**   **Biological Pesticide:** **1**, **6**

1 [Factual Question]

The author writes, "As a result, some countries, including the United States, have banned the use of organochlorines."

2 [Negative Factual Question]

The safety of biological pesticides is not mentioned in the passage.

3 [Rhetorical Purpose Question]

About DDT, the author mentions how many lives it has saved around the world. Thus the author is describing its effectiveness.

4 [Fill in a Table Question]

According to the passage, chemical pesticides are not permitted to be used in some places, may harm people and animals, and have four primary types. As for biological pesticides, they may keep pests from reproducing, and they may use pheromones.

Summarizing

Pesticides kill all kinds of pests. There are two main types: chemical and biological pesticides. There are four types of chemical pesticides. They typically kill pests. Many, such as DDT, are lethal, but some have been banned because they may be harmful to humans and other animals. Nowadays, many people prefer biological pesticides. There are three types of these. Biological pesticides do not always kill pests. Sometimes they merely drive them away. All around the world, pesticides such as DDT are commonly used.

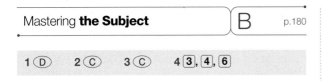

1 [Factual Question]

The author notes, "Smith wanted to be a surveyor, not a geologist. He began his career working in coal mines and on canals. However, while working, he noticed some layers of rocks in the mines and canal cuttings. Each layer was distinct and appeared to be composed of different types of rock."

2 [Sentence Simplification Question]

The highlighted sentence notes that Smith observed exposed rocks in various places that he traveled to around the country. This is best described in answer choice ⓒ.

3 [Vocabulary Question]

When Smith's ideas were co-opted by others, his ideas were taken by people.

4 [Prose Summary Question]

According to the passage, Smith realized that each layer of rock represented a different geological era. In addition, Smith's 1815 map of Great Britain was an improvement of his 1799 map. And Smith's maps were important to geologists and people working on various projects.

Summarizing

> William Smith was a geologist from England who lived in the 1700s and 1800s. Smith noticed different layers of rock in places around the country. He realized that each layer came from a different age in the Earth's past. He started making maps of these rock layers. In 1799, he made a small map. But in 1815, he produced a large map that made him famous. His maps were useful to geologists and many others and helped in the future study of geology.

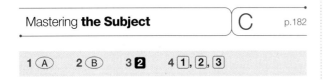

1 [Reference Question]

The "their" that have surface areas that are not as old as those of others places are the maria.

2 [Inference Question]

The small sizes of simple impact craters make it possible to infer that they are caused by relatively small objects from space.

3 [Insert Text Question]

The sentence before the second square mentions that the moon's lack of an atmosphere prevents objects from burning up before they strike the moon. The sentence to be inserted compares this with what happens to objects that enter the Earth's atmosphere.

4 [Prose Summary Question]

According to the passage, there are three classifications of lunar impact craters. In addition, lunar impact craters greatly vary in size. And asteroids, meteors, and comets all strike the moon.

Summarizing

> The moon has been struck by numerous objects from space. These include asteroids, meteorites, and comets. These impacts have left craters on its surface. The craters range from one kilometer to more than 2,000 kilometers in diameter. They also vary in shape. This is caused by the size and speed of the objects impacting the moon. There are three main types of impact craters: simple, complex, and impact basin craters. The diameters, depths, and shapes of these craters are all different from one another.

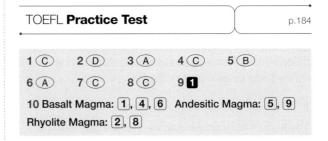

1 [Vocabulary Question]

When magma surfaces, it emerges onto the ground.

2 [Negative Factual Question]

The passage notes that magma often comes to the surface; therefore answer choice ⓓ cannot be correct.

3 [Vocabulary Question]

The viscosity of a substance refers to its thickness.

4 [Reference Question]

The "it" that cools is the lava.

5 [Factual Question]

About basalt magma, the author writes, "It has a lower silica and gas content than the other two magma types."

6 [Rhetorical Purpose Question]

When discussing the eruption of andesitic magma, the author mentions, "When the eruption is more explosive, a high stratovolcano—a cone-shaped volcano—may be the end result."

7 [Factual Question]

The author notes, "Volcanic eruptions caused by it can either be flowing—like basalt magma—or more violent, explosive eruptions."

8 [Factual Question]

It is written, "On account of its high level of gases, rhyolite magma is highly explosive and may cause massive eruptions."

9 [Insert Text Question]

The sentence before the first square mentions that parts of volcanoes may be blown away when they erupt. The sentence to be inserted provides an example of when this happened.

10 [Fill in a Table Question]

According to the passage, basalt magma has high levels of iron and calcium, may produce cinder cones, and may be up to 1,200 degrees Celsius. As for andesitic magma, it may produce a stratovolcano, and it can cause slow-moving or violent eruptions. And rhyolite magma may cause a pyroclastic flow, and it has the highest viscosity of all three types of magma.

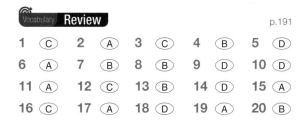
Vocabulary **Review** p.191

1	C	2	A	3	C	4	B	5	D
6	A	7	B	8	B	9	D	10	D
11	A	12	C	13	B	14	D	15	A
16	C	17	A	18	D	19	A	20	B

Chapter | **08 Environmental Sciences**

Mastering **the Question Types** A p.194

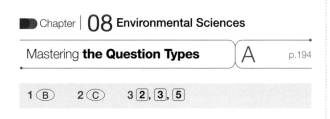

1 B   2 C   3 ②, ③, ⑤

1 [Vocabulary Question]

When water displaces other water, it causes the water to shift.

2 [Rhetorical Purpose Question]

The author notes which effects the fall turnover has on the water in deep lakes.

3 [Prose Summary Question]

According to the passage, the three layers of water form again during the spring turnover. In addition, the layers may vanish because of cold wind and less sunlight. And a lake's layers disappear during the fall turnover.

Summarizing

Deep lakes have three layers: the epilimnion, the thermocline, and the hypolimnion. The epilimnion has the most oxygen while the hypolimnion has the least. As the wind blows the water on top of the lake, it circulates. The lower two layers do not circulate. When the weather becomes colder, the layers all disappear. This is the fall turnover. Then, water circulates through the entire lake. This replenishes the oxygen level of all of the lake's regions. As the temperature gets warmer, the layers return. This is the spring turnover.

Mastering **the Question Types** B p.196

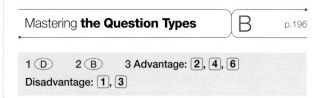

1 D   2 B   3 Advantage: ②, ④, ⑥
Disadvantage: ①, ③

1 [Inference Question]

The author writes, "This creates energy that is cheap, clean, and reusable." Thus it is implied that geothermal energy does not create any pollution.

2 [Negative Factual Question]

The author writes, "Its primary drawback is that it is only useful in places where it is located."

3 [Fill in a Table Question]

According to the passage, the advantages of geothermal energy include that it is renewable, it does not cost much, and it is clean. As for its disadvantages, it may have to be accessed in dangerous areas, and it must be used where it is created.

Summarizing

Geothermal energy uses heat from inside the Earth. People

use it to make electricity and to heat buildings and homes. It makes a cheap, clean, and reusable form of electricity. For heating, it involves piping water underground to heat it and then sending the water back aboveground. Geothermal energy is not used much nowadays. It cannot be transported to other places, and it is not accessible in all places. Since it is available for use near volcanoes, it can also be dangerous to access.

Mastering **the Question Types**   C   p.198

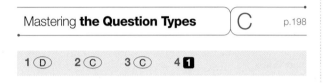

1 ⓓ   2 ⓒ   3 ⓒ   4 **1**

1   [Sentence Simplification Question]

The highlighted sentence notes that fish and other animals get harmed when water is lost from rivers, lakes, and streams. This is best described in answer choice ⓓ.

2   [Reference Question]

The "they" that can be harmed over time are roots.

3   [Factual Question]

The author writes, "When water levels are reduced, the soil may have salt levels that are higher than normal. Most plants are unable to grow well in soil which is too salty."

4   [Insert Text Question]

The sentence before the first square mentions that groundwater supplies may become depleted. The sentence to be inserted mentions that it may take years for the groundwater supplied to recover.

Summarizing

One effect of irrigation is that water is moved from one place to another to support crops, yards, or other landscapes. There are also some negative effects. For instance, water is removed from sources such as rivers, lakes, and streams. This can harm animals such as fish. Groundwater supplies may also be depleted. The weather in the irrigated areas can become rainier, too. Soil salinization and waterlogging can take place as well. These both can cause problems for vegetation growing in some areas.

Mastering **the Subject**   A   p.200

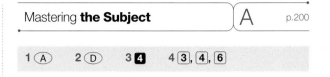

1 ⓐ   2 ⓓ   3 **4**   4 **3**, **4**, **6**

1   [Vocabulary Question]

Something that does not retain water well does not keep much of it.

2   [Factual Question]

The passage notes, "Soils with higher percentages of clay are more densely packed so are better able to resist erosion. They also retain water and nutrients well, which makes them ideal for growing plants."

3   [Insert Text Question]

The sentence before the fourth square mentions that darker soil is usually the most fertile soil. The sentence to be inserted then explains that farmers prefer growing their crops in that soil.

4   [Prose Summary Question]

According to the passage, soil is composed of different amounts of minerals, water, air, and organic materials. In addition, the excessive use of fertilizers can make soil become less fertile. And clay's characteristics make it fertile.

Summarizing

There are many factors involved in the creation of soil. Because of this, some soils become fertile while others do not. There are four basic components in soil: minerals, water, air, and organic matter. There are three main types of soil texture: sand, silt, and clay. Sand is the least fertile. Clay is the most fertile. Soil can also be different colors depending on its content. In general, dark soil is very fertile. Fertilizers, pesticides, and a lack of rain can all harm the soil.

Mastering **the Subject**   B   p.202

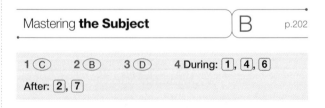

1 ⓒ   2 ⓑ   3 ⓓ   4 During: **1**, **4**, **6**
After: **2**, **7**

1   [Reference Question]

The "these" that may kill impurities are chemicals.

2   [Sentence Simplification Question]

The highlighted sentence notes that some people

believe the chemicals used when filtering the water make it not be pure. This idea is best described in answer choice Ⓑ.

3 [Rhetorical Purpose Question]

The author mentions, "A third process some use is reverse osmosis. This involves forcing water through a membrane at high pressure. In doing that, the membrane filters out any impurities."

4 [Fill in a Table Question]

According to the passage, during the filtration process, water is given chemicals to make it colorless, it is run through screens to capture impurities, and it may be treated with various chemicals. After the filtration process, water is filtered by some people in their homes, and it is released into the public drinking system.

Summarizing

> People need clean water in order to survive. So the water must be purified at a plant. There are several steps. Water goes through screens and is treated with various chemicals. These make the water clean and colorless. Once it is released, people can access it in their homes. But some people further purify their water by using filters in their homes. Many people around the world get sick from drinking unpurified water. Some even die because of impurities in the water that harm them.

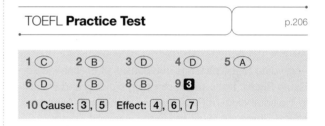

Mastering **the Subject**   C   p.204

1 Ⓑ   2 Ⓑ   3 Ⓓ   4 ①, ④, ⑥

1 [Reference Question]

The "they" that require a temperature that is not too hot or too cold are crops.

2 [Inference Question]

About the Anasazi, the author writes, "This was the fate of the Anasazi people. They lived in what is today the southwestern United States around a thousand years ago. At one time, the Anasazi's land received plenty of rainfall, and they led comfortable lives. Then, conditions changed. For some reason, rain began falling less often. The Anasazi's crops died, and they were forced to depart their ancestral homelands." It can therefore be inferred that they no longer live in the Southwestern United States.

3 [Negative Factual Question]

Melting ice is mentioned as a possible reason people will have to move in the future. But it is not mentioned as having forced people to move in the past.

4 [Prose Summary Question]

According to the passage, the Anasazi had to move away when their crops failed. In addition, the Dust Bowl forced farmers to leave their land. And some people believe melting ice could change millions of people's lives.

Summarizing

> The environment can often change. This can disrupt the lives of people and sometimes force them to move to other lands. When the environment changes, it can negatively affect farming. This happened to the Anasazi people. Their once-fertile land received less rain. Their crops died, so they moved away. In the 1930s, the Dust Bowl in North America ruined the land, so farmers and their families moved. Some people fear that melting ice could raise ocean levels. This would greatly disrupt lives all around the world.

TOEFL **Practice Test**   p.206

| 1 Ⓒ | 2 Ⓑ | 3 Ⓓ | 4 Ⓓ | 5 Ⓐ |
| 6 Ⓓ | 7 Ⓑ | 8 Ⓑ | 9 ❸ | |

10 Cause: ③, ⑤   Effect: ④, ⑥, ⑦

1 [Negative Factual Question]

According to the passage, El Nino occurs every two to seven years. Its effects, however, do not last that long.

2 [Rhetorical Purpose Question]

The author notes, "One reason is that a cold ocean current—the Humboldt Current—runs along the Pacific coast of South America."

3 [Inference Question]

The author writes, "The winds originate in the south-central Pacific and usually blow in a westerly direction. This pushes warm water toward the southwestern Pacific." Since the winds blow to the west, it can be inferred that sailing west with the wind is easier than sailing east against the wind.

4 [Vocabulary Question]

When cold water mingles with warm water, it mixes with the water.

5 [Sentence Simplification Question]

The highlighted sentence notes that thermometers in the Pacific Ocean let scientists know about the changing water temperatures. This is best explained in answer choice Ⓐ.

6 [Factual Question]

It is written, "This can cause a decrease in the number of fish there. Accordingly, during El Nino, the fisheries of South America suffer major losses."

7 [Factual Question]

The author writes, "However, during El Nino, the warmer water results in more evaporation. In turn, more rain falls on the land," and, "Even some parts of Africa may endure droughts while other regions there receive heavy rainfall."

8 [Factual Question]

The passage notes, "Meteorologists refer to this as La Nina. During this time, weather conditions return to normal."

9 [Insert Text Question]

The sentence before the third square describes the weather conditions in South America. The sentence to be inserted emphasizes that it is not just South America, however, that is affected by El Nino.

10 [Fill in a Table Question]

According to the passage, the causes of El Nino include South Pacific trade winds stopping blowing and water in the southeastern Pacific warming. As for El Nino's effects, there are fewer fish in the water off South America, there is more rain than normal in western South America, and places far from South America get changing weather.

Vocabulary Review

p.213

1	Ⓓ	2	Ⓐ	3	Ⓒ	4	Ⓑ	5	Ⓑ
6	Ⓓ	7	Ⓐ	8	Ⓒ	9	Ⓐ	10	Ⓐ
11	Ⓑ	12	Ⓓ	13	Ⓐ	14	Ⓒ	15	Ⓐ
16	Ⓑ	17	Ⓑ	18	Ⓒ	19	Ⓒ	20	Ⓓ

Part C

Experiencing the TOEFL iBT Actual Tests

Actual Test 01

p.217

1 Ⓓ	2 Ⓑ	3 Ⓐ	4 Ⓓ	5 Ⓑ
6 Ⓐ	7 Ⓒ	8 Ⓐ	9 **2**	
10 **2**, **5**, **6**				
11 Ⓑ	12 Ⓒ	13 Ⓐ	14 Ⓓ	15 Ⓒ
16 Ⓐ	17 Ⓓ	18 Ⓑ	19 **1**	
20 Cause: **3**, **4**, **7** Effect: **2**, **6**				
21 Ⓓ	22 Ⓐ	23 Ⓒ	24 Ⓓ	25 Ⓑ
26 Ⓓ	27 Ⓐ	28 Ⓓ	29 **2**	
30 **2**, **4**, **6**				
31 Ⓑ	32 Ⓒ	33 Ⓓ	34 Ⓓ	35 Ⓒ
36 Ⓐ	37 Ⓐ	38 Ⓓ	39 **4**	
40 **1**, **2**, **6**				

1 [Sentence Simplification Question]

The highlighted sentence notes that organisms in the deep sea must adapt to their surroundings, so they have adaptations found in no other animals. This idea is best described in answer choice Ⓓ.

2 [Factual Question]

The passage reads, "Some deep-sea creatures are predators. Therefore, they attack and feed on other organisms living in their area."

3 [Rhetorical Purpose Question]

The author mentions how tubeworms use chemosynthesis in order to survive deep under the water.

4 [Vocabulary Question]

When something is a chore to do, it can be difficult to accomplish.

5 [Inference Question]

The author notes, "Most of the fish living deep below the surface are small. They are typically less than half a meter in length. This means they require much less food and oxygen than do larger fish." It can therefore be inferred that smaller fish survive more easily than do larger fish.

6 [Factual Question]

The author writes, "Instead, most deep-sea fish have gelatinous bodies with non-rigid skeletal structures. This enables them to float yet avoid being crushed by the ocean pressure."

7 [Negative Factual Question]

The author notes, "Seeing is difficult in the total darkness of the ocean depths since the sun's light cannot penetrate that deep." Thus fish deep underwater cannot possibly rely on the sun's rays to see.

8 [Vocabulary Question]

Another word for undoubtedly is surely.

9 [Insert Text Question]

The sentence before the second square notes that some species of fish use bioluminescence to create their own light. The sentence to be inserted names a fish—the lanternfish—that relies on this method.

10 [Prose Summary Question]

According to the passage, fish such as the anglerfish use bioluminescence to create their own light. In addition, many fish in the deep sea have jellylike bodies that keep them from being crushed by the water pressure. Finally, some deep-sea organisms live near underwater vents to get heat and nourishment.

11 [Sentence Simplification Question]

The highlighted sentence notes that nationalism, the gap between the upper and lower classes, economic problems, and bad harvests all contributed to the revolutions of 1848. This is best described in answer choice Ⓑ.

12 [Inference Question]

The passage notes that Napoleon's armies "rampaged across Europe." It can be implied that Napoleon led his armies to victory throughout Europe.

13 [Factual Question]

The author writes, "A major legacy of the French Revolution of the late 1800s was nationalism. Nationalism—the feeling of belonging to a nation and having pride in it—motivated the French armies under Napoleon as they rampaged across Europe. Nationalist feelings spread from France and had become powerful forces by the mid-1800s."

14 [Negative Factual Question]

The Austrian Hapsburgs are mentioned in the passage, but no other families that ruled countries in Europe are mentioned.

15 [Rhetorical Purpose Question]

The first sentence that mentions Sicily reads, "The troubles began in Sicily in 1848." The author therefore mentions Sicily to show where the revolutions of 1848 began.

16 [Vocabulary Question]

When the French king abdicated, he stepped down from the throne and quit as the monarch.

17 [Vocabulary Question]

An uprising is a revolt.

18 [Factual Question]

The author mentions, "Their nationalist feelings and desires for independence would eventually help cause World War I, which began in 1914."

19 [Insert Text Question]

The sentence before the first square notes that people wanted a role in the government and rights and freedoms granted by constitutions. The sentence to be inserted points out that their inspiration was the American Revolution and the independence the American people had gotten.

20 [Fill in a Table Question]

According to the passage, the causes of the revolutions of 1848 included the economic suffering of common people, the desire of minorities for more autonomy, and the fact that the lower classes wanted to help run their countries. As for the revolutions' effects, they included constitutions being written in some places and the French undergoing a change in their government.

21 [Vocabulary Question]

Unfeasible ideas are ones that are unworkable.

22 [Sentence Simplification Question]

The highlighted sentence notes that it was not surprising that the Soviet Union launched the first space station since it had also put the first satellite and person into space. This is best described in answer choice Ⓐ.

23 [Factual Question]

The passage reads, "The Soviets had hoped that *Salyut 1* would remain in orbit perpetually. However, it only stayed in orbit for around six months before it plummeted to the Earth."

24 [Rhetorical Purpose Question]

The author writes, "They also used some space stations, particularly *Salyut 3* and *Salyut 5*, for military purposes."

25 [Inference Question]

In writing, "Its astronauts performed a wide variety of experiments, including learning how the human body reacted to being in space for a long time," the author implies that some of the astronauts on *Skylab* had long-term stays in space so that they could conduct experiments on how their bodies reacted.

26 [Negative Factual Question]

There is no mention in the passage of why the Americans abandoned *Skylab* for a period of several years.

27 [Factual Question]

The author notes, "When first launched, *Mir* was a single module. However, it contained several docking ports, so additional modules were launched into space and connected to it. These modules contained equipment for studying the Earth, for conducting astrophysics, and for doing materials-science work."

28 [Reference Question]

The "it" that has remained in service until the present day is the *International Space Station*.

29 [Insert Text Question]

The sentence in front of the second square notes *Skylab* weighed around 75,000 kilograms. The sentence to be inserted makes a comparison in stating that the Soviet modules weighed around 18,000 kilograms. Thus the two sentences go well together.

30 [Prose Summary]

According to the passage, *Mir* had several modules for experiments and stayed in space for fifteen years. In addition, seven *Salyut* space stations made successful orbits and conducted various missions. Finally, *Skylab*'s crews did many experiments, such as on effects of long-term stays in space.

31 [Factual Question]

It is written, "First, land bridges appeared between large land formations. These allowed people to travel to places they could not access prior to the ice age."

32 [Factual Question]

The author writes, "During an ice age, large amounts of seawater freeze. This causes ocean levels to drop."

33 [Inference Question]

When discussing how the first humans arrived on Australia, the author notes, "The debate on this issue is ongoing." Thus it can be inferred that the manner of the first humans' arrival is not known for sure.

34 [Vocabulary Question]

A pristine land has been untouched by humans.

35 [Rhetorical Purpose Question]

The author discusses terminal moraines to explain their significance: Their presence indicates how far south an ice sheet traveled.

36 [Factual Question]

The author writes, "The most obvious changes were the thousands of lakes that currently dot the Northern Hemisphere. The ice sheets gouged huge holes, which were subsequently filled by water when the sheets melted and retreated."

37 [Negative Factual Question]

There is no mention of drumlins being located in Scandinavia.

38 [Reference Question]

The "they" that left a lasting legacy are the ice sheets.

39 [Insert Text Question]

The sentence in front of the fourth square notes that people were living all around America and had their own civilizations by the time the Europeans arrived. The sentence to be inserted begins with the phrase "they had also," which shows that the sentence will provide more information about these different tribes.

40 [Prose Summary]

According to the passage, ice sheets can change how the Earth looks by making drumlins and terminal moraines. In addition, without the land bridge from New Guinea that formed during an ice age, Australia would have been unpopulated. And the land bridge connecting Asia and America let people populate the Americas.

| 1 C | 2 D | 3 B, D | 4 A | 5 D |
| 6 A | 7 C | 8 B | 9 **1** | |

10 **1**, **4**, **5**

| 11 A | 12 A | 13 C | 14 D | 15 C |
| 16 C | 17 C | 18 C | 19 **4** | |

20 Senses: **1**, **7**, **9**   Stealth: **6**, **8**   Speed: **2**, **3**

| 21 B | 22 D | 23 A | 24 B | 25 C |
| 26 A | 27 C | 28 C | 29 **2** | |

30 **1**, **3**, **5**

1 [Sentence Simplification Question]

The highlighted sentence notes that agriculture took a long time to develop in Northern Europe after being introduced from Southern Europe 5,000 years ago. This is best described in answer choice ⒸC.

2 [Rhetorical Purpose Question]

The author writes, "Later, the Romans introduced large-scale farming on their extensive estates, but the dissolution of the Roman Empire in the fifth century resulted in a return to subsistence farming."

3 [Factual Question]

The passage reads, "Serfs planted crops in long rows called furrows, which had small ridges between them. Typical crops were wheat, barley, oats, rye, and legumes, which included beans, peas, and lentils." It also notes, "Most animals were held in common and foraged on communal grounds," and, "Chickens, pigs, cows, and sheep were typically raised by serfs and provided milk, meat, and wool."

4 [Vocabulary Question]

When animals foraged, they grazed on the land and ate the vegetation there.

5 [Negative Factual Question]

There is no mention in the passage of the amount of crops that serfs harvested each year.

6 [Reference Question]

The "they" that were bronze while later ones were iron were metal shoes.

7 [Inference Question]

In writing, "Crop yields were perhaps five times less than in modern times, and famine was a constant danger," the author implies that crops could yield poor harvests that resulted in some people starving.

8 [Factual Question]

The passage reads, "Sometime during the late feudal period, farmers introduced the three-crop system—a form of crop rotation—which played an important part in increasing crop yields," and, "A third section was left fallow to allow the land to recover some of its nutrient levels."

9 [Insert Text Question]

The sentence before the first square mentions that legumes added nitrogen to the soil. The sentence to be inserted points out that nitrogen is a valuable nutrient that can be used by other crops later.

10 [Prose Summary Question]

According to the passage, the three-crop system improved crop yields by adding nutrients to the soil. In addition, the horse collar and the horseshoe made using horses for farming easier. Finally, serfs planted various crops and raised several kinds of livestock.

11 [Vocabulary Question]

Carnivorous animals are meat-eating ones.

12 [Factual Question]

The author writes, "Predators employ a wide variety of methods to find, track, and kill their prey." Then, the rest of the paragraph describes many of these skills.

13 [Rhetorical Question]

The author writes, "The eyes of most predators are in the front of each one's head. This gives them binocular vision and depth perception. They can see animals directly in front of them and from far away, and predators can judge the distance to these animals."

14 [Sentence Simplification Question]

The highlighted sentence notes that crocodiles and alligators sneak up, grab their victims, drown them, and then eat them. This process is best described in answer choice ⒹD.

15 [Negative Factual Question]

There is no mention of tusks anywhere in the passage.

16 [Inference Question]

The passage reads, "Lions have even been known to attack baby elephants. In a display of teamwork, some lions hold the young animals down while others kill it." By noting that lions attack baby elephants, it can be inferred that they will not attack a full-grown one.

17 [Vocabulary Question]

Enhanced senses have been heightened.

18 [Factual Question]

The author notes, "Some species of herd animals, including water buffaloes, place their babies in the center of a moving herd. This offers their young some measure of protection from predators."

19 [Insert Text Question]

The sentence before the fourth square mentions that sharks are fast swimmers. The sentence to be inserted mentions that fish cannot get away from them, so they get eaten.

20 [Fill in a Table Question]

According to the passage, examples of animals using their senses are eagles having exceptional vision, sharks detecting blood in the water, and predators using depth perception. Examples of animals using stealth are hawks and eagles swooping down on their victims and alligators hiding in the water. Examples of animals using speed are cheetahs running down fleeing animals and sharks swimming very quickly.

21 [Inference Question]

The author notes, "Among the three, the Aztecs were perhaps the most powerful." Thus it can be inferred that the Inca Empire was not as strong as the Aztec Empire.

22 [Factual Question]

The author writes, "Later, in 1427, the Mexica people joined two other tribes to create the Aztec Alliance, which soon became the Aztec Empire."

23 [Vocabulary Question]

Something that is in a vicinity is in a region.

24 [Sentence Simplification Question]

The highlighted passage notes that the Aztecs did not have to garrison soldiers in many conquered lands since the people there were no longer a threat to them. This idea is best described in answer choice Ⓑ.

25 [Inference Question]

The author writes, "While the Aztecs had some measure of civilization, they were warriors at heart." The author therefore implies that the Aztecs enjoyed fighting in battles.

26 [Rhetorical Purpose Question]

The author explains the purpose of flower wars by writing, "The Aztecs referred to these events as flower wars. Some historians believe flower wars also enabled the Aztecs to train their warriors in combat and to allow members of the lower classes to advance to higher ones by showing bravery in battle."

27 [Factual Question]

The author writes, "They were joined by many tribes, whose people despised their Aztec overlords."

28 [Factual Question]

It is written, "Outbreaks of smallpox and typhus killed off most of the people. The Aztecs and other tribes lacked natural defenses to these illnesses. By the start of the 1600s, most Aztecs had died from disease."

29 [Insert Text Question]

The sentence before the second square mentions that the Aztecs had none of the advantages that the Spanish had. The sentence to be inserted states that the Aztecs were defeated because of their lack of modern weaponry.

30 [Prose Summary Question]

According to the passage, the Aztecs fought and defeated most of their neighboring city-states. In addition, the Aztecs had a hierarchy complete with a strong warrior class. And the Aztecs were defeated by the Spanish, who used their superior technology.

MEMO

MEMO

TOEFL®
MAP

New TOEFL® Edition

Reading

Intermediate